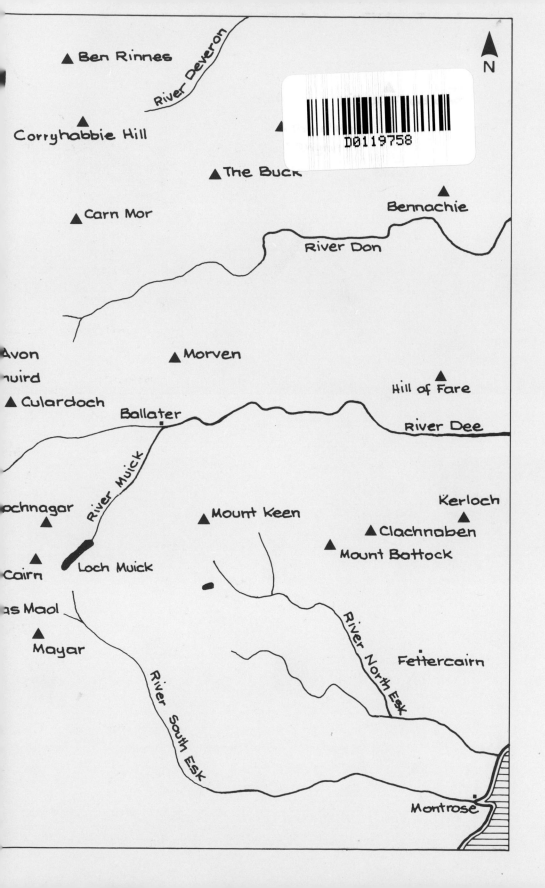

N

Ben Rinnes

River Deveron

Corryhabbie Hill

The Buck

D0119758

Bennachie

Carn Mor

River Don

Avon
nuird

Morven

Hill of Fare

Culardoch

Ballater

River Dee

ochnagar

River Muick

Kerloch

Mount Keen

Clachnaben

Loch Muick

Mount Battock

Cairn

as Maol

Mayar

River North Esk

Fettercairn

River South Esk

Montrose

Scottish Mountaineering Club
District Guidebooks

THE
CAIRNGORMS

Series Editor: D J BENNET

Published by
The Scottish Mountaineering Trust

THE
CAIRNGORMS
LOCHNAGAR AND THE MOUNTH

Adam Watson

Scottish Mountaineering Club District Guidebook

PUBLISHED BY THE SCOTTISH MOUNTAINEERING TRUST: 1992
© THE SCOTTISH MOUNTAINEERING CLUB

First Edition 1928
Reprinted 1931
Second Edition 1938
Third Edition 1950
Fourth Edition 1968
Fifth Edition 1975
Sixth Edition 1992

British Library Cataloguing in Publication Data
Watson, Adam
  Cairngorms: Cairngorms, Lochnagar and the
  Mounth. - 6th Rev Ed
  I. Title
  796.5

  ISBN 0-907521-39-8

Front cover: Loch Avon and Beinn Mheadhoin *W. D. Brooker*
Back cover: Derry Cairngorm from Beinn Mheadhoin *D.Scott*

Book design by Donald Bennet
Maps drawn by Jim Renny
Production by Peter Hodgkiss
Typeset by Westec, North Connel
Colour separations by Par Graphics, Kirkcaldy
Printed by Pillans and Wilson, Edinburgh
Bound by Hunter and Foulis, Edinburgh
Distributed by Cordee, 3a DeMontfort Street, Leicester, LE1 7HD

CONTENTS

ILLUSTRATIONS

PREFACE

Any guidebook to a wild area such as the Cairngorms should not be so detailed that it seriously reduces the visitors' feeling of wonder and exploration by themselves, which is the best joy that wild country can give. Hence this guide is not over-peppered with numerous map grid references, times and other figures like a railway timetable.

The main aim is to give an introduction to the area's potential for serious hillwalkers, while at the same time giving readers a flavour of what is unique or unusual about the Cairngorms as compared with other hill districts in Scotland. That flavour includes a fair amount of the area's human history and distinctive social culture, including the local pronunciation of place names. It also includes summaries of the remarkable geology and landforms which make up so much of this varied hill country, and on the wildlife whose home it is.

May the Cairngorms and their wildlife always remain grand and serene. Let us feel wonder, peace, inspiration and humility in their presence. Let us leave no obvious mark or mess behind, so that those who come in future to the Cairngorms will find them as challenging, beautiful and wild as we have been priveleged to find them.

The author is grateful to Roger Everett for his comments on the sections on Climbing, Jim Renny who has drawn a new set of maps for this book, Lucy Burnett for typing and Donald Bennet for general guidance. Thanks are also due to those whose photographs are in this book, and who are named in the list of illustrations.

Adam Watson, Crathes

THE CLIMBER AND THE MOUNTAIN ENVIRONMENT

With increasing numbers of walkers and climbers going to the Scottish hills, it is important that all of us who do so should recognise our responsibilities to those who live and work among the hills and glens, to our fellow climbers and to the mountain environment in which we find our pleasure and recreation.

The Scottish Mountaineering Club and Trust, who jointly produce this and other guidebooks, wish to impress on all who avail themselves of the information in these books that it is essential at all times to consider the sporting and proprietory rights of landowners and farmers. The description of a climbing, walking or skiing route in any of these books does not imply that a right of way exists, and it is the responsibility of all climbers to ascertain the position before setting out. In cases of doubt it is always best to enquire locally.

During the stalking and shooting seasons in particular, much harm can be done in deer forests and on grouse moors by people walking through them. Normally the deer stalking season is from 1st July to 20th October, when stag shooting ends. Hinds may continue to be culled until 15th February. The grouse shooting season is from 12th August until 10th December. These are not merely sporting activities, but are essential for the economy of many Highland estates. During these seasons, therefore, especial care should be taken to consult the local landowner, factor or keeper before taking to the hills.

Climbers and hillwalkers are recommended to consult the book HEADING FOR THE SCOTTISH HILLS, published by the Scottish Mountaineering Trust on behalf of the Mountaineering Council of Scotland and the Scottish Landowners Federation, which gives the names and addresses of factors and keepers who may be contacted for information regarding access to the hills.

It is also important to avoid disturbance to sheep, particularly during the lambing season between March and May. Dogs should not be taken onto the hills at this time, and at all times should be kept under close control.

Always try to follow a path or track through cultivated land and forests, and avoid causing damage to fences, dykes and gates by climbing over them carelessly. Do not leave litter anywhere, but take it down from the hill in your rucksack.

The increasing number of walkers and climbers on the hills is leading to increased, and in some cases very unsightly erosion of footpaths and hillsides. Some of the revenue from the sale of this and other SMC guidebooks is used by the Trust to assist financially the work being carried out to repair and maintain hill paths in Scotland. However, it is important for all of us to recognise our responsibility to minimise the erosive effect of our passage over the hills so that the enjoyment of future climbers shall not be spoiled by landscape damage caused by ourselves.

As a general rule, where a path exists walkers should follow it and even where it is wet and muddy should avoid walking along its edges, the effect of which is to extend erosion sideways. Do not take short-cuts at the corners of zigzag paths. Remember that the worst effects of erosion are likely to be caused during or soon after prolonged wet weather when the ground is soft and waterlogged. A route on a stony or rocky hillside is likely to cause less erosion than on a grassy one at such times.

Although the use of bicycles can often be very helpful for reaching remote hills and crags, the erosion damage that can be caused by them when used 'off road' on soft footpaths and open hillsides is such that their use on such terrain must cause concern. It is the editorial policy of the Scottish Mountaineering Club that the use of bicycles in hill country may be recommended on hard roads such as forest roads or private roads following rights of way, but is not recommended on footpaths and open hillsides where the environmental damage that they cause may be considerable. Readers are asked to bear these points in mind, particularly in conditions when the ground is wet and soft after rain.

The proliferation of cairns on the hills detracts from the feeling of wildness, and may be confusing rather than helpful as regards route-finding. The indiscriminate building of cairns on the hills is therefore to be discouraged.

Climbers are reminded that they should not drive along private estate roads without permission, and when parking their cars should avoid blocking access to private roads and land, and should avoid causing any hazard to other road users.

Finally, the Scottish Mountaineering Club and the Scottish Mountaineering Trust can accept no liability for damage to property nor for personal injury resulting from the use of any route described in their publications.

Cairn Gorm from the Forefinger Pinnacle below the Shelter Stone Crag

Introduction

This book covers North-east Scotland from its arctic-like high plateaux to its coast. The area is bounded on the west and south by the Inverness-Perth road, and on the east and north by the North Sea and the Moray Firth.

NAMES OF THE HILL-RANGES

The book has been named mainly after the Cairngorms, the great central dominating hill-range in the north-east Highlands. Within the main Cairngorms massif from Aviemore to Braemar and from Glen Feshie to Glen Gairn, 30 kilometres from east to west and 25 from north to south, you will find magnificent remote hills and a wealth of river, loch and forest scenery that cannot be matched elsewhere in Britain. Although we are so used to the name *'the Cairngorms'*, it is a nickname. These hills are Am Monadh Ruadh or the red hill-range, distinguishing them from Am Monadh Liath or the grey hill-range west of Spey. The name Am Monadh Ruadh is still known among the oldest folk of Strath Spey, but long ago outsiders had replaced it with the Cairngorms on maps and in guidebooks. They transferred the name of the best-known hill in the massif, Cairn Gorm, to the massif as a whole.

The other main hill-range is the long chain running from Drumochter in the west almost to the sea just south of Aberdeen. Many maps and books have given its name as *'the Grampians'* , but although children have to learn this at school, they do not learn it at home and nowhere is it used in local rural speech. Some map-makers have confused the issue by printing *'Grampians'* over the Cairngorms and Strath Don hills as well. As this name has often been used on maps to take in the Ben Alder and Perthshire hills far to the west of our area, it is unsuitable for this book. The old local name was Am Monadh, the hill-range commonly called The Mounth, often spelled *'munth'* in old documents and still pronounced *'munth'* today by local people. It survives in the local names of the old *'roads'* or paths that cross it, such as the Cairn o' Mount, the Firmounth, the Capel Mounth, the Tolmount, etc. and in their collective term *'The Mounth Roads'*.

PLACE NAMES

The rule, as in all the SMC Guides, is to follow the latest Ordnance Survey maps for their spelling of place names. In some cases, long-established local usage differs greatly from what appears in the OS maps, and the book mentions a few examples. However, as it would be confusing for a guidebook to give names very different from the OS maps, the OS names are used except where the map has obvious printers' errors. Another slight difference from the maps is that this guide omits the Gaelic vowel accents on the names; these accents are often inaccurate on the OS maps, but in any case their function is not understood except by Gaelic speakers and they are not necessary for finding locations.

In most of the hills of Moray and Nairn, and to the west of Corgarff, Balmoral and Glen Shee, the names are virtually all Gaelic in origin. Around Strath Don, Glen Muick and Glen Isla, many are corruptions of Gaelic and difficult to decipher, with a few in north-east Scots and English. Next to the lowlands around Huntly, Banchory and Angus, many are north-east Scots or English, and the rest from Gaelic or Pictish. This book gives many names of corries, burns and glens which are not on the OS maps. Most of them are still used locally, but a few have virtually died out. Publication here should help to keep them alive, as well as being useful to visitors for describing locations in these hills more precisely.

This guide gives English meanings of Celtic place names only where there is reasonably good evidence for doing so. Place-name research has its own standards and discipline like any other field of research, and it is reprehensible to ignore these and give meanings without doing the necessary hard work. Many writers have ignored them and produced absurd derivations that defy local pronunciation and Gaelic grammar and usage, and this has often brought Scottish place-name study into disrepute.

A.MacBain (1890) *Badenoch: its history, clans and place names.* A careful collection by an expert. Later reprinted 1922 in *Place Names Highlands & Islands of Scotland.*

J.Macdonald (1899) *Place Names of West Aberdeenshire.* New Spalding Club. A pioneering list.

J.Milne (1908) *Kirkmichael (Banffshire) place names.* CCJ 5, 93. A good list of map names, but some rather speculative meanings.

W.J.Watson (1916) *Some place names in the Cairngorm region.* CCJ 8, 133. Very good but short.

W.J.Watson (1926) *History of the Celtic Place Names of Scotland.* Includes interesting history and derivation of some words from the Cairngorms region.

F.C.Diack (1944) *Inscriptions of Pictland.* 3rd Spalding Club. Valuable material on place names, local Gaelic and local Gaelic poetry.

S.Gordon (1948), reprinted (1972) *Highways and Byways in the Central Highlands.* Authoritative glossary and list by W.J.Watson.

W.M.Alexander (1952) *The Place Names of Aberdeenshire.* 3rd Spalding Club. A very good list.

C.P.Will (1963) *Place Names of Northeast Angus.* Covers Glen Esk, Lethnot and Edzell. A pioneering list, but many of the suggested meanings are speculative.

A.Watson & E.Allan (1984) *The Place Names of Upper Deeside.* Aberdeen Univ. Press. A comprehensive list.

NAME PRONUNCIATIONS

The most accurate pronunciations are given by older local people who have lived all their lives in a small area and whose parents also lived there. Many of those who know the area well as climbers nevertheless err when pronouncing some place names. Coming from temporary visitors, such errors may seem ignorant or even patronising to those who belong to this hill country. A feature of this guide is to give many of the local pronunciations in parentheses. As it is impossible to describe Gaelic pronunciations accurately without the International Phonetic Alphabet, this guide gives no more than approximate versions of how some of the place names are pronounced by the local people. The following indicates pronunciations:

ai	-	gain	igh	-	high
aw	-	dawn, got	ng	-	hung
ch	-	loch	o	-	pole
e	-	get	oi	-	boil
ei	-	height	ow	-	howl
i	-	hit	u	-	but
y	-	you			

'-indicates stress on the following syllable, e.g. under'stand

LANGUAGE

The climber can understand and enjoy a piece of hill country better if he knows something of the people who live there and appreciates something of their speech, life and history. Gaelic was the language of all but the coastal strip and Aberdeen till the 13th century. It survived as a living tongue west of Ballater till the early 1900s, and in Speyside, Atholl and Inverey well into this century. The people of Spey and Atholl now speak English with a Highland intonation, and occasional words of Gaelic or Scots origin. The language of the folk of Dee, Don and Deveronside now is the north-east Scots dialect, strongly influenced by the farming people of lower Aberdeenshire. It contains many words of Gaelic origin and also a large number of Norse origin, many of them like modern Norwegian. If you are a visitor, remember that this north-east Scots, and not English, is the language these people are at home with. The folk of the Angus glens speak a slightly different variety of Scots, more influenced by the speech of Dundee, Perth and Strath More.

HISTORY

The history of the people in this hill country is a vast subject with much literature. The chapters of this book give some brief pieces of historical information which relate mainly to the hills rather than to the region as a whole. References are given below for the reader who wishes to know more. In addition, the various village guide booklets describe many historical events in the inhabited valleys.

'Glenmore' (1859) *Highland Legends*. Includes old legends and Gaelic poetry from Spey, Avon and Dee.

J.Grant (1861) *Legends of the Braes o' Mar.* A racy account on old legends in the previous three centuries.

J.G.Michie (1872) *Deeside Tales.* Local history since the 17th century, and 19th century way of life. Selective but good story-telling.

W.Scrope (1883) *Days of Deer-Stalking in the Scottish Highlands.* Descriptions and historical material about Atholl.

A.MacBain (1890) *Badenoch: its history, clans and place names.* Later reprinted (1922) in *Place Names Highlands & Islands of Scotland.* A good, careful collection; much on the Cairngorms massif.

J.G.Michie (ed) (1901) *The Records of Invercauld.* New Spalding Club. Collections of old Invercauld Estate records, with detailed documentation.

W.M.Smith (1904) *The Romance of Poaching in the Highlands.* Accounts of some well known poachers of Mar and Atholl.

T.Sinton (1906) *The Poetry of Badenoch.* An excellent collection of the Gaelic poetry not just of Badenoch but also Braemar and Atholl.

T.D.Miller (1925) *Tales of a Highland Parish: Glen Shee.* Local story telling.

W.D.Simpson (1943) *The Province of Mar.* A good account of local history, emphasising castles.

S.Gordon (1948) reprinted 1972 *Highways and Byways in the Central Highlands.* A useful book which collates many old legends and descriptions of historical events in Atholl, Spey and Dee, including many long quotations, which are otherwise available only in scarce old books.

V.Gaffney (1960) *The Lordship of Strathavon.* 3rd Spalding Club. Contains detailed notes on shielings in Strath Avon.

I.F.Grant (1961) *Highland Folk Ways.* Authoritative account on old ways of life, much of it from Speyside, by the originator of Am Fasgadh Museum at Kingussie.

F.Wyness (1968) *Royal Valley.* Useful book on Deeside history, drawing on a wide literature.

S.Piggott & W.D.Simpson (1970) *Illustrated Guide to Ancient Monuments. Vol 6, Scotland.* A booklet with detailed summaries of all the sites and a list of further reading.

Useful articles in CCJ are in Vol 2: *The Braemar Highlands after the '45; 6: Tales told in Rothiemurchus; The Cairngorm parishes and the (old) Statistical Account of Scotland; Rights of Way in Braemar and Glen Tilt in 1840-50; 10: The Canadian lumber camps in the Cairngorms; 12: James Downie, Guide; The Glen Doll Right of Way Case;* and 14: *Braemar of old: extracts from a Highland diary.*

V.Gaffney wrote a short account on *Shielings of the Drumochter* in Scott. Stud. 11, 91, with two old maps. The article by I.H.Adams on *The historical geography of Glenfernate 1460-1968* in Ann. Rep. Scott. Fld Stud. Ass. (1969), 17, is a short study of the old settlements and their depopulation.

LAND USE

Man's land use greatly affects one's ease of walking and also the appearance of the hills. Foresters have made impenetrable woods on many lower slopes, but forest roads usually give some access to the hill above. On the higher and western deer forests the stalkers burn the heather to give the deer a young bite, often in fires of up to 40 hectares; this makes for easy walking. On the grouse moors - such as in Strath Don - the fires are usually small, often in long narrow strips, giving a unique appearance to this kind of landscape, which shows best when a light dusting of snow shows up the contrasting patchwork pattern. On some of the lower northern and eastern moors where the keepers have burned little in recent years, the heather is now very rank and many young trees are colonising by natural regeneration.

PUBLIC TRANSPORT

Rail and bus services in rural Scotland are poorer than they were, but planes, taxis and post-buses are more readily available. Details of rail and bus services change frequently, and it is not the function of this guide to duplicate such information. Readers should apply to travel agents, railway stations, bus stations and tourist offices for current details.

ACCOMMODATION

With the continuing growth of tourism in the Highlands there is a wide choice of accommodation throughout the area covered by this guidebook, whether it be hotels, caravans, cottages and hostels, or the simpler joys of wild camping and bothy dwelling. However, it should be borne in mind that many of the hostels and caravan sites and even some hotels are closed during winter. An indication is given in each chapter of this book of the accommodation available in each area, but it is not the function of this guide to give detailed information on accommodation. Readers should apply to tourist offices for details. Some towns and larger villages such as Braemar produce their own guidebooks which give information on local accommodation and other tourist facilities.

The Scottish Youth Hostels Association has several hostels in the area, and the relevant ones are noted in each chapter. Wild camping is possible widely in the glens and on the mountains, but campers should bear in mind the law regarding camping and should seek permission if camping in the vicinity of farms, crofts and other habitation. (The relevant law is that it is an offence to camp or light a fire on private land without the landowner's permission). No camping is allowed in most woodland areas because of fire risks. In such places and in the lower valleys, it is best to go to the organised camp sites or to camp at the farms which allow it.

There are numerous remote cottages, once occupied by shepherds and stalkers, but long since abandoned and fallen into disrepair. Many of these cottages have been renovated by, among others, the Mountain Bothies Association, and with the landowners' permission these bothies are now available as simple shelters for climbers and walkers. They usually have no more than four walls and a roof with little furniture inside, but do provide dry spartan accommodation. They are not suitable for large parties, and during the stalking season they should not be used without the owners' permission. The cardinal bothy rule is that no damage should be caused to the building, and no litter left in or near it. Take your litter home in a plastic bag, and leave the place as clean as you found it.

On the lower hills and grouse moors there are many stables, shooters' lunch huts, outhouses and boathouses, most of which have no locks; these have not been described individually as they are too numerous to mention and as they lie in country that hillwalkers use mainly for day-trips rather than for longer stays. Above all, they are not traditional bothies long used by many walkers. Hence the quickest way to have them locked or demolished by the estates would be to publicise them in this or any other guidebook. In the area there have been several forcible break-ins of unoccupied houses and lodges by hillwalkers, and in one case this let to immediate destruction of an excellent bothy which had been used by the culprits.

MAPS

It is assumed that the readers of this book will also have and be able to read suitable maps for hillwalking. The recommended maps are the Ordnance Survey 1:50,000 metric maps, of which the most recent edition is the Landranger Series. These maps have sufficient detail for the needs of hillwalkers. There are 1:25,000 maps which show fine detail, but each one covers only a relatively small area of 20 x 10 kilometres. However, the Ordnance Survey's 1:25,000 Outdoor Leisure Map, *High Tops of the*

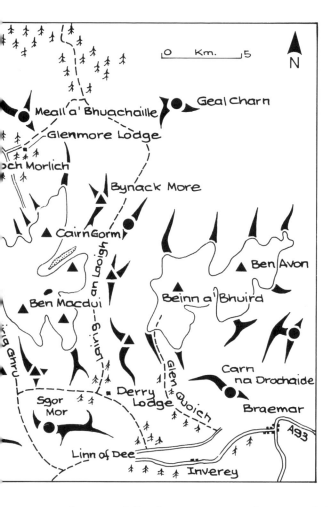

Cairngorms, is very useful, covering 26 x 21 kilometres and showing the whole Cairngorms massif except the eastern Cairngorms east of Glen Derry.

The names and spellings used in this book are taken from the 1:50,000 maps except where there is an obvious printer's error. Summit and other heights are taken from Ordnance Survey 1:10,000 and 1:25,000 maps, which are more up to date than the 1:50,000 maps in this respect. Thus there are some instances where heights in this book do not agree with the 1:50,000 Landranger Series maps.

The Landranger Series has been quite recently revised and most maps are up to date in their showing of features such as forests, tracks, paths and footbridges. There are, however, a few instances where newly planted forests are not shown, and walkers should be aware of this. There are also a few cases where the Ordnance Survey has not been able to keep up with changes in paths and tracks, especially the appearance of some and disappearance of others.

SKI TOURING

The region covered by this book, the snowiest in Britain, offers the best skiing. Some fine ski tours were done here in the early years of the sport (SMCJ 10, 345; 12, 253; and 16, 196). For instance, in March 1913 a party crossed Cairn Gorm and Ben Macdui on skis, on their way from Aviemore to the Derry, returning to Spey over Carn Ban Mor and Sgoran Dubh. H.MacRobert described Scottish snow for skiing and suitable skiing places in the Cairngorms (SMCJ 21, 379). One of the pioneers, H.J.Butchart, wrote an accurate and remarkably far-sighted description for the early editions of this guide. An early attempt in the 1930s to make Braemar a ski centre failed because of a lack of snow in very mild winters. More people took up skiing after 1945, and the sport grew rapidly in the late 1950s. This led to the new road, chairlifts and cafes being built at Cairn Gorm in 1960-61, a chairlift at the Cairnwell by the Glenshee

Chairlift Company in 1962, and many developments at both centres since, as well as at the Lecht in the 1980s and early 1990s. As the main ski centres are well known and described fully in tourist publications, there is no need for further mention here. However, the new lifts and other facilities have been noted briefly in the chapters below, as some may find them useful starting points for walks or ski tours.

Walking on skis offers a different way of exploring the hills, corries and glens in winter, and the following section describes some of the area's potential for it. During severe winters with heavy snow you may get good ski touring from November till May, and exceptionally from October till June. In most years, however, good heavy snowfalls in November and December are often followed by great thaws and even January snowfalls may be unreliable. Indeed, in the mildest years such as 1964 and 1990 there may be far less snow on the hill in January or February than in June of other years. In mild years a continual succession of snowfalls, thaws and freezings may last most of the winter, producing temporary stretches of skiing only on some weekends, often on poor sticky or crusty snow, or on dangerously icy snow with a surface almost like rough concrete. However, in most years from February to April there is plenty of good snow on the higher hills and corries.

If you are skiing wholly on the lower hills and glens up to 750m, or are starting in the glens and then climbing over the hills with skis on all day, you can very rarely do so in mild years like 1964 or 1990. However, in hard winters like 1955 and 1963, excellent conditions for skiing occur on the lower slopes and glens from December to March. In 1951, which was the longest winter in the Cairngorms since 1943, one could ski in the glens from late November till late April. If you are content to carry your skis up snowfree glens or lower slopes, there will usually be good skiing higher up from February to May every year, except in the mildest winters. However, as this merely forms a variant of hillwalking up snowfree ground combined with downhill running on narrow drifts, it is not further described here.

During heavy snow, especially in long hard winters like 1963, you can get fine touring on the lower hills such as Kerloch, Mount Battock, Geallaig Hill and the hills of Cromdale and Glen Esk, but you cannot depend on it for long if the winter is average or mild. The Ladder Hills, Morven, Mount Keen, Drumochter and the Glen Clova hills offer good conditions frequently in January to March of most winters. The lower hills in the Cairngorms massif, such as Sgor Mor and Beinn Bhreac, likewise give good ski touring then, and in deep snow the pine woods of Ballochbuie, the Derry, Dubh Ghleann and Rothiemurchus are magnificent when visited on ski. These lower grounds become attractive on short mid-winter days as they are so accessible.

On the higher hills of Glen Feshie and the Mounth between Glen Ey and Glen Doll, good ski touring usually lasts into the spring, and on the even higher Cairngorms above 1100m you will then get a great variety of excellent touring. After climbing to the summit, you should make for certain places where the snow has drifted in and usually gives a good downhill run.

Skiing down to Coire an Lochain below the cliffs of Cairn Lochan

From November to early February the days are so short and the weather so often stormy that ski tourers or hillwalkers who head for the highest summits should leave early in the morning and be prepared for very severe weather. Beautiful weather can, however, come at any time in winter, with frost, blue skies and much calmer air than in summer; then you can feel too hot skiing in your shirt sleeves. At these times, ski touring from powdery white glens up through snow-laden pines to the highest ground shows the Cairngorms at their finest: waves of frozen hills stretching for many miles and great cliffs plastered white or creamy in thick ice, snow and hoar frost. In April and May the storms can be as bad as in December, but with long hours of daylight and usually more reliable weather, you often have days when it is like a scene in the high Arctic, with strong sun, deep blue skies, bright colours on thawed patches of vegetation, a beautifully uniform snow surface, and the odd ptarmigan croaking loudly on its chosen snowfree patch.

Unless you are going to ski only on the lower hills, it is safer to use Vibram-type soles on skiing-cum-climbing boots rather than downhill ski boots or ski-touring boots with flat soles; these give a far better grip on steep slopes if you have to take your skis off. You should carry an ice axe and crampons on any route where even a small part of the tour lies on steep slopes or places that are often icy, such as climbing down into or up out of the Lairig Ghru and Coire Dhondail. Try to avoid steep slopes in any case because of the risk of avalanches, a risk which is heightened when you have the skis on your feet.

Timing and difficulty are often much worse than in summer, but sometimes can be much easier; it all depends on the snow conditions that you meet. There are at least 40 recognisably different kinds of surface, varying from exhausting plodding in deep powdery snow to hard ice. Which ones you meet, and the extent of them, will govern how well and fast you can ski and thus how long you will take. During the winter, the risk of a fall on skis when you are moving much faster than walking speed is obviously far greater than a fall when walking on foot. This risk becomes heightened by the fact that the·skis enable you to penetrate into country far from roads and houses, and thus far from safety, in conditions when anyone plunging in on foot could never get far out. Forget, therefore, about fine skilled technique, and ski downhill not as if you are beside the thronged Coire Cas ski grounds, but as if you stand in the middle of the Greenland ice cap.

There is no point in listing here all the routes of ascent or descent on cross-country ski tours; most of the walking routes described later in the book are suitable, the only difference being that the skier on his descent should if possible include one of the better downhill runs. Some of these are mentioned in the skiing sections of the individual chapters below.

One way of giving a brief sketch of the possibilities is to describe some of the more notable tours done in the area since 1945. Many have crossed Cairn Gorm and Ben Macdui from Spey to Dee and vice versa. Such cross-country tours are good, as it is finer to start in one valley and finish in another without going over the same ground twice. The next best alternative involves a return to your starting point, but on a different round tour into new ground. Special precautions, however, should be taken for such tours right across or around a massif, in particular the need for good navigation.

Fewer have come on skis over Cairn Toul and Braeriach from Spey to Dee or vice versa, though this makes one of the finest tours in the Cairngorms. Ben Avon and Beinn a' Bhuird have been crossed several times. The four highest tops of Cairn Toul, Braeriach, Cairn Gorm and Ben Macdui were traversed on skis in a day by N.D.Clark in January 1953 from Glen More back to Glen More, by the writer in April 1958 from Luibeg back to Luibeg, and in March 1972 by W.D.Brooker, D.Grieve and J.M.Taylor from the top of the Cairn Gorm chairlift to Glen Feshie. In April 1962 the six highest tops, including these plus Beinn a' Bhuird and Ben Avon, totalling 61km, with 55km on skis, were crossed from Invercauld to Derry Lodge (A.Watson, SMCJ 27, 348). This 'Six Tops' tour has since become a classic ski-mountaineering route for Scotland.

The longest day tour from west to east in the region, for 48km, started at Gaick Lodge and ended at the Derry in April 1951 (A. Watson, ECJ 2, 186). The longest continuous tour so far recorded, lasting 4½ days, was accomplished by M.and J.Slesser in March 1970; starting at Glen Clova, they crossed to Drumochter on a tough tour in bad weather and poor snow (SMCJ 29,322). Many fine but shorter tours have been done elsewhere in the area, for instance from Drumochter to Gaick, Cairnwell to Inverey, Luibeg to Kingussie by Glen Feshie, Glen Clova to Lochnagar, the Cairnwell to Lochnagar and Ballochbuie, and the Cairnwell to Loch Muick via Broad Cairn.

Much touring in the Cairngorms has been done with light wooden skis and their plastic or fibreglass replacements, and with the heavier modern downhill skis whose bindings allow heel-lifting. Immediately after heavy falls of powder snow that have not been accompanied by gales to pack it down, even on skis you can sink in up to the calf or the knee, which is very tiring. Snow shoes then become valuable, allowing you to go on top of the snow. They are particularly handy for walking in the forests and lower glens after deep snow. On the high tops, they are useful when there is deep powder but not a uniform enough cover to make skiing easy. Traditional Canadian-type snow shoes and the new plastic ones have both been used successfully in the Cairngorms. The plastic ones withstand rough wear from granite boulders sticking through the snow better than does the gut of the traditional type, but the old-time shoes are better after deep snowfalls in the glens.

M.Slesser (1970) *Scottish Mountains on Ski.* Describes in detail some routes in the area covered by this District Guide.

W.D.Brooker (1972) *The other side of the hill.* Aberdeen Ski CJ 1972-73, 20. A good summary mainly on the Cairngorms, particularly useful for its detailed information on equipment.

D.Bennet & B.Wallace (eds) (1987) *Ski Mountaineering in Scotland.* The best book on the subject, and describes many routes in the Cairngorms as well as giving a useful historical account.

MOUNTH ROADS AND RIGHTS OF WAY

The many long-distance paths across the Mounth and other hills were once much used for travelling and cattle droving, and most of them are now rights of way. For walkers they are one of the area's finest assets. Some have become very popular today but others are seldom visited. This book emphasises their qualities, as many of them offer fine ways of exploring the remote, secluded and less well known of our areas of wild country.

G.M.Fraser (1921) *The Old Deeside Road: Aberdeen to Braemar: including the Mounth Passes over the Grampians.* The best detailed account of these old routes in Deeside.

A.R.B.Haldane (1952) *The Drove Roads of Scotland.* The best account on the droving, its economics and history, and way of life, including much material from north-east Scotland.

G.M.Fraser's article on *The Mounth Passes over the Grampians,* Scott. Geog. Mag. 36, is also useful, and W.M.Alexander's *The Mounth Roads* in Scott. Gaelic Stud. 5, 154.

Our rights of way are a valuable heritage; everyone has the right to walk there without obstruction at any time of the year. In many cases the original path or drove road may have disappeared through lack of use, but the right remains so long as once every 20 years (the prescriptive period) someone walks along it. A public right of way is defined as a right of passage, open to the public, over private property by a route which is more or less well-defined. Rights of way can be of three types: vehicular routes, drove roads and footpaths. Only the two latter categories are of much relevance in the rough terrain of the Cairngorms and both confer right of passage for walkers. A drove road also confers a right of way on horseback, or leading a horse. It is generally considered that a pedal cyclist has the same rights as a pedestrian, but this has not been definitely established in law.

The essential elements of a right of way are that it should at some time in the past have been in continuous use for a period of not less than 20 years; that its use is a matter of right and not due to tolerance on the part of a landowner; that the right of way must connect two public places, or places to which the public habitually and legitimately resorts; and that it must follow a more or less well-defined route. It is not at present considered that mountain tops can be regarded as public places; if they were, many of our mountains could be considered to have rights of way to their summits. As regards the definition of a well-defined route, it is not necessary that there should be a visible track, rather that it should be established that the public has followed a more or less consistent line during the period in question. Minor deviations such as might be required following the raising of the level of a loch do not invalidate a right of way. It is to be hoped, however, that walkers along rights of way will have regard for the legitimate interests of those who live in the country and earn their living there.

For further information the reader should refer to the booklet *Rights of Way, A Guide to the Law in Scotland*, published by the Scottish Rights of Way Society Limited, 10/2 Sunnyside, Edinburgh EH7 5RA.

The use of mountain bicycles is on the increase, both as a sport in itself and as a means of enabling hillwalkers and climbers to reach remote mountains more easily. There is increasing evidence that the use of mountain bicycles erodes footpaths, particularly in wet and muddy patches. It is therefore the policy of the authors of these guidebooks to recommend the use of bicycles only on 'hard' tracks such as forest roads and private estate roads following rights of way, where their use can cause only negligible damage. It should be borne in mind, however, that the legal position about cycling along a right of way is not clear. As stated earlier in this section, it is considered that a cyclist has the same right as a pedestrian, but this is not absolutely certain. It may be diplomatic, therefore, to seek permission before cycling along a private road.

Carnachuin Bridge in Glen Feshie on the right of way to Braemar

MOUNTAIN RESCUE

There are several mountain rescue posts and teams in the area. In the event of an accident or a person missing, one member of the party should go to the nearest telephone and contact the Police who will begin a rescue or search. If an injured person must be left alone while you summon help, it is vitally important before leaving to write down a six-figure map reference of the location for the information of the rescue team, and to mark the position well, for instance by a rope spread out over boulders or by some other means. The casualty should be left with a torch or whistle to attract attention.

TIMES

Naismith's formula (SMCJ 2,136) is very useful, one hour for every 4½ kilometres, plus one minute for every 10m of climbing (one contour line to the next on the 1:50,000 map). A special note of warning is that in bad weather with mist, gales or heavy rain, on icy frozen slopes, and above all in deep snow with or without drifting snow and mist, you should forget about Naismith's formula. In bad conditions one level mile can easily take one hour, or even more. Big packs also slow a party.

LONG HILL WALKS

The six main hills in the Cairngorms have attracted many hillwalkers keen on breaking records. Though this sport does not appeal to the writer, a few details are given here as it involves some historical interest and provides as worthwhile an experience to its devotees as any other sport. In June 1908, H.J.Butchart and four others from Aberdeen, who started from Loch Builg at midnight, covered a 45 kilometres, 2700m 'round' of the six tops of Ben Avon, Beinn a' Bhuird, Cairn Gorm, Ben Macdui, Cairn Toul and Braeriach, to the now non-existent Lower Bothy of Einich. J.Beattie, W.D.Hutcheon and G.Shand did the same round during June 1932 in 16 hours 15 minutes. Then, in July 1932, R.P.Yunnie and party completed the alternative easier route from Ben Macdui by Braeriach to Cairn Toul and Corrour Bothy in 14 hours 45 minutes (CCJ 13, 99). In the summer of 1933, W.D.Hutcheon and G.Shand next cut the time for this easier alternative to 13 hours 25 minutes (CCJ 13, 191). E.F.Johnston greatly reduced it to 11 hours 10 minutes on 31 July 1960 (CCJ 17, 210). This was then beaten by V.C.Wynne-Edwards who, in his sixties, covered the same route in 9 hours 34 minutes in September 1968 (CCJ 17, 273).

Eric Beard did some very fast hills walks. On 12 June 1967 he climbed Braeriach, Cairn Toul, Ben Macdui, Cairn Gorm and Beinn a' Bhuird from Glenmore Lodge back to Glenmore in 15 hours, a considerably longer route than the others. In 1963 he went round the four highest Cairngorms in 4 hours 41 minutes from and back to Glenmore Lodge, travelling by the gap at Creag a' Chalamain to Braeriach, Cairn Toul, Ben Macdui and Cairn Gorm. Many have climbed these same four tops from Rothiemurchus and from the Derry. For a good walker, 12 hours will give plenty of time to stop and enjoy the scenery, but anything less than 10 is a race.

The longest walk continuously into new country was done very leisurely with a tent by J.Duff. When a policeman at Braemar, he decided to get to know his enormous beat better by walking round its perimeter. The route covered just over 160 kilometres, for 7½ days walking round the main watershed of the Cairngorms and the Mounth from Carn an Fhidhleir to Lochnagar, and then along the subsidiary watershed by the Crathie-Gairn hills. P.D.Baird once leisurely walked 121 kilometres round all the 22 Munros - i.e. separate hills over 3000 ft or 914m in the Cairngorms - during 2½ days, camping and studying snow patches en route and also claiming a new record of having smoked his pipe on top of each Munro (CCJ 17, 75).

One of the greatest of walkers was Lord Kennedy. *The Times* of 31 August 1822 tells how he, as shooting tenant of Fealar near Glen Tilt, wagered 2000 guineas that he would, in one day, shoot 40 brace of grouse at Fealar, and then ride 140 miles on a horse to Dunnottar near Stonehaven and back to Fealar. He won the bet on 12 August. Starting to shoot at 04.15, he completed the 40 brace by 08.56, changed his clothes and ate, mounted his horse at 09.30 and rode the 70 miles to Dunnottar by 14.00. After resting an hour, he reached Fealar again at 19.56. Later that evening he even rode to Braemar, arriving at 22.00, thus adding another 14 miles. Perhaps even greater was the wager he made one night at Blackhall near Banchory, when Sir A.L.

Hay bet Lord Kennedy £2500 that he would get to Inverness before him. 'Off they started at nine o'clock at night in their evening costume, thin shoes and silk stockings. Sir Andrew Leith Hay went by the coach road via Huntly and Elgin. Lord Kennedy, with Captain Ross as umpire, struck straight across the Grampians. Amid pouring rain they walked all night, next day, and the next night, reaching Inverness at 6 a.m. on the third day. Sir Andrew Leith Hay, who had chosen the longer but far more comfortable route, did not arrive till four hours later.' If, as is likely, Lord Kennedy went by the Lairig Ghru, Aviemore and Tomatin, the distance was 100 miles in 35 hours; he would have had a road from Banchory to the Linn of Dee and again from Aviemore to Inverness (CCJ 3,312).

ROCK, SNOW AND ICE CLIMBS

For climbing routes on rock, snow and ice, the region is now covered by the SMC guidebook *The Cairngorms Rock and Ice Climbs*, which describes and illustrates the many routes that have been done. Another SMC Climbers' Guide - *North-East Outcrops* - covers coastal routes and small inland crags. These guides are comprehensive and contain clear photographs and diagrams. There would therefore be no point in trying to duplicate any of this material here. Instead, the intention is merely to give a brief sketch of the chief features of each main cliff and to note a few of its routes and their history, concentrating on the classics. This will help the serious hillwalker to appreciate better these grand cliffs. Sporting routes to the plateaux are also noted.

The grading in the SMC Climbers' Guide to the Cairngorms is the normal British system of Easy, Moderate, Difficult, Very Difficult, Severe, Hard Severe, Very Severe (VS), Hard Very Severe (HVS) and Extremely Severe (the last-named subdivided into E1, E2, E3, E4, E5 etc with increasing severity). Grades I to VI indicate increasing difficulty for climbs in winter conditions. The SMC Climbers' Guides give full details of these gradings.

The SMC guidebook *The Cairngorms Rock and Ice Climbs* includes a useful historical survey of the exploration of climbs in the area. Tom Patey's article *Cairngorm Commentary* (SMCJ 27, 207) is recommended for its witty history of the great surge of exploration which began on the crags after 1945 and led to publication of the first edition of the SMC Climbers' Guides.

The sections on rock, snow and ice climbing in this District Guide emphasise summer rock. This will help the average hillwalker, who is usually a summer visitor to the Cairngorms and not a winter walker or climber, to identify some of the more interesting or popular climbs. Most winter hillwalkers are also snow and rock climbers to some extent and well aware of the Climbers' Guides. Thus, although a few notes have been given here on some of the finer winter routes, it would be outside the function of this book to give much space to these; the reader who wishes more should refer to the appropriate Climbers' Guide. However, in passing it is important to emphasise that this lesser space does not mean lesser interest. The very opposite applies, as the Cairngorms and Lochnagar are the most dependable hills for snow and ice climbing in Britain.

Unlike summer rock climbs which do not differ very greatly whether wet or dry, the same routes in winter vary enormously from one day to another, depending on the current conditions. Gullies with rock pitches can be smoothed out into easy snow climbs, or in cold snowless winters can be a series of difficult giant ribbons of ice. Routes that are wet, grimy and vegetated in summer, and thus not recommended then - as in many gullies, chimneys, and on faces with green mossy ledges - become very fine climbs in winter. The hard lower pitches of some ridges and buttresses may be buried so much under deep snow that you can step across on to the rocks high up the route. Easy rock may become ensheathed in a slippery film of icy verglas, or a few days later may turn into dry rock with powdery snow filling the cracks and ledges. The snow can be firm and reliable, or a great variety of unstable types; hardly any two days are the same, and you frequently encounter marked changes in snow type and reliability within even one day. The cornices on these hills are often massive, giving formidable problems of tunnelling or other means of escape to the plateau for a party that has completed all the difficulties of the actual route on the cliff. There are scores of different kinds of snow and ice, and only experience enables you to assess and know their qualities and dependabilities. Some of the big gullies like the Black Spout on Lochnagar and the spouts of Coire Sputan Dearg can give good safe glissades for experienced winter mountaineers, but in other conditions these gullies become dangerous avalanche slides of unstable powder, heavy wet snow, or wind slab, and next day can change to tough reliable hard snow.

H.A. Alexander (1928) *The Cairngorms*. SMC District Guide. Later editions 1938, 1950, 1968.

W.H. Murray (1947) *Mountaineering in Scotland*. Two chapters in this classic book describe Lochnagar and the Cairngorms.

J.H.B.Bell (1950) *A Progress in Mountaineering*. Good pioneering chapters on the Cairngorms, Cairngorms granite and climbing on Lochnagar.   ·

T.Patey (1971) *One Man's Mountains*. Some well-written chapters by the North East's greatest climber, published posthumously.

A.Fyffe (1987) *Cairngorms Winter Climbs*. A wide selection to the best winter climbs in the region in booklet form. Cicerone Press

The Cairngorms Rock and Ice Climbs (1990). Current SMC guide covering the Cairngorms massif and Lochnagar in comprehensive detail, by A.Fyffe & A.Nisbet. The original series, now out of print, was issued in two volumes in 1961-62, written by M.Smith. The present guide covers all summer and winter climbing routes.

K.Howett (1990) *Rock Climbing in Scotland*. A selected guide. Constable.

T.Prentice (1992) *The Climbing Guide to Scotland*. A gazetteer of climbing areas. Crowood Press.

At the top of Y Gully in Coire an Lochain

The SMC Climbers' Guides to *Creag Dubh and Craig-a-Barns*, and to the *North-East Outcrops* cover most climbs on lower ground, but are now out of print. They are to be re-published as the following new editions:

N.Morrison (ed) *North-East Outcrops*. SMC Climbers' Guide to be published 1993. Includes coastal cliffs from Kincardineshire to Morayshire, and inland valley crags such as the Pass of Ballater.

K.Howett et al. *Highland Outcrops*. SMC Climbers' Guide to be published 1994. Will include Craig a Barns, Creag Dhubh, Strath Spey and lower Badenoch crags, Glen Nevis, Ardverikie and Glen Lednock.

CORRIES AND PLATEAUX

The corries and the high arctic-like plateaux excel as two of the most wonderful features of the Cairngorms country. Some previous books on the area tended not to do justice to the wealth of corrie scenery, and wrote of featureless or dull plateaux. This guide puts more emphasis on the richness of corries and on the attractions of the many plateaux, which are unique in Britain. A particularly interesting point is that, on the plateaux of the high Cairngorms, the general appearance of the land-scape, the landforms, the soils, weather, vegetation, invertebrates and birds are all much more akin to stony hill ground in high-arctic Canada, Iceland, or the arctic tip of Norway than they are to the Alps, the Caucasus or the Rockies. Sir Henry Alexander, author of the first edition of this guide, wrote of the high plateaux, 'Not less impressive than the corries, the cliffs, and the dark lochs are the great wastes of shattered stone and sand which form the summit plateaux and ridges of these mountains, and on which only a few of the hardiest Alpine plants maintain a footing. Here are the largest areas of lofty ground in these islands where the forces of nature - frost and heat, snow and rain, wind and tempest - work with a power and a violence undreamed of at lower heights. The very bareness of these mountain-tops is on a majestic scale, and it forms one of the elements in the massive grandeur and repose which are the distinguishing characteristics of the Cairngorms. The first fleeting impression made by these mountains may be one of disappointment, for their appeal is not of the picturesque or obvious kind; but, as one explores them and wanders among them, the magnitude of everything begins to reveal itself, and one realises the immensity of the scale upon which the scene is set, and the greatness and dignity and calm of the Cairngorms cast their spell over the spirit.'

MUNROS, CORBETTS AND OTHER HILLS

In each chapter, each Munro or separate hill over 3000ft (914.4m) is mentioned as such. Only a selected few of the large number of Tops over 914m are described; the latest edition of Munro's Tables should be consulted for the others. All hills regarded as Corbetts (summits between 2500ft (762m) and 3000ft (914.4m), and with a drop of at least 500ft (152.4m) between each listed hill and any adjacent higher one) are also noted. This Guide also describes some noteworthy lower hills that are well worth climbing. Those who wish more detail on the Munros and Corbetts should consult *Munro's Tables*, *The Munros*, and *The Corbetts and Other Scottish Hills* - three books published by the Scottish Mountaineering Trust.

MOUNTAIN SAFETY

There are many basic lessons of common sense, good judgement and safety which every hillwalker, climber and ski tourer should learn before venturing into any kind of mountainous or upland country anywhere. As these lessons have been described in detail in various handbooks on technique and the Mountain Codes, there is no need to mention them here. The point of this section is wholly to mention features which occur in the Cairngorms but which do not necessarily apply and often do not apply elsewhere. Most of these lessons stem from the special peculiarities or characteristics of the Cairngorms. So, paradoxically, the features which make these hills so special, attractive and enjoyable are the very same features which can in other circumstances make them a place where people easily become lost, injured, or can die.

One feature which the high Cairngorms share with Ben Nevis is that the tops rise higher than elsewhere in Scotland. This means more likelihood of mist, stronger gales, heavier falls of rain and snow, and colder temperatures than on lower hills. Often a drop of only 150m from the summit at over 1200m takes you into conditions that, though still stormy, become so dramatically better than where you have just been that it is like entering another world. Because of the greater height of these 4000 footers (1200m) and the big areas above 1100m, you are more likely to encounter a greater variety of snow and ice conditions on a single outing than on other hills. This means in turn a greater risk of meeting icy snow or deep powder on the higher ground, on days when all the lower hills below may be largely free of snow. You will find it common in mild winters to see little or no snow low down, and yet with the gentle slopes of the highest plateaux under snow so icy that crampons are the only safe way of progressing even on almost flat ground. There is also a greater risk of being soaked in rain or sleet on the lower slopes (which greatly reduces the insulation of clothing) and then later that day freezing higher up.

One of the area's main characteristics is the long distances to the higher hills and their cliffs, with consequent feelings of great space, complex country and remoteness. In most British hills you are usually only a short distance from a road or house, and so can usually get down to safety quickly by plunging downhill. In the Cairngorms you may be up to 16 kilometres from an inhabited house or a road, separated from it by miles of plateaux and slopes that may involve travelling uphill as well as down. These great distances and the lack of shelter are reasons why bad weather is more serious here than in more dissected steeper hill country. Even in the lower but fairly unsheltered long open glens, winds with sleet or cold rain have killed some people with inadequate protective clothing, by wetting them to the skin and destroying the insulation of their clothing; this has happened even as early as September.

Dusk on Lochnagar, looking towards Broad Cairn

Even once you are down off a higher hill into a glen, you usually have many miles to go along uninhabited glens, moors and lower hills before you reach a house or road.

Very few of these glens and lower hills support scrub or trees, so you cannot quickly warm up or dry out, as in the Rockies and many other mountain ranges, by dropping quickly to the tree line and then lighting a fire. Another feature is that the plateaux, slopes and glens are so smooth-sided and vast that you can seldom get quickly into good shelter behind a ridge, corrie or steep stream-side, as you can commonly do in the more dissected hills of western Scotland and most mountain ranges elsewhere.

Because of these vast smooth slopes, the wind has free play during storms, whirling the loose snow off big areas of exposed open plateau or moor into a dense storm of drift within a few metres of ground level, even when no snow is actually falling. Equally. if you are in any slightly sheltered place on these plateaux or moors, the snow coming off square miles of ground will start to rest instead of continuing to blow above the ground. It visibly piles up, quickly covering your skis or boots. At the edges of steep slopes it also quickly builds bigger cornices than on most Highland hills, which form an extra risk. Another consequence of the large snow depths that pile up on steep slopes is the greater likelihood of avalanche.

Because the ground is so open, visibility tends to be worse than in most other hills during a storm. A characteristic of smooth slopes and wide plateaux is that they contain fewer landmarks. In the dissected western hills and the Alps you seldom travel far without coming to ridges or other obvious features. Visibility in a blizzard or thick mist is mainly a matter of having some object, even the odd stone, for the eye to latch on to. With a general snow cover and mist on the high plateaux of the Cairngorms, particularly bad 'white-outs' develop where it is hard to know if you are going uphill or downhill. As soon as you reach bouldery ridges, even if snow largely covers them, the visibility and your speed and confidence rapidly improve.

The plateaux are often swept by gales and winds of hurricane force, especially in winter. The writer has often seen small gravel blowing in the wind and plants torn out by the roots, and the strongest man can be blown right over and thrown on the ground, or reduced to crawling on all fours. Of course this happens equally on other Scottish high hills, but in the Cairngorms the consequences are more vital as you may have to travel so much further to get safely out of that wind.

When a gale is accompanied by thick storms of ground drift, or worse, by heavy falling blizzards plus ground drift, or worse still by mist as well, conditions can be extremely serious on the plateaux, making it suffocating and difficult to breathe, hard to open your eyes, impossible to see anything beyond your own feet, and unable to communicate with your party except one at a time by cupping an ear and shouting into it. In these respects the blizzards of the Cairngorms can be as bad as anywhere in the world (see also *Shelter* by P.D.Baird CCJ 17, 184). They can be severe not only on the high plateaux but also on the lower plateaux and moors which, in deep snow, are often even more lacking in landmarks than the high Cairngorms.

The important rule here is to learn to assess the weather throughout every day, even if you are just on a summer stroll, until the habit becomes second nature. There can be nothing ghoulish in doing this. An experienced hillman does it not remotely with possible death or injury in mind, but the better to understand and become part of his environment and so enjoy his days on the hill more. It is useful to learn the meaning of the radio or TV low-ground forecasts, to know how they relate to the weather at higher altitudes in the Cairngorms, to telephone for local and more accurate forecasts, and to learn your own weather lore by reading and local experience. Also, a board at the top end of the car park at Coire Cas gives the latest local forecast of weather for the upper part of Cairn Gorm, including wind direction and speed. Unless you are in mist all day, you will see signs of bad weather coming hours before it actually hits you, and can take common sense action accordingly. For instance, in the Cairngorms a rapid greying of the blue sky is a sign of impending bad weather, and a wide ring round the sun is a fairly sure sign of heavy rain or snow in the Highlands within 12 to 24 hours, though fortunately it often hits only the western hills and does not get through as far east as the Cairngorms. A sudden and sustained change of wind from south, south-west or west to any other direction will quickly bring much colder air to the Cairngorms in winter, apart from a few rare exceptions that you should not rely on; within two hours, easy wet snow can turn into frozen icy sheets. There are many other useful tips about weather in the area, but of course most of these apply elsewhere in Scotland as well.

In a Cairngorms storm the most important aim should be to reach sheltered lower ground as quickly as you can. Above all, do not battle into a gale, especially a snow-laden gale. It exhausts, numbs the mind, and can easily kill. In any case, there is here a simple practical point. Given a storm or hurricane on the plateau, which is not an uncommon event in winter, the strongest and fittest man may be unable to walk even a single metre into the wind, just because of its force. The best plan should therefore be to get the wind flat on your back or at least at one side of your back, and use it to help you along. Even though buffeted uncomfortably, you will travel fast, breathe far more easily, see better, and soon be taking an escape route off the hill. There are always a number of options and escape routes from any place in the Cairngorms. The best one will be different on different occasions; it all depends on wind direction and various other conditions of the moment. The important thing is not to be influenced by having arranged to be back at some scheduled place or time because you have booked a youth hostel or train ticket, a mistake that has led to a few deaths in the area.

One feature which the Cairngorms share with oceanic hills and subarctic hills near coasts is the big fall in temperature with increasing altitude, which is often far greater than in continental mountains. Especially in April to May, it may be a pleasant sunny breezy day at Loch Morlich, warm enough to bask or sleep in the sun. At 1200m, out of the 'rain shadow' in the wide valley below, it can be a roaring gale, snowstorm and dense fog, 9 °C colder or worse.

To assess snow conditions underfoot is not easy. The penalties for failure are greater in the Cairngorms than elsewhere in Scotland. Many have become exhausted by ploughing to the knees or even to the waist in powdery snow, while carrying heavy packs. Here again the long distances and the flat or uphill stretches of these hills tell heavily; on steep slopes you can soon plunge downhill even in deep snow. Few things are more tiring than floundering for miles in deep snow; the speed of the strongest man on flat ground can be reduced to only one kilometre per hour, even with skis on, and without skis can be so dreadfully slow and exhausting that any long journey becomes impossible.

Cross-country routes in snow, starting on Spey and going right over the hills to finish on Dee, or vice versa, or crossing the higher parts of the Mounth, are the most risky walking routes in the Cairngorms region. Elsewhere, and on any individual hill in the Cairngorms, all you usually have to do if bad weather hits you is turn and walk quickly down the way you came up. But on cross-country treks you are always heading into new conditions which may as easily get worse as better, and your route to safety may well involve having to climb uphill on ground not yet seen. You cannot assess this by looking from your morning base; after snowfalls there will often be light hard-packed snow on one side of the Cairngorms but deep heavy powder on the other side. This is something you cannot see until you get to the other side, by which time you may be in trouble. An early start in winter should be common sense

On Cairn Lochan, looking towards Braeriach and Sgoran Dubh

on a long trek; it is crucial to be off the exposed plateaux and the steep hillsides below them by mid afternoon and at the very least well down a sheltered lower glen by dusk. In bad weather you should aim to be at your bothy, car or on a good road while daylight lasts.

For rock and ice climbers the risks are far greater than in other British hills. If a climber has an accident, he will have a very long wait for help as it is so far for a fit member of the party to go to the nearest house or telephone. If you start a hard climb late in the day and finish in fading light or darkness, you take a big risk as the weather may have become much worse during the climb. Once you are off the cliff and on to the plateau, tired and perhaps relaxing mentally at getting safely off the climb, you may have to fight a storm in the dark. Here the early start and sensible anticipation of weather become imperative.

Another special feature of the Cairngorms is that the hill burns roar down in flood during heat waves at the end of a long wintry spell. Then, the vast accumulation of snow on the plateaux and corries melts rapidly and funnels into narrow burns. High streams that are gentle, shallow and meandering during the rest of the year - or even earlier that day in the morning's hard frost - turn into deep, fast, roaring torrents. The snow bridges over these streams become rotten, needing careful testing. You should avoid the snow covered ice over the high lochans in early summer; be particularly careful here, as you can often walk on to one of these lochans without realising it exists, so uniform is the cover of rotting spring snow. The fact that many streams in the area funnel into narrow glens draining big areas of plateau higher up adds another danger in summer and autumn. After torrential downpours, huge quantities of rain over the great plateaux concentrate into tiny burns, which rise in spate more quickly than most burns in other parts of Scotland. Good examples are the Gaick burns, Tarf, Eidart, Caiplich, Allt an Dubh Ghlinne, Mark and Lee.

There has been talk of improving hill safety by erecting lines of cairns over the plateaux of the Cairngorms (for a rebuttal, see B.H.Humble, SMCJ 28, 286), by building strings of huts over the plateaux with flashing lights and sounding devices, and by issuing radios and full survival gear to parties. If accepted, these and other such innovations may well make inexperienced people who would not otherwise climb the more remote hills, take the risk of venturing far out. They might well go with a feeling of security that would be false and could be fatal. It would then take only one human error or technical failure for an irreversible chain of serious troubles to set in. The Feith Buidhe disaster in 1971 is a type case. No rural place can be completely safe; some have died during blizzards even on lowland Aberdeenshire farmland beside public roads. People can continue to enjoy the special character of the Cairngorms in reasonable safety, providing they are made safe for the hills.

H.R.Spencer (1961) *Storm on Macdhui.* CCJ 17, 214. Describes a summer day when it stayed very hot and sunny on low ground but when a storm came very rapidly to the high plateau, with dense mist, torrential rain and violent gales.

G.Tiso (1968) *First footin'. A New Year avalanche.* SMCJ 29, 34. A graphic personal account of a serious avalanche accident at Loch Avon.

A.Watson & J.Duff (1973) *Lessons to youth parties from the Feith Buidhe disaster.* Climber & Rambler 12, 282.

E.Langmuir (1985) *Mountain Craft and Leadership.* Gives a detailed summary on safety in the Scottish hills.

R.Barton & D.S.B.Wright (1985) *A Chance in a Million? Scottish Avalanches.* A good survey of their history and their causes.

Some Noteworthy Accidents, by John E.M.Duff, BEM

Accidents. The first recorded mountain accident was the 'Loss of Gaick' in early January 1800, when Captain John MacPherson of Ballachroan ('The Black Officer') and four others were overwhelmed in bed in a hut near Gaick Lodge by a snow avalanche. All died. A selection of other noteworthy accidents is given below.

Christmas 1804. Five soldiers out of a party of seven died of exposure in the Lairig an Laoigh in a snowstorm, while walking from Edinburgh to their homes in Abernethy for Christmas leave.

January 1928. Thomas Baird and Hugh Barrie died of exposure in Gleann Einich after being overtaken on Braeriach by a snowstorm.

January 1933. Alistair Mackenzie and Duncan Ferrier died of exposure on Cairn Gorm in a storm.

September 1950. James Mackay drowned while crossing the Dee in spate at Corrour. One of his companions, William Pinkerton, died of exposure later that day near the Pools of Dee.

March 1951. Donald McConnach was killed when he walked over a cornice on Beinn a' Bhuird in a 'white-out'.

January 1959. Five men who had set out from Braemar to Glen Doll by Jock's Road on New Year's Day died of exposure in a snowstorm.

April 1960. Nigel Milne and Jean McBain became overtaken by a sudden snowstorm on Cairn Gorm and died of exposure. One body was found near the Lairig an Laoigh path and the other near the Castle rock on the Ailnack.

March 1962. William Garland became lost while skiing on Cairn Gorm in bad weather. Two nights and almost three days later he was found alive near Loch Avon, although meanwhile the weather had been cold with a north wind and bad visibility. On one of the days he had climbed uphill, but slipped and then rolled and fell a long way without injuring himself. After being found and having been given hot drinks, he was able to climb up Coire Raibeirt in deep snow without help.

December 1964. Alexander Mackenzie, Alexander MacLeod and Robert Burnett were buried by a wet snow avalanche on Beinn a' Bhuird, Mackenzie and MacLeod being killed. Burnett was dug out, still conscious but badly frostbitten, after 22 hours.

April 1965. Stewart Turnell and Kenneth Macdonald, who were teenage members of a party of Army Cadets, died of exposure in Glen Derry after the group had been overtaken by bad weather on Beinn a' Bhuird. Several other members of the party were near to death when found, but recovered.

July 1967. John Birss fell on Braeriach and suffered a compound fracture of the leg. He improvised a makeshift splint and crawled for 12 hours to the Lairig Ghru, where he was found next day, 18 hours after the accident.

February 1969. John Dempster and James Wallace died of exposure on Lochnagar after trying to complete a climb on Eagle Buttress at night in a snowstorm.

February 1969. A large avalanche in Coire Cas carried down a party of nine. Some were seriously injured, but none died.

November 1971. Five teenage schoolchildren and an 18 year-old trainee instructress died of exposure at an emergency bivouac in a blizzard at Feith Buidhe, 500 paces east of Lochan Buidhe on the Cairn Gorm-Ben Macdui plateau. A 15 year-old schoolboy and a 20 year-old instructress survived, although both were badly exposed and frost bitten.

March 1976. A party of two men and one woman, all in their 20s, set off from Glen Doll for a round trip of about 10 miles to Cairn Damff. Near Loch Esk, in worsening weather, the woman was unable to continue, and one man stayed with her while the other went for help. The messenger lost his way and became trapped in the ravine of the ice-bound White Water. He eventually managed to escape, but by this time was so weak that he was barely able to surmount a deer fence near Glen Doll Youth Hostel. He finally arrived at the Hostel about 20 hours after setting off. During the extensive search for the other two members of the party, a snow-trac broke through the ice of a frozen lochan, the crew narrowly escaping through the roof panel. Six days after the party set off, the two bodies were found, both probably having died during the first night.

March 1980. An experienced ski-tourer was found dead in Lairig Ghru on the slopes below Sron na Lairige, having possibly skied over the edge in a white-out.

January 1984. On 20 January, four male walkers aged 19 to 24 failed to locate Jean's Hut and camped. The weather further deteriorated on 21st. Possibly either the tent blew down, or they decided to abandon it and walk out. In blizzard conditions three died en route of exposure, one by one. The fourth, aged 21, walked out exhausted on the morning of 22nd. The subsequent search was hampered because many of the rescue team members were storm-bound.

November 1985. A walker left the Lecht Ski Centre to walk to Glenmore, leaving his (road) map in his car, and carrying nothing. He walked via Inchrory to beyond Faindouran, then returned there at dusk. Alarmed by mice in the building, he then walked east down the Avon in the belief he was heading for Nethy Bridge. He was eventually found near Inchrory, safe and well.

March 1986. Winds of over 156 mph caused a series of alarms concerning students under assessment for SMLTB Certificates on the Cairn Gorm - Ben Macdui plateau. Only sound hillcraft prevented serious consequences.

April 1986. During a search for skiers lost from Glenshee Ski Centre, two members of a rescue party fell through a cornice in a white-out, and fell and slid 150m into Caenlochan Glen, suffering shoulder and back injuries.

March 1989. Following a sudden thaw, a solo climber triggered off an avalanche on Lochnagar where Shallow Gully and Central Buttress meet. He was swept away, along with another solo climber and another pair of climbers on Central Buttress. The rope of this pair held, and they were left hanging one on each side of the buttress. A second pair of climbers on Central Buttress were struck by the avalanche, the leader taking the full force. His rope broke and he was swept away, dying soon after from his injuries. His partner, protected by a rock outcrop, was not dislodged. A third pair of climbers on the buttress were unaffected by the avalanche.

August 1989. A father with his daughter of 8 and son of 11 set off from Linn of Dee to walk to Coire Cas car park, with no compass. They went via Loch Etchachan and possibly Ben Macdui, and became lost after being overtaken by bad weather. All three were suffering from exposure, and the girl, unable to continue, was left on the west slopes of Coire an Lochain with her brother while the father tried to get help. They were reported overdue by the mother, and searchers found first the father and then the children. The father and son survived, but the daughter died.

January 1990. One of two climbers preparing for a climb in Coire na Ciche, Beinn a' Bhuird, saw a powder avalanche about 100m above him. Shouting to his companion, he took shelter behind a boulder and was protected from the avalanche, which passed over him. His companion was struck and swept 30m, suffering a broken leg.

September 1990. After traversing Beinn a' Bhuird, a mountain biker fell off his machine near the Sneck, injuring his ankle.

Although the Cairngorms have their share of rock climbing and snow and ice climbing accidents, the word 'exposure' crops up again and again, especially with young people; in fact, 43 out of 104 deaths between 1950 and 1990 occurred from exposure. Very often this kind of accident starts off when a party leaves base with insufficient or inadequate clothing, subsequently is overtaken by bad weather (not necessarily snow) and gets lost because of inefficient navigation. This leads to the classic exposure syndrome of demoralisation, exhaustion and hypothermia, which can kill very rapidly, and especially quickly with children or young people.

The decision to modify a route or to turn back, although often difficult, is of crucial importance. The writer has information on 37 exposure deaths since the year 1800 in the Cairngorms area, up to 1975. Of these, 28, or almost 76%, are attributable to the party failing to turn back when they met bad weather, because they were determined to stick to a previously planned route. Long trips can be dangerous, especially in winter conditions. This is partly because the heavy load necessary for such an undertaking becomes so tiring. Also, people outside may not realise that a party has got into difficulties until it is overdue at the end of the trip, after perhaps several days have already passed.

Avalanches are more common than has generally been supposed. There is some evidence to suggest that airborne avalanches occasionally occur, for example on the steep slopes on the north side of Loch Muick, where a reliable observer has reported extremely fast-moving avalanches. After the Loss of Gaick in 1800, contemporary accounts relate that the bodies of the victims were found mangled and widely scattered, and some of the debris of the hut lay 500 yards away, again suggesting something much more destructive than the usually fairly slow-moving ground avalanche; indeed so terrible was the destruction that local people believed it to have been the work of the Devil. Cornices feature quite often in accidents, and many gully-climbing parties in thaw conditions have become avalanched by a collapsing cornice. Some gullies such as Raeburn's Gully on Lochnagar have been the scene of several accidents like this. Several people have died or injured themselves by walking over cornices, usually in bad visibility. Slopes of hard snow are especially inviting and dangerous to the inexperienced, and many serious injuries have occurred when individuals lost control while glissading and were dashed headlong into boulder fields below.

The corniced edge of Coire an t-Sneachda

In addition to the fairly straightforward if perhaps technically difficult rescues such as known accidents on cliffs, the vast area of the Cairngorms occasionally gives rise to extremely large and prolonged searches for people who have completely disappeared. Some of these last for months and at their peak they involve hundreds of searchers. Notable examples are: Hugh Barrie in 1928 - 3 months; the Glen Doll tragedy in 1959 - 10 weeks; Nigel Milne and Jean MacBain in 1960 - 8 weeks; Dr Fischer in 1960 - many weeks, not found; Brian Goring in 1967 - 8 weeks.

Occasionally, bodies have been found but never identified. The most bizarre of these incidents occurred on the south face of Ben Avon on Tuesday 20 September 1938. A stalker on the beat which includes the remote Allt an Eas Mhoir was searching for a wounded stag, when in the stream he found a badly decomposed human head. A short distance upstream lay the remains of a man, dressed in what appeared to have been a dark suit with a light check. On the bank a plain walking-stick was found, and then a brown leather attache case containing a pair of pyjama trousers, two collars, a toilet roll, a pair of scissors, a box of safety matches and a handbill referring to Simpson's Two Day Tours. On a ledge of rock sat a razor, shaving brush, soap, comb, toothpaste and toothbrush, with a bowler hat nearby. It was estimated that the man had been dead for at least six months. No clue to his identity could be found apart from the fact that the two collars bore the name of an

Aberdeen firm. **Despite intensive** police enquiries, the man's identity has never been established.

In recent **years, incidents** involving gliders, hang gliders and para-gliders, and more noticeably, **mountain bikers,** have been occurring, reflecting changes in recreational use of the **Cairngorms.**

The mountain rescue service should not be confused with the ski rescue services which work during the winter and spring at Cairnwell, Cairngorm and the Lecht ski centres, usually only on the heavily used piste areas.

Lists of mountain accidents and incidents are published annually for the Cairngorms area in the SMC Journal.

WEATHER

The prevailing wind is south-westerly, bringing moist and usually mild air from the Atlantic. As the Cairngorms lie far to the east, they get half or less of the precipitation received by hills just in from the mainland's Atlantic seaboard. The average precipitation on the lower ground in Deeside and Speyside reaches only 70 to 90cm, hardly any more than on the east coast at Aberdeen. These wide main valleys lie in a 'rain shadow' and often bask in sunshine when it is raining and cloudy on the hills on either side, but the narrower valleys like Glen Esk get little of a rain shadow. On the tops of the high Cairngorms, the total precipitation is much heavier, roughly 225cm a year according to a recent figure based on readings from the weather station on Cairn Gorm.

The Cairngorms stand exposed to winds from north around to south-east, which are the main snow-bearing cold winds in Scotland. This is the reason why coastal Aberdeenshire gets far more snow and frost than Skye, and also why the Cairngorms in most years become the snowiest hills in Scotland. As they lie in the centre of Scotland their climate tends to be more continental, with warmer summers and colder winters than on the coasts round about. This again gives more frost and snow in winter, which makes the Cairngorms so attractive for snow and ice climbing and for skiing. You can see this continental effect even very locally as you move in from the east coast. Even with snowfalls coming from the east, the snow line drops lower in altitude as you go inland; the decrease is particularly rapid from east to west along the Hill of Fare and on the hills between Cairn Mon Earn and Glen Dye. You will see the same effect as you go inland up Glen Esk or in the Moray hills.

In the bottoms of deep basins the dense colder air flows downwards on very still nights, producing much harder frosts than on the hilltops. These frost pockets often feature in the news because of their low temperatures, and the area covered by this book has most of Britain's frostiest places: Glen Livet, Grantown, Glenmore Lodge, Aviemore, Braemar, Glen Shee, Tarfside, and Balmoral. Early-morning winter temperatures below - 18 °C are not uncommon there, and temperatures of - 29 °C have been recorded. You will frequently hear the snow squeak under your boots or feel your hands sticking slightly to metal; both happen below - 5°C. During windless sunny days in winter, the cold air stays in the valley bottoms, sometimes producing a frosty fog, while up on the tops it feels much warmer. If you see deer right up on the high ridges in deep snow, this is a good sign of these special conditions.

Usually, however, it becomes much colder as you climb; this is virtually always the case if any wind blows, even with a light wind. P.D.Baird's observations from 1250m on Ben Macdui, 900m above Braemar, showed average temperatures that usually sank about 7°C lower, or 2.2°C per 1000ft (300m) of altitude. In any one month, however, especially in April-June, they could be 9°C lower. The hills are far windier than lower down, and Baird found that wind speeds on Ben Macdui were usually double and sometimes treble those in the valley. Weather instruments, since they were put up on Cairn Gorm, have proved this to be one of the most windy places in the British records, along with some exposed places on coastal islands.

The weather varies a great deal locally. During spring and early summer, and sometimes at other seasons, it may be fairly calm in the valley and yet with a very strong, dry, warm, Föhn-like wind blowing down the lee slopes of the moors and higher hills. Subsidences of dry air on to the summits during anticyclones, and cold winds that are katabatic (due to convection when air drops in altitude as it flows down hillsides) sometimes produce locally violent winds on fine sunny days. Exceptionally, these reach hurricane force and may cause a blizzard of ground drift, when there is virtually a calm day only two kilometres away on ground only 100m in altitude lower down. These severe conditions sometimes occur even in the glens, and can arise suddenly and with little or no warning.

The likelihood of snow increases rapidly as you climb. The average number of days per year with snow falling amounts to about 10 at Dartmoor, 20 in Skye, 50 near Aviemore and about 100 at the top of the chairlift on Cairn Gorm. The average number of mornings with snow lying also increases as you go up, 20 in Skye, 30 near Aberdeen, 60 at Braemar, 100 at 460m at the Derry, and over 150 above 600m at the Derry. Like other Scottish hills, the Cairngorms can have rapid thaws in winter with warm Atlantic winds, but less so than in the far west. In summer you are more likely to get snowfalls here than on any other British range. Snowfalls occur during most years in June and September, during some years in July, and rarely in August; these may involve heavy falls of 30 cm or more, usually with drifting and frost. In May, blizzards can be frequent and very severe. In some years the maximum snow depth above 1100m occurs in mid or late May, but in most years in April. With May storms, the glens and lower hills below 600m usually stay clear, but occasionally, as in 1973, the glens receive a fall of 30cm, with drifting. In 1971 a June snowfall lasted a week on the high Cairngorms.

Much precipitation on the higher hills comes in mist, which in frost condenses on to stones, cliffs, or the existing snow surface as frozen rime. This builds into fantastic frost feathers, and in long snowy winters into a plating a few metres thick. Mist or hill fog also become far more frequent as you climb, but these hills are much less misty than at the same altitude in western Scotland.

In the Cairngorms region you can often use weather information and local experience of it to your advantage. When a wind is dumping heavy rain on Drumochter or Cairn Toul, bright sun often shines on Beinn a' Bhuird, Ben Avon and Mount Keen. These changes can be very local; for instance, when heavy rain and mist from the south-west enshroud the Cairnwell, you may enjoy bright sun as near as at Morven. But the east is not always best. The heavy low mists and sweeping rain or snow over lower Deeside and Lochnagar with winds from north-east to south-east will often give beautiful weather in the upper Spey and Glen Feshie, or even at Derry Lodge. In summer anticyclones, prepare for the weather becoming far hotter than at the coastal strip which may even be enshrouded in cold fog; shade temperatures of 27 °C are not uncommon. Because of these higher temperatures, thunderstorms occur more frequently in such weather than nearer the east coast.

The importance of weather for mountain safety is described under that heading. The frequent and rapid worsening of weather, as well as being a risk to the incompetent or unobservant, form part of the ever-varying character of our hills that is one of their great attractions. Also, the weather can change equally fast for the better, and indeed faster if you are already in the cloud and cannot see the change coming. If you stand in cloud or snowstorm which suddenly clears up to show blue sky and sun and unearthly bright colours on vegetation and stones, it is far more exciting than any day of blue sky from morning to night.

P.D.Baird (1967) *Weather and snow on Ben Macdhui.* CCJ 17, 147. An account of his observations at a weather station near the top of Ben Macdui.

F.H.W.Green (1981) *Climate and weather.* A fairly detailed account on the climate of the Cairngorms in a chapter in *The Cairngorms*, by D.Nethersole-Thompson & A.Watson (1981).

GEOLOGY

The main rock of these hills, as indeed of a vast area to the west and north-west, is schist; it covers nearly all the Morayshire hills, and with only a few interruptions much of the Strath Don hills and the great block of hill country on the Mounth from Drumochter to Glen Esk. Once having been sediments of limestones, sandstones and shales lying on the gneiss underneath, they became metamorphosed or greatly changed by heat and pressure when great movements of the earth 500 million years ago folded them into huge schist mountains. Vast masses of granite formed either from molten rock coming up from far below or from melting of the bottom of the hot folds themselves. These granites make up the high Cairngorms, Lochnagar and Broad Cairn, the Mounth from Mount Keen to Cairn Mon Earn, a big mass at the Hill of Fare and Bennachie, and smaller patches at Geallaig, Ben Rinnes and other hills.

Millions of years later, weather and water wore down these huge peaks to their foundations, more sediments were laid down in layers, and in turn erosion wore these down selectively. The result that you now see is a mere remnant, composed of much of the schist foundation of the folded mountain range plus the masses of once-molten granite that are included in the foundation. Less commonly you also see some smaller intrusions of other rock that have been emplaced into the granite and schist. Some of the intrusions, earlier than the granites, have been metamorphosed to form epidiorite, whereas others which were later than the granites form narrow dykes and sheets. The metamorphic rocks make up fairly continuous narrow bands, such as those formed by the limestone and epidiorite stretching from Blair Atholl past Ballater to Portsoy. The later sedimentary cover has remnants which appear in the sandstones of the Hopeman and Pennan sea-cliffs and the conglomerates of Fowlsheugh.

The geologist goes to places on cliffs, lumps or slabs where the bedrock outcrops on the surface. He then classifies this bedrock by its crystal size, gross appearance and chemical composition. He cannot see most of the bedrock, so has to infer what probably lies under the ground between one cliff or rock outcrop and another. By comparing with many places elsewhere in the world where the layering and the folds can be seen more clearly, he reconstructs the layering and folding that probably went on here. He has to think in terms of three dimensions of rock, based on scattered outcrops on the two-dimensional surface. It is easier to grasp the geological story if you can try to visualise the Cairngorms in three dimensions too, when you come to look at a geological map or read a detailed article or book on the geology.

The massif of the high Cairngorms is a very large foundation mass of granite, which accounts for the infertility of that hill-range. The Lochnagar granite consists of a much smaller circular lump, surrounded by rings of schist and some diorite; this makes it a more fertile massif for vegetation and animals than the Cairngorms. Other big masses of granite occur from Mount Keen to Cairn Mon Earn and from Aberdeen through the Hill of Fare to Dinnet and Bennachie. Geologists classify the schists into two kinds. The Moinian or Central Highland granulites were sandstones which have been metamorphosed by heat and pressure into a fairly uniformly-coloured, layered rock with even sized grains; it covers the Morayshire and Drumochter-Atholl hills. The Dalradian schists further east are far more varied and have given rise to the fertile black and calcareous schists, and the sparkling mica schists.

The local rock greatly affects the appearance and scenery of an area. Granite weathers fairly uniformly as it varies little in its make-up and hardness; one result is the even weathering and typically massive, smoothed slopes so characteristic of the Cairngorms. The scenery in Glen Clova and just east of Braemar, with its more variable schists, diorites and gneisses, looks quite different and more 'western', showing many rocky bluffs as well as a more grassy vegetation. The schists, diorites and gneisses form cliffs with many small, stable holds for climbing, whereas the granite tends to wear uniformly into smooth slabs and faces where the few holds are rounded. Climbing on granite is therefore partly a matter of guile where you use friction to work up chimneys, cracks and slabs, whereas on the schist it involves delicate footwork on the many small holds and a greater choice from the many face routes available. On the coastal cliffs, the contrast appears again with the granite of Longhaven and the small holds on the Dalradian schists east of Macduff. Granite is not always uniform in a corrie, however, as it does not wear uniformly beside fractures and joints. You will find a good place to see this variable weathering and rock appearance near the Mitre Ridge in the Garbh Choire of Beinn a' Bhuird. Some of the granite there looks pale, worn, smooth and sandy-looking, from top to bottom of the cliff. Nearby, masses of darker, harder rock with many cracks also continue from top to bottom of the cliff, and project outwards from the plateau at the Mitre Ridge and Squareface.

The hill Cairn Gorm has given us the name of the smoky quartz crystals which occur there and on many other granite mountains. These 'cairngorms' are usually brown, but blue varieties exist. In the 19th century, many made a

The Shelter Stone Crag

living by searching for these gems in the gravel in the streams of the Cairngorms, or breaking up veins of white quartz on the open hill with hammers. In the 1960s, the bulldozers at Coire Cas dug up a few fine specimens, but the veins on the open hill are largely worked out, and the big trade in 'cairngorms' for Scottish jewellery now depends a lot on stones imported from Brazil. One of the biggest-ever 'cairngorms' is the 5lb one at Invercauld House. There are interesting articles on stones in No. 2 of The Deeside Field in 1925 by A.W.Gibb on *Cairngorms and other local gemstones*, and W.M.Alexander's *The stones of our district* in CCJ 12.

G.S.Johnstone (1966) *British Regional Geology: the Grampian Highlands. 3rd ed.* A good summary for those with a little knowledge of geology. Summarises previous literature.

G.S.Johnstone (1981) *Geology*. In *The Cairngorms*, by D.Nethersole-Thompson & A.Watson. A chapter on the geology of the Cairngorms, Lochnagar and much of the Mounth.

The detailed Geological Survey Memoirs on this region were published from 1896 to the 1910s, and can be seen in the bigger libraries. They are: The Geology of Upper Strathspey, Gaick and the Forest of Atholl (explains sheet 64 of the geological map), The Geology of the District of Braemar, Ballater and Glen Clova (sheet 65), The Geology of Mid Strathspey and Strathdearn (sheet 74), and The Geology of West Aberdeenshire, Banffshire, etc (sheet 75).

LANDFORMS

One of the characteristics of the region is the large area of plateau. The highest level just below 1200m includes all the grand high plateaux of the Cairngorms massif, but the lower plateaux around 800-900m at Drumochter, Gaick, east of Glas Maol, and Clova-Glen Esk, and at 600-750m at Caiplich, north-west of Tarfside, the Ladder Hills, and Cromdale Hills are far more extensive. Before the Ice Age, rivers had cut into these plateaux, producing many smooth steep valleys like upper Glen Gairn. Apart from Spey and Deveron, which run north-east along similar lines in the underlying rocks, the main rivers cut across the lines of the rocks, going south-east off the Angus hills and east at Dee and Don.

The Cairngorms are the best place in Britain for seeing a great variety of tors. These tors and the many patches of deeply rotted rock at the surface are thought to have developed in a warmer and wetter climate than today.

The glaciers later cut into the gentle rolling hills and valleys, producing many steep, rocky hillsides and great cliffed trenches as at Loch Avon, Gleann Einich, upper Glen Clova, Caenlochan and Glen Geusachan. Other ice-cut trenches broke right through a hill mass, as at the Lairig Ghru and between Gaick and Stronphadruig, and several others diverted rivers like Avon, Feshie and Tarf to flow in completely new directions and add to a different river in a different county. The ice wore over many lower hills, which became eroded rocky lumps with ice-smoothed sheets of rock on the side next to the oncoming ice; Craigendarroch and the little hills south of the Burn o' Vat are good examples of these 'roches moutonnes'. The great ice sheet, which probably covered the highest summits, generally moved eastwards, a fact confirmed by the finding of 'erratic' boulders of rock originating from bedrock far to the south-west. Meanwhile, small corrie glaciers went on cutting and formed the grand corries and corrie cliffs that we see today.

Many of the landforms which now make the scenery so varied were formed by rivers flowing beneath and roaring off the huge melting ice-sheet as it began to retreat and thin with the milder climate. These rivers cut the dry cliffed gullies so common in the region; many are small, like the one between Clachnaben and Mount Shade, or even smaller, but some are big, such as Clais Fhearnaig, the Burn o' Vat, and several between the Lairig Ghru and the Eag Mhor of Dorback. Other rivers dumped great masses of gravelly ridges and hillocks along the sides of the wasting lumps of ice. A smaller number of gravelly ridges were once moraines dumped by the ice itself, sometimes forming a low wall across a glen or along its sides.

After the ice-sheet disappeared 10,000 years ago, a few corrie glaciers continued to form moraines. David Sugden and Sheila Rapson have tried to date these moraines in the corrie floors by measuring the diameter - and by assumption the growth rate - of patches of the yellowish-green lichen, *Rhizocarpon geographicum*, on the boulders. (Geomorphologists have used the growth of this lichen in the Arctic and in the Alps to estimate when the boulders were last free of ice.) From this evidence they concluded that the moraine in Garbh Choire Mor of Braeriach may have held glacier ice as recently as the Little Ice Age in the 17th to 19th centuries.

These dates of presumed recent glaciation tally with known advances of the glaciers in Scandinavia and Iceland, and with known periods of worse climate, hard winters, poor harvests and sometimes famines in Scotland itself. Travellers in the Cairngorms at these times gave the impression of seeing large snowfields or snow-capped hills in summer, terms we would scarcely use today. However, in a few summers today, when the snow does lie very extensively, as in 1951, or in 1967 when scores of small patches survived through to the next winter, one can easily see how near the Cairngorms are to having permanent snow caps or glaciers. Probably a drop of only 2 °C in mean temperature would be needed for this to happen again.

Since the ice-sheet melted 10,000 years ago there have been warmer climates, but nevertheless cold enough to form great stone polygons on flat ground, like those in the Arctic. Stone-banked lobes and stone stripes are common on slopes. Other relics of colder times are the huge boulder fields on the plateaux and high ridges, torn by frost and thaw from the ice-smoothed bedrock. However, you can still see where small stone polygons and stone stripes are forming in gravel. Usually the finer soil lies in the middle of the polygon, whereas in the stripes running straight downhill in gravel, the dark soil forms a pattern with a long line of fine gravel next to each line of soil. These often form in spring when movements of stones and gravel due to alternate freezing and thawing are so common. Another type on well vegetated flat high ground, which is very common on low land in north Iceland, occurs in parts of the Cairngorms as a regular pattern of hummocks about 30cm across, with hollows between them. Also, alternate freezing and thawing continue to eat away the cliffs, causing rockfalls, new screes and new exposures of virgin pink granite for the weather to work on.

There are other forms of recent erosion in the Cairngorms. One is the blowing of gravel during gales, another the hagging of peat, and a third is caused by deer or people moving soil or tearing off vegetation under their feet as they walk along. A commoner kind is erosion by water. In heavy rain storms, you may have the alarming experience of watching the ground around you visibly disappearing downhill, especially on the sparsely-vegetated high tops. Water action by massive thawing of big snow fields in early summer often washes out gravel which piles up further down as cones and ridges, often on top of the snow. During the heaviest rain storms, as in 1956, water roars down some hillsides, gouging out a trench up to 3m deep and throwing large masses of gravel and boulders hundreds of metres downhill. You can see some of these trenches well in Glen Geusachan. River floods cause other great deposits of wash-out gravel and boulders, as in Glen Luibeg and beside the Allt Mor by the bridge carrying the ski road to Cairn Gorm.

A.Bremner (1912) *The Physical Geology of the Dee Valley.* 1921 The Physical Geology of the Don Basin. Pioneering exploration on local landforms.

J.B.Sissons (1967) *The Evolution of Scotland's Scenery.* A good book on landforms for those with a little knowledge of geomorphology. Covers all Scotland but some information on the Cairngorms region.

D.Sugden (1981) *Landforms.* In *The Cairngorms,* by D.Nethersole-Thompson & A.Watson. An up to date chapter on the landforms of the region, fairly detailed but written for the lay reader.

S.C.Rapson (1990) *The age of the Cairngorm corrie moraines.* SMCJ 34, 457.

There are also good articles in the Scott. Geog. Mag. by D.L.Linton on river captures (Vols 65, 67, 70) and Problems of Scottish scenery (67), and by P.D.Baird & W.V.Lewis on the Cairngorm floods in 1956 (73). In 1935, A.Bremner published detailed notes on the lochs of the Dee basin in The Deeside Field (No. 6).

SOILS

Soil is a part-living, part inorganic medium which supports most terrestrial plants and animals. Different rocks break down into soil of very different fertility, depending on the rock's lime content but also on the size of the weathered rock grains. However, this can be modified by very local fertile patches or strips of lime-rich rock even on the poorest masses of granite. It has also often been modified by glacial drift. For instance, some ground over granite includes many boulders and gravel deposits which have been dumped there by ice flowing from schist, limestone or diorite hills nearby. An example occurs north of Crathie, where the hill is much richer than ground in the middle of a vast tract of pure granite, such as in upper Glen Dee. Deposits of thick acidic peat may also keep the roots of plants far from the fertile mineral soil which may be lying above lime-rich rocks underneath. Nevertheless, the soils usually reflect the fertility of the underlying rocks. The soils on the granites of the Cairngorms, Lochnagar and Mount Keen are thinner, more acid, more gravelly and thus more infertile than on the schists of the Mounth. On the schists you will also see far less bare unvegetated gravel than at the same altitude on the granite. The lime-rich patches of limestone near Braemar and Tomintoul, of diorite near Crathie, Glen Tilt and Moine Bhealaidh, and of epidiorite in Glen Muick and on Morven, are even more fertile. You will see spectacular changes from heather to grass where rich and poor rocks make contact, as in Glen Builg near Inchrory, on the slopes north of Craig Derry towards the Glas Allt Mor and on the grassy nose at the foot of Glen Baddoch.

The farmland on the granite generally looks poorer and stops lower down the hillside than over the richer rocks; this is why the farms of Strath Don are higher and better than on the granite north of Lochnagar. On the granite of Balmoral, the Cairngorms and Glen Tanar, sheep have never done well and no sheep are now run there. Sheep occur on nearly all other hills and moors except in winter; on the most fertile ones such as around the Glas Maol, upper Glen Callater and Glen Fearnach, the land is renowned for its hill sheep. Hares, voles, moles, red grouse and ptarmigan in most years live at much higher numbers on hills with rich rocks, as around the Cairnwell, than on the granite. So do dunlins, golden plover and meadow pipits.

In the Cairngorms there is a great variety of soil types. Soils have formed there since the last ice left the ground below as a plantless desert without life, 10,000 years ago, but mostly since 7500 years ago. At one extreme, the boulders and screes have been colonised so far only by bacteria and a few lichens which are the first steps in soil formation. On the highest ground about 1200m, severe winds, frost, the short growing season, and in dry periods the lack of water in the well-drained grit, depress plant growth. Tiny pockets of soil here and there support a few sparse mosses and flowering plants, but most of the ground is like a desert, covered with stones, bare gravel or sand. In some places, woolly fringe moss and crowberry have begun to blanket the rocks and form a sparse soil. The bare gravelly plateaux and ridges are covered by a well-drained granite grit, with a thin infertile soil below in which soil organisms and organic matter occur sparsely because plants are so few. A similar type has developed at altitudes below 1100m, with a thicker layer of organic matter lying underneath it. This organic layer often becomes more complete in the more sheltered hollows where snow lies long and where mat grass forms a continuous cover of vegetation. All these hill soils are very acid and infertile, except where lime-rich 'flushes' or springs pour out water rich in calcium and other minerals; you can often spot these places by their bright green appearance and luxuriant vegetation.

On the moors and lower hills the plant cover is usually complete and the organic layer underneath has grown much thicker. The acidity and the washing out of minerals by water reduce the ability of 'decomposer' soil organisms to break down the material from dead plants. The resulting accumulation produces a build-up of peat. On well-drained ground it is called a peaty podzol, with a thin layer of black peat and a reddish hard iron pan below which forms a barrier to roots and water and often causes waterlogging. Thick peat builds up in the poorly drained hollows, in places up to 3m. These thick blankets cover vast tracts from 450-750m and some flat ground up to 900m. Deposits even as little as 30cm thick are rare above 900m, but small patches occur up to 1000m. A similar but less peaty kind of podzol has developed under the pine woods, and less acid, browner soils without peat under birch woods. Good places for you to get to know more about local soils are now common-place in the gravel quarries, bulldozed vehicle tracks, new cuttings on public roads, and gravel slips on river banks. There you will see the different layers or 'horizons' that the soil consists of, clearly exposed in vertical section.

An up to date, more detailed but readable account on the soils of the hill country of the Cairngorms is given in R.Heslop's chapter in *The Cairngorms* by D.Nethersole-Thompson & A.Watson (1981).

VEGETATION

One of the most outstanding features of the region is the variety of its arctic-alpine vegetation. In the Cairngorms massif the special snow-patch vegetation is richer in its extent and number of species than anywhere else in Britain. It also has a remarkable variety, depending on the length of snow cover. Under the longer-lying patches as at Garbh Choire Mor, a sparse brownish or blackish-looking vegetation of tiny mosses and liverworts grows on largely bare soil, with the granite bedrock showing its virgin colour, mostly uncolonised by lichens. Under the less prolonged cover in the snow hollows on the Ben Macdui plateau, where snow usually lies till August, some flowering plants grow such as dwarf cudweed as well as the mosses. In many hollows of the Cairngorms snow lies into June and July; here you will find a vegetation dominated by mat grass, and other grasses in some places where patches of fertile soil occur.

The high Cairngorms and Lochnagar are unique in Britain for the size and variety of their great plateaux and ridges of wind-swept granite grit where the snow usually blows off, sparsely dotted with the three-leaved rush which also grows commonly in subarctic areas. Where the snow lies longer on slightly less exposed ground on the plateaux and open high slopes, the circumpolar dwarf willow commonly creeps low over the ground. Over the schists, where soils are more fertile than over granite, the plateaux tend to be covered with a complete coat of vegetation, mainly composed of stiff sedge mixed with woolly fringe moss. The drier eastern plateaux, such as on the Glas Maol, have more lichen and less woolly fringe moss. Boggy streams with wide, braided, shallow channels dotted with mosses are a special characteristic of the highest plateaux in the Cairngorms above 1100m, and occasionally occur down to 850m.

On the lower slopes from 600 to 750m, where snow cover is decreasing, blaeberry dominates the small deep hollows that hold the snow longer; the top of the Cairnwell road is a good place to see this. On the windswept gravelly ridges up to 900m a prostrate mat of heather forms the main vegetation. The bouldery or stony slopes from 600 to 1100m, where snow usually blows off, support a sparse heath of blaeberry and crowberry, with pure crowberry on some exposed dry boulder fields.

The arctic-alpine vegetation of the crags is outstanding, especially on the fertile lime-rich crags of Glen Doll, Glen Callater, Caenlochan and the head of Gleann Einich. On a single hill, only Ben Lawers is better in Britain, but as a whole hill-range, the Lawers group lacks the great variety of the Cairngorms or especially that of the

Mounth between the Glas Maol and Glen Clova where rare arctic willows and many other uncommon species grow in fair abundance locally.

For both plants and animals, you will often see a big change around 750m, where you pass from an obvious arctic-alpine zone with many screes and much blaeberry and crowberry, down into a less stony moorland zone dominated by long heather. The point of transition varies from 600 to 900m, depending on snow cover, exposure, and kind of ground; you see it well in Glen Clunie at the foot of Meall Odhar or on a shelf on the Cairnwell uphill from the top car park. The transition also involves a change from ptarmigan to red grouse.

On the moorland zone below there is again a varied flora on lime-rich crags near Tomintoul and elsewhere. On patches of well drained fertile soil in the glens you see bright green turfy grasslands, Glen Lui being a good example. Many were once farmed or used for summer cattle grazings, but now are grazed mainly by deer and hill sheep; they make excellent walking. On the poorer, more peaty soils in some of the flat glens like the middle part of Glen Derry, and on the peaty tops of some flat low hills, you will also see grassland, but of a poorer sort with much purple moor grass, deer grass and cotton grass. The walking becomes much heavier on the softer, hummocky surface, except by the well drained burn-sides where you often come upon short turf again.

By far the main vegetation on the moorland slopes consists of heather. Mixed through it grows much sedge, rush, bog asphodel, cotton grass, purple moor grass and cross-leaved heath on the wetter western hillsides and on poorly drained bogs in the drier east. On blanket bog, where the peat is a metre or more thick, the abundant cotton grass gives a special greyish-brown colour to the hills. You will find this blanket bog on very shallow slopes. In places it has eroded into peat hags with some of the most difficult walking in the region as well as some of the hardest navigation in bad weather. You see this country well on the Glen Dye side of the Cairn o' Mount, on the low hills between Tarfside and Glen Muick, the Ladder Hills, and some of the Atholl-Gaick upper moors.

Much of the drier moorland, as in Morayshire, Banffshire, Donside, lower Deeside and Angus is dominated by a fairly uniform sward of heather, which colours whole hillsides a warm pink in August and September. On well drained fairly fertile dry ground, such as in lower Glen Clova and at the Muir of Dinnet, bell heather, bearberry and petty whin are mixed through the heather, along with various other flowering plants. When you visit the higher fertile moors such as north of Crathie, you will see that more blaeberry, cowberry, bearberry and scrub juniper are the signs of greater fertility. The less fertile moorland slopes support a much more uniform sward of heather. Places to watch out for are the bright green mossy flushes of Sphagnum on all these moors; a step into them can land you up to your chest or deeper in a quagmire.

Most of the moorland is artificial, maintained as open heath by burning, grazing, and tree-cutting. This produces economic benefit in grouse and deer for the estates and in sheep and cattle for the hill farmer. There are a few patches of forest left up to 600m, with scattered small trees up to 670m. In the peat bogs you will see plenty of roots up to these heights on now treeless moors. Forests and scrub would spread over all this ground again if burning and stock grazing were stopped; you can see the process at work on the Muir of Dinnet and on Geallaig Hill west of Ballater. Burning and grazing have wiped out most of the forests, and have completely obliterated hill scrub as a common type of vegetation, apart from a few scattered good stands of juniper on many moors, such as at Morven Lodge. In subarctic and arctic countries a dense scrub of dwarf birch and willow, up to lm high, spreads above the tree-line and sometimes in tongues or patches uphill, occupying the land between the trees and the prostrate ground vegetation of the arctic-alpine zone. In Scotland it has virtually disappeared from the open hill, but the Cairngorms region retains the best relict patches of it in Britain, on craggy ledges in the Glen Doll hills away from the mouths of sheep and deer. It also has a few good though very small patches of dwarf birch and willow in other glens.

The boreal forests of pine and birch give this region much of its outstanding character. Especially in Strath Spey, the great natural forests of Abernethy, Rothie-murchus, Glen Feshie, Glen More and Dulnain together make up the biggest area in Britain that is largely timbered with natural forest. The junipers grow tall in these woods, and they and the plants under the trees add to the boreal character; examples are the abundant chickweed wintergreen and creeping lady's tresses, and the rarer St Olaf's candlesticks and twin flower.

The literature on vegetation is now extensive, particularly in recent years when much ecological research has been done in the region. Only general reviews or else semi-popular yet authoritative treatments are mentioned below; however, these give references to the many definitive papers with the original data, for anyone who wishes to read further.

J.G.Roger (1956) *Flowering plants of the Cairngorms.* CCJ 17, 57.

J.Raven & M.Walters (1956) *Mountain Flowers.* New Naturalist. Two chapters on the Cairngorms and a third on the early pioneering botanists.

H.M.Steven & A.Carlisle (1959) *The Native Pinewoods of Scotland.* The best book on the old woods, with two chapters on the Cairngorms.

A.Watson (1977) *Wildlife potential in the Cairngorms region.* Scott. Birds 9, 245. Reviews what is there and what could be there if land practices changed.

D.A.Ratcliffe (1981) *The Vegetation.* A long chapter in *The Cairngorms,* by D.Nethersole-Thompson & A.Watson. Describes vegetation in all parts of the region, including also some hills to the west, such as Creag Meagaidh, Monadh Liath and the Ben Alder range.

Dotterel nesting on the tundra of the high Cairngorms

WILD ANIMALS

The region is unique in Britain for the richness of wild animals in its relict boreal forest and on the arctic-alpine tops. On the high ground of the Cairngorms massif lies a fairly large area of natural habitat largely untouched by man. Many species of insects, spiders, and other invertebrates on that high ground also thrive on lowland, good examples being the big harvestman *Mitopus morio* and the shiny dark beetle *Carabus problematicus*, let alone the house fly, the cleg and the midge! However, many of the hill invertebrates have a largely arctic distribution. Some species are rare, such as the high-arctic sawfly *Amauronematus abnormis* which has been found in Britain only on the Braeriach plateau, feeds on least willow and has flightless females. The arctic weevil *Otiorrhynchus arcticus* is more common, as are the dung beetle *Aphodius lapponum*, the water beetles *Agabus arcticus* and *Dytiscus lapponicus*, and the ground beetles *Amara alpina* and *Miscodera arctica. Zygaena exulans* the mountain burnet, a moth common in Lapland, has been found in Britain only on high ground south of Ben Avon. These examples show that for insects the Cairngorms are a piece of the Arctic in the middle of Scotland, remaining as a relic from colder, glacial times.

The arctic affinities are rich for birds also. The ptarmigan, most arctic of birds, has its main Scottish centre in the hills of the Cairngorms region, where its populations live at a higher density than anything recorded in the Arctic. Another arctic bird - the snow bunting - nests on the higher Cairngorms among boulder fields near big snow wreaths and mossy flushes, in higher numbers than on other Scottish hills. The dotterel nests on the vast arctic tundras of northern Siberia and Lapland, and also here; most dotterels nesting in Britain are on the Cairngorms and the Mounth. You may see this beautifully-coloured little plover, so confiding when breeding that the old folk used to call it *An t-amadan mointich - the moss fool -* on the high bare grasslands and gravelly tracts of the highest plateaux. Since 1950, many bird watchers have seen a snowy owl on the Ben Macdui - Cairn Gorm plateau in several years. Although dunlins and golden plovers also nest on low moors in Britain, their world distribution is mainly arctic, and so it comes as no surprise to find that they breed over much of the arctic-alpine zone in the Cairngorms; in some years they are particularly abundant on the Mounth. In autumn and spring the high passes and valleys become good places for seeing migrating northern birds, especially wild geese, redwings, fieldfares, some wild duck and a variety of small birds.

The lower hills and moors below the arctic-alpine zone in the Cairngorms are now of some international importance for the conservation of peregrine falcons. Almost everywhere in its vast world range the peregrine has declined dangerously because of contamination with insecticides and other pollutants. In many places like the Arctic where these chemicals are not used, the peregrines pick them up by having to migrate south in winter to where they are widely applied. Our peregrines in the North-east Highlands can stay at home in winter, as their prey is so abundant on these less contaminated hills. The golden eagles here also became less contaminated than in western Scotland where for some years they picked up poisons from eating dead sheep treated with chemical dips.

A few scattered pairs of greenshanks nest on the boggy glens and forest bogs. On some of the lower moors, red grouse and mountain hares reach very high population densities, and a big variety of other moorland birds nests here. Particular features are the good stocks of black grouse, snipe, curlews, golden plover and other waders, the nesting hen harriers on lower moors, and the many goosanders up the high open or wooded glens. Wild cats now breed fairly commonly on moors and in woods over the whole region except on farmland and on the highest tops, and foxes occur throughout. Red deer also live throughout the area except on farmland, some woods, and some eastern moors, at a high density. A special feature is the many roe deer that live on the open lower hills and moors all the year round, even up to nearly 600m.

In the natural pine woods, the area excels in Scotland for its many crested tits in Spey and Moray, and its nesting Scottish crossbills of Spey, Moray and Deeside. For siskins, lesser redpolls, capercaillie, and red squirrels, it contains some very good habitats with high densities. Other interesting species, which are typical of the northern boreal forest of Scandinavia and Russia, do not breed regularly or commonly. However, their occurrence in the Cairngorms in spring, with records of nesting for most of them, shows that the remnants of boreal forest here do attract them. Examples are the redwing, fieldfare, brambling, waxwing, green and wood sandpiper, Temminck's stint, whimbrel, spotted redshank, red-spotted bluethroat, goldeneye, whooper swan and Slavonian grebe. Some of these occur at boreal forest bogs and forest lakes, where again the area is unique for Britain in its richness.

The variety of the forest shows again in the fact that, here also, many typically southern or central European summer migrants occur or breed near or at their northern Scottish limit. They do so in pine and birch woods as in their Scandinavian boreal-forest habitats, not in habitats more like England; the wryneck, garden warbler, chiffchaff, blackcap and pied flycatcher are a few examples.

Southern marsh-birds also occur here near their northern limit for Britain, namely the grasshopper warbler, spotted crake and marsh harrier. For variety of forest and loch birds, Spey is slightly richer than Dee, but for moorland and arctic-alpine ground slightly the other way round. The Spey ospreys have become a big tourist attraction. On the rivers, ringed plovers, common terns and oystercatchers nest right to the centre of Scotland.

To entomologists, the Strath Spey woodland zone is one of the most exciting places in Britain. In the boreal forests of pine and birch and on the nearby moorlands they have found a rich group of boreal species, with many rare insects and some species new to science. Others are common and characteristic of the old forests, like the red wood ants, which have not yet colonised and formed their great mounds in the new pine woods in lower Deeside near Banchory, but which live abundantly in new plantations next to the old forests.

In 1954, domestic reindeer from Swedish Lapland were introduced to a low forest bog in Glen More. They did not thrive, but a later introduction to a fenced area that included some windswept hill on Airgiod-meall was successful. They are often on the northern corries of Cairn Gorm and on the high plateau towards Ben Macdui.

A fairly detailed review describing the wild animals of the region is in *The Cairngorms* by D.Nethersole-Thompson & A.Watson (1981), with separate chapters on insects, fish, birds and mammals. A.Watson's *Hill birds of the Cairngorms* in Scott. Birds 4, 179, summarises information on the birds from tree-line upwards.

NATURE CONSERVATION

The region of the Cairngorms, Lochnagar and the Mounth is outstanding for its very large continuous areas of high country resembling the Arctic, its great tracts of natural pine and birch forest and forest bogs, and the soils and wildlife of plants and animals that go with them. For these features it is certainly unique in these islands. Of course you can see relict pine forest and arctic-like summits in other parts of Scotland, but nowhere else in Britain is there any other region which contains such a variety and extent of these habitats and their associated wildlife. It is also unique in Scotland for the great extent and variety of its lochs, lime-rich crags and vast tracts of moorland and glen. Many naturalists have come here for generations, and the

An isolated survivor of the Caledonian pine forest facing Braeriach at the foot of Gleann Einich

area's value for scientific research also ranks very high. It has now become essential to plan so that the most outstanding or easily damaged features of this hill country are safeguarded, and so that interested folk who go there in future will enjoy them as much as we do. If there are to be big new developments for large numbers of people who simply want open-air recreation but not necessarily the special kinds of it available in the Cairngorms, they should be put in parts of the country that are not outstanding or fragile.

It was for these reasons that the Nature Conservancy declared its large National Nature Reserve in the Cairngorms massif, another at Caenlochan-Clova, smaller ones at Morrone near Braemar and at the Muir of Dinnet, and Sites of Special Scientific Interest in the east Cairngorms, the Ladder Hills and elsewhere. Apart from Invereshie and Inshriach which the Nature Conservancy (now Scottish Natural Heritage) have owned, these reserves entail agreements with the landowners, which have to be periodically renewed. The Scottish Natural Heritage agency has to be consulted and its agreement secured before any developments on these National Nature Reserves are allowed; therefore it has power to object to developments which threaten the integrity of the reserve, such as new roads or ski lifts. It also gives advice to planning authorities and the Secretary of State for Scotland about planning applications for developments in nature conservation areas.

The reserves are much used for scientific research by the Institute of Terrestrial Ecology, universities, and others, mainly in ecology. Most of this is aimed at getting a better understanding of wildlife and its environment; as new problems keep cropping up which may possibly threaten the area, the Scottish Natural Heritage agency will thus be in a stronger position to take reliable decisions about them and manage the whole area better.

One good reason for keeping a close watch on new roads and other developments in an outstanding area like the Cairngorms is that no one can say now what important information the researchers may turn up in the future. For instance, the interesting work by D.Sugden leading to suggestions of possible glaciation in the Cairngorms in the 17th - 19th centuries could not have been attempted if the necessary research material - in this case the small corrie moraines - had been disturbed by bulldozers for roads or other developments. Sometimes it is not enough just to maintain things as they are, and active management of habitats or wildlife may be needed. For example, some forests have decayed so far that the lack of regeneration due to excessive deer numbers eating the young seedlings led the Nature Conservancy to fence off plots and plant trees from local seed. Deer stalking by the owners still goes on, and indeed the shooting of deer is necessary to prevent marauding of deer to other people's ground where they are a pest to farmers and foresters.

The Scottish Natural Heritage agency welcomes people, provided they do not abuse the land and the rights of future generations by picking or digging plants, leaving litter, allowing dogs which are untrained to wildlife to roam free, and lighting fires in dry weather. The agency has a base and office at Achantoul, north of Aviemore, in a building also used by the Meteorological Office and the Cairngorm Mountain Rescue Team. The wardens will gladly give you advice and information, including leaflets on the Cairngorms Reserve, and you should tell them if you see any damaging behaviour or hear of any proposal likely to threaten the area. Other nature reserves with access to the public are owned by the Royal Society for the Protection of Birds at Abernethy including Loch Garten, upper Glen Avon, and the fen marshes at Loch Insh.

CONSERVATION OF WILD LAND AND LANDSCAPE

The beauty, wild landscape and scenery of the Cairngorms are a great attraction for tourists, and to many people give priceless physical enjoyment, mental renewal and peace. Some parts of the high ground are real wilderness, and the native forests also have much wilderness character. However, the landscape quality of some parts of the area has been much reduced by new vehicle tracks, chairlifts, poorly designed hotels and other developments. There are plans for further developments, and the huge increase of countryside recreation threatens the beauty that people come to see.

Conservationists have no desire to halt all development or to prevent downhill skiers or any other recreational group from enjoying their sport. What they suggest is that every group such as downhill skiers can have most of that they want, without entailing the free-for-all of development which would completely spoil the sport or interest of some other group such as climbers, walkers and cross-country skiers. This is the point of planning. With the increase of pressures on the hills, future climbers cannot have the same freedom as in the past. People can motor, camp, boat, fish or walk anywhere they like and still have nature and wild land and no conflicts with the interests of others, but only if a very few of them are doing it. As a few grew to a great many after 1945, so did locked gates in the Cairngorms region become the rule, low-ground bothies become demolished by the owners because of vandalism, theft and litter, and camping become restricted.

The Countryside Commission for Scotland, which was set up in 1968, merged in 1992 with the Nature Conservancy Council for Scotland to become the Scottish Natural Heritage agency. It works with local authorities to plan for recreation in the countryside and to advise the Government on the payment of grants for recreation projects.

W.H.Murray (1962) *Highland Landscape, a Survey*. A far-sighted book describing areas of outstanding landscape, including two chapters on the Cairngorms and Balmoral Forest.

A.Watson & N.Bayfield (1973) *The need for a conservation code for the hills*. Recreation News Suppl. 10, 7. Describes some of the conservation problems due to more people on the hills, and gives a simple code for visitors. Based on experience in the Cairngorms.

Countryside Commission for Scotland (1978) *Scotland's Scenic Heritage*. Describes the National Scenic Areas of the Cairngorms, Deeside & Lochnagar, and River Tay (Dunkeld).

K.Curry-Lindahl, A.Watson & R.D.Watson (1982) *The Future of the Cairngorms*. North-East Mountain Trust. Summarises conservation problems and suggests some solutions.

J.Crumley (ed) (1988) *Cairngorms at the Crossroads*. Scottish Wild Land Group. Well illustrated articles on the conservation problems of the Cairngorms.

J.W.H.Conroy, A.Watson & A.R.Gunson (eds) (1990) *Caring for the High Mountains - Conservation of the Cairngorms*. Centre for Scottish Studies & Natural Environment Research Council. Proceedings of the Conference on Conservation of the Cairngorms. Contains papers on nature conservation, landscape conservation, human impact, and local social and economic problems.

Countryside Commission for Scotland (1991) *The Mountain Areas of Scotland*. Reviews the problems and suggests proposals intended to help solve them.

J.Crumley (1991) *A High and Lonely Place. The Sanctuary and Plight of the Cairngorms*. A strong plea for the wild landscape and its wildlife.

SELECTED BIBLIOGRAPHY

There is such a vast literature on this district that only a brief sketch can be given here. An early record of a visit to the Cairngorms is from 1618, in The Pennyless Pilgrimage of John Taylor the 'Water Poet'. Travelling from Glen Esk over the Mounth at Mount Keen. he came to Braemar, saw 'Mount Benawne' and watched the Earl of Mar's hunt. Carrying on to 'Ruthen' in 'Bagenoch' presumably by Glen Feshie, and to Darnaway, he then headed south by 'Stroboggi' and the 'Carny Mount to Breekin'. P.H.Brown reproduced his tour, in *Early Travellers in Scotland,* an interesting book reprinted again in 1973. Blaeu's *Atlas Novus*, published at Amsterdam in 1654, contains maps by Scottish geographer Robert Gordon of Straloch. They were based on work by Timothy Pont, including a notably accurate description of the region in Latin, which was translated centuries later by C.G.Cash (CCJ 5, 196; and 6,18). Gordon's map mentions Carn-gorum, Bini bourd, Bin-Avin, Bini vroden, L. Avin and L. Garr.

The next general traveller was Pennant in 1769. In his *Tour of Scotland* (1774) he wrote of the 'naked summits, many of them topped with perpetual snow'. The Statistical Account (1791-99) describes all the parishes, each written by the parish minister, and gives much information on the district, especially on the local people and their life. Around 1786, Col T.Thornton, game shooter, in his *Sporting Tour* (1804) visited Strath Spey, climbed Sgoran Dubh (p 157), and first used the term 'Cairngorms', referring to the 'Aurora peeping over the immense Cairngorms'. In 1796 the Hon Mrs Murray Aust crossed Drumochter to Aviemore, and during 1801, in her *Companion and Useful Guide to the Beauties of Scotland* (1810), she writes how she returned to Rothiemurchus, 'that most enchanting place', climbed Cairn Gorm, and visited Loch Einich. She then rode through Lairig an Laoigh and advises 'all travellers, in search of uncommonly fine scenery, not to omit visiting every part of the district called Braemar, the charms of which have hitherto been unheard of, and unseen, except by the very few'.

Some pioneering scientific descriptions of the Cairngorms appear in the *General View of the Agriculture of Aberdeenshire* (1811) by the Rev G.S.Keith, who in 1810 climbed some of the hills with a barometer to measure their height (p 102); his account was reprinted in 1968 in CCJ 17, 238. In 1814, G.F.Robson published his *Scenery of the Grampian Mountains*, a book with 40 etchings, descriptive notes and a map, on the hills from Ben Lomond to the Cairngorms, including 11 on 'Lochan-y-Gar' and the Cairngorms, and later he published an edition with coloured plates in 1819. Artists in those days often exaggerated the steepness of the hills, but most of his etchings look fairly reasonable, all catch the mystery of these hills, and the descriptive notes show an observant eye. Lord Cockburn's *Circuit Journeys* (1837-54) speaks enthusiastically of the view from the Inverness road west of Carrbridge, 'the approach to Aviemore becomes interesting soon after the waters begin to flow Speyward, till at last the full prospect of these glorious Cairngorms, with their forests and peaks and valleys, exhibits one of the finest pieces of mountain scenery in

Britain'. From her base at Balmoral, Queen Victoria climbed Ben Macdui, Lochnagar and other hills, and wrote lovingly and in observant detail about some of this country in her *Leaves from the Journal of Our Life in the Highlands*, published in 1868.

Walking from Aberdeen to the hill, and thinking nothing of striding out across Scotland from Aberdeen to his home in the far west, Prof W.MacGillivray did much exploration of the Cairngorms and Deeside hills. His book on *The Natural History of Dee Side and Braemar*, published in 1855, is a fascinating account by this all-rounder, covering geology, plants, animals, pioneering ecological descriptions, the hill folk and their way of life. *The Guide to the Highlands of Deeside*, appearing in 1831, and again in 1869 as the *New Deeside Guide* by J.Robertson, was the first guidebook in our area, but did not describe the hills in any detail. Of more interest to walkers is *The Cairngorm Mountains*, published in 1864 by historian J.H.Burton; it gives some description of these hills and appreciates the value of fine scenery in Scotland.

Some later books and publications are listed below. In addition, since 1893 the Cairngorm Club in Aberdeen has published a Journal which contains a large amount of material about our region that is important for anyone with a serious and wide interest in the area. From the late 1940s till 1964, the Etchachan Club in Aberdeen also printed or duplicated a Journal with much information on the area, especially on the post-war exploration of rock and ice climbing. The Deeside Field Club has published issues of The Deeside Field with interesting papers on topography and a great variety of subjects on Deeside. Only general literature is described below; other more specialist papers are noted under the separate sub-headings of this Introduction and in the Further Reading at the end of each chapter. Only books that the author considers authoritative and worth reading have been mentioned, so as to save space; much of the huge literature available is largely repetitive.

A.I.McConnochie (1885) *Ben Muich Dhui and His Neighbours*. (1890) *Bennachie*. (1891) *Lochnagar*. (1893) *Deeside*. (Prob. 1897) *Queen Victoria's Highland Home and Vicinity*. (1898) *The Royal Dee*. (1900) *Donside*. (1902) *Strathspey*. (1902) *Guide to Aviemore and Vicinity*. A series which includes some good descriptions of the hills, glens and local history. Several were reprinted in the 1980s.

E.Grant (1899) *Memoirs of a Highland Lady*. A personal account of local life in Rothiemurchus in the early 1800s.

W.Forsyth (1900) *In the Shadow of Cairngorm*. A general book on life and traditions in Abernethy and Strath Spey.

G.M.Fraser (1921) *The Old Deeside Road*. Good descriptions of old roads, bridges and villages in Deeside.

S.Gordon (1925) *The Cairngorm Hills of Scotland*. A 20th-century classic, one of the best books for fine descriptions of the Cairngorms massif, with much information on traditions and wildlife.

V.A.Firsoff (1949) *The Cairngorms on Foot and Ski*. A mainly personal account of the author's journeys in the Cairngorms massif.

J.R.Allan (1952) *North-East Lowlands of Scotland.* A book on farmland, town, people and way of life.

C.Gibson (1958) *Highland Deerstalker.* Memories of a deer stalker from upper Glen Clova and Glen Muick, written by a friend.

J.Walton (ed) (1960) *Glen More. National Forest Park Guide.* A booklet on the Glen More Park and nearby ground, with useful bibliography.

H.L. Edlin (ed) (1963) *Forests of North-East Scotland.* Brief chapters describing scenery, geology, vegetation, wildlife, landscape, history, and other aspects of the entire region, not just of the forests.

British Association (1963) *The North-East of Scotland.* A survey of the natural features of the whole area including the hills, climate, rocks, soils, plants and animal life, in addition to human history, population changes, local dialects and other aspects of human culture. Although the chapters are brief, this is the best general introduction to the region, its main features, and its people. Mostly a semi-technical style and content.

D.Fraser (1966) *Discovering Angus and Mearns.* Includes information on topography and local history.

Technical Planning Group (1967) *Cairngorm Area.* A Scottish Office survey of skiing potential and possible tourist development. Urged many new roads through Tilt, Feshie and other glens and on to a few hills, and new ski lifts on various hills. Largely ignored the conservation-wilderness case. It made proposals for huts and paths without consulting mountain rescue organisations; these proposals are dangerous for hill safety.

T.Weir (1970, 1972) *The Scottish Lochs. Vols 1 & 2.* Fine photographs of many lochs in the Cairngorms, plus brief descriptions of them and the surrounding country.

A.Gray (1970) *The Big Grey Man of Ben Macdhui.* A book giving detailed case histories.

R.Smith (1980) *Grampian Ways.* Melven Press. Describes walks over the Mounth tracks.

D.Nethersole-Thompson & A.Watson (1981) *The Cairngorms,* Melven Press, Perth. A book on the history, physical background, natural history, sport, conservation and future of most of the area covered by this District Guide, but omitting Moray and Nairn and the North-east lowlands and coast.

CHAPTER 1

Speyside, Moray and Nairn

Meall a' Bhuachaille	810m	991 115
Geal Charn	821m	090 127
Ben Rinnes	840m	255 354

Speyside is one of Scotland's longest, most varied, and beautiful hill valleys. This chapter emphasises the finest part, Strath Spey - the wide valley in the middle reaches of the Spey - but includes the hills of the lower reaches, the counties of Moray and Nairn, and that part of the Findhorn catchment east of the A9 road from Perth to Inverness. The *Central Highlands* District Guide covers those parts of Speyside west of the A9.

There has been some erroneous comment on the name Strath Spey. The name Spey Valley has been criticised as an anglicisation which it is, and some say it should be Strath Spey. However, to local indigenous people Strath Spey is the wide valley between Nethy Bridge and Aviemore, and above Aviemore lies Badenoch. The name Speyside covers the whole catchment from source to mouth.

The upper stretches of the Spey from Newtonmore to Kincraig are prone to flooding, giving rise to the district's name of Badenoch ('badinach) from Gaelic Baideanach or drowned land. Upstream from Loch Insh lies a huge marsh, where the river drops only 15m of altitude in a distance of 20 kilometres. Badenoch's two main villages - Newtonmore and Kingussie - nestle below the lower wooded slopes of the Monadh Liath. The name Newtonmore comes from the English translation of Baile Ur an t-Sleibh or new town of the moor, the nearby Kingussie being Cinn a' Ghiuthsaich (keen'yoosee) or end of the pine wood.

The valley widens below Aviemore, with Rothiemurchus stretching away far to the east, and spreads even more at Boat of Garten and Nethy Bridge. Here the huge sweep of flat forest, moorland and low hills rolling out to Dorback in the east and to the Monadh Liath in the west gives a feeling of great space, more like a valley in Sweden or Canada than one in Scotland. These lower hills are seldom visited by climbers, but to the walker who likes exploring new upland country which still retains a strong link with its past despite the big influx of outsiders, this countryside offers one of the most varied and interesting tracts of any in Scotland.

From this whole district the Cairngorms show their north and west sides as a single great front, so there are many places in the flattish valley below where you

ACCESS

The A9 Perth-Inverness road and adjacent railway give easy access to Newtonmore and Kingussie in upper Speyside, and the A96 and nearby railway from Aberdeen to Inverness cross the lower Spey east of Elgin. From the lower Spey, public roads go up both sides of the river to Kingussie. The road from Aviemore via Coylumbridge ('koilyum') to Loch Morlich and the Coire Cas ski area gives good access to the north side of the Cairngorms massif. The central part of Speyside from Kingussie down to Nethy Bridge, centred on Aviemore, has long been a good base for the northern and western parts of the main Cairngorms massif, and is now the main base for people going into the massif. Boat of Garten, Nethy Bridge and Grantown, all at about 200m, lie further from the Cairngorms than Aviemore, but make very good centres for visiting Abernethy and the other forests, lochs, and lower hills and moors of Strath Spey.

PUBLIC TRANSPORT

Rail: Perth-Inverness stopping at Aviemore and other stations.
    Aberdeen-Inverness stopping at Elgin and Forres.
Bus: Perth-Inverness stopping at Aviemore.
    Grantown via Aviemore to Coire Cas ski area.

ACCOMMODATION AND BOTHIES

In Speyside there are many hotels, boarding houses, and houses offering bed and breakfast, as well as restaurants or cafes in all towns. Aviemore has many facilities, including shops for outdoor clothing. Glenmore Lodge is the Scottish Sports Council's base for courses in climbing, canoeing and other outdoor sports, and also offers self-catering accommodation. Ardenbeg Bunk House at Grantown-on-Spey provides private bunkhouse accommodation. There are youth hostels at Aviemore, Kingussie, Glen More and Tomintoul.

The SMC's Raeburn Hut is at 636 909 on the A889 8 kilometres from Dalwhinnie, and the Ladies Scottish Climbing Club hut of Milehouse at 839 043 near Kincraig. The Edinburgh section of the Junior Mountaineering Club of Scotland has a hut called Jock's Spot at 667 947 midway between Laggan and Newtonmore, and the Mountaineering Council of Scotland has Mill Cottage near Feshiebridge, at 844 047. Visiting climbers who are members of mountaineering clubs may make bookings to stay in these huts through their club secretaries. Ryvoan Bothy near Glen More is at 006 115.

MAPS

Ordnance Survey 1:50,000 Sheets 27, 28, 35 and 36

can have magnificent views of these hills. The great dark green carpet of Rothiemurchus Forest makes a fine foreground. Some especially good viewpoints from the low ground are from the railway station or high in the tall hotels at Aviemore, from the Nairn road between Lochindorb and Duthil, from the A9 road west of Carrbridge, and best of all the nearer view from the end of the public road at Whitewell, where the great forest of Rothiemurchus makes a wonderful setting.

GEOLOGY, LANDFORMS AND WILDLIFE

The Moine granulites or schists dominate the Monadh Liath, the moors and hills of Moray and Nairn, and the hills of Cromdale. Patches of limestone occur near Ord Ban and in Strath Avon, and granite at Ben Rinnes. This district contains some of the

The northern slopes of the Cairngorms from Rothiemurchus Forest

best examples of cliff-sided glacial meltwater channels in Scotland, as at the Eag Mhor near Dorback and at Stac na h-Iolaire south of Mam Suim. Loch Morlich and most of the other lochs in the area occur because the glaciers dumped gravel and boulders which dammed up the water coming from the hills after the ice had all melted. The great conical hillocks south-west of Loch Morlich, called the Sidhean, are fine examples of one type of glacial landform. At the forest edge near the road to Cairn Gorm, the broad back from the Allt Mor to Airgiod-meall is one of the largest glacially formed ridges in Scotland; the burn of Allt Mor has cut through it, and big landslides which were caused during spates show well the kind of gravelly material making up the ridge. Floods since 1950 have dumped much of the gravel from this landslide near to where the road to Cairn Gorm crosses the bridge over the Allt Mor.

For wildlife, Strath Spey is a place for superlatives. The natural pine forests are bigger and more varied than anywhere else in Britain and generally in a better state of regeneration, so the flora and fauna that go with the boreal pine forest are also richer here than elsewhere. Strath Spey has the best set of forest lochs and forest bogs in Britain. Loch Insh (Gaelic innse, 'eensh), or meadow loch and its neighbouring marsh are now a reserve run by the Royal Society for the Protection of Birds. The marsh is an outstanding example of a northern fen, which supports a rich bird life. The loch also contains many char, a northern fish relict of colder climates. The RSPB reserve at Loch Garten is famous for its ospreys, and their Abernethy reserve for its native pine forest.

HISTORY

The upper Spey by Newtonmore was the country of Clan MacPherson, and Badenoch was also part of the ground occupied by the confederation of the 'super-clan' Chattan ('chatan). There is a clan museum at Newtonmore. For those interested in learning about the life and history of the folk of Badenoch and Strath Spey, a good place to visit is the Highland Folk Museum of Am Fasgadh at Kingussie, which was founded by Dr I.F.Grant, an expert on Highland folk tradition and social organisation. A pictorial presentation is offered at the Landmark Centre at Carrbridge, which also has a nature trail, films and an excellent selection of books on Highland topics. It was at Ruthven near Kingussie in 1736 that James MacPherson was born, later to become well known as the man who wrote the book *Ossian* with its Celtic legends.

Up in the rocks on the face of Kennapole Hill near Loch Gamhna is a cave called the Cat's Den. Here 'Black Sandy' Grant, who had attacked and badly injured a Speyside drover, lay hidden for a while, but later had to emigrate to America and is said to have become the ancestor of President Grant. Near there, the little parish church of Rothiemurchus nestles among trees below the road from Insh to Inverdruie. In the graveyard lies a flat stone on which rest five cylindrical stones. The inscription commemorates Farquhar, who led the Shaws in combat on the North Insh at Perth in 1396, and tradition has it that anyone moving the five stones will be cursed. Once some reckless youths risked the curse by moving the stones, and before the year was out they were all dead. On the flat ground nearer the river stands the Doune, old home of Elizabeth Grant, who wrote *Memoirs of a Highland Lady;* first published in 1899, it gives a good account of Highland life in the early 1800s.

In 1728, much of the woodland of Abernethy was sold to the York Buildings Company for iron smelting. The Company went bankrupt but introduced new methods of tree extraction, sawmilling and timber floating to the area. Since then, Abernethy, Glen More and Rothiemurchus have all been exploited for timber. The timber floating, which lasted until the mid 1800s, was a special feature of life in Strath Spey, well described by Elizabeth Grant in her *Memoirs*. The point where the River Luineag ('looeenak) leaves Loch Morlich is the site of the old sluice gates that were used in the days of timber floating. After the cut logs had been dragged to the river side, the sluice gates were opened and the flood swept the logs down to the sawmills at Inverdruie or into the Spey. There the timber floaters made rafts with the logs and guided them down to the shipbuilding yards at Kingston on the Moray Firth.

In Glen More an old legend spoke of a giant spectre, the Lamh Dhearg or red hand, who offered battle to belated travellers through the woods. At the far end of the glen, Ryvoan Pass forms part of the old Rathad nam Meirleach or road of the thieves. The reivers from the traditional marauding clans of Cameron and MacGregor from the west Highlands used this track when heading for the lowland farms and returning with their spoil. Leaving Feshiebridge, the caterans struck along the south side of Loch an Eilein through Rothiemurchus, and next along the south side of Loch Morlich to Ryvoan. From here the thieves' road went through the top of the Nethy woods at Loch a' Chnuic to the Eag Mhor, and then by Dorback to Tomintoul.

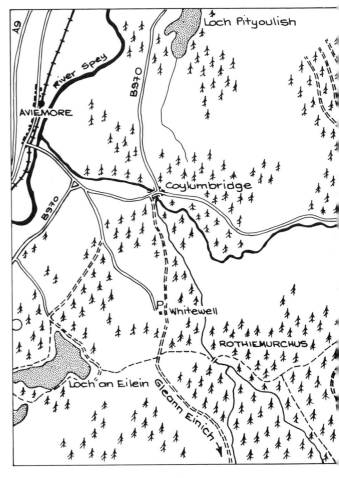

At Lynachork near Tomintoul, where Rathad nam Meirleach comes over the hills from Nethy, a great feat of eating occurred in the early 1800s. A wandering preacher called Nicol ate a whole sheep at Abergeldie on Deeside about 1840, and at Lynachork he ate a peck (two gallons) of raw meal and cream. When the meal began to swell inside him he was in great pain and cried 'Raip me an row me or I'll rive!' (Rope me and roll me or I'll burst!) So they bound him with straw ropes, the safeguard that had to be taken in these contests!

Just up from Lynachork the rocky gorge of the Water of Ailnack comes out at Delnabo. A cave in the gorge is named after Seumas an Tuim or James of the Hill, who was the subject of an old Gaelic poem, given in the book *Highland Legends*.

THE HILLS

Meall a' Bhuachaille (*myala'vooachil, hill of the herdsman*) (810m)
This conical hill is the highest of the Kincardine Hills on the north side of Glen More, and looks well from Abernethy to the north. The best route is from Glen More, where cars can be parked 150m beyond the Scottish Sports Council's Glenmore Lodge. A gravel track then leads through the woods, past An Lochan Uaine and through the Ryvoan Pass to Ryvoan Bothy. A path turns west from the bothy and goes to the top of Meall a' Bhuachaille (5½ kilometres from Glenmore Lodge, 480m ascent). The broad ridge continues for 3½ kilometres to the north-west of the summit, giving grand views of the Cairngorms across the foreground of Glen More and a fine

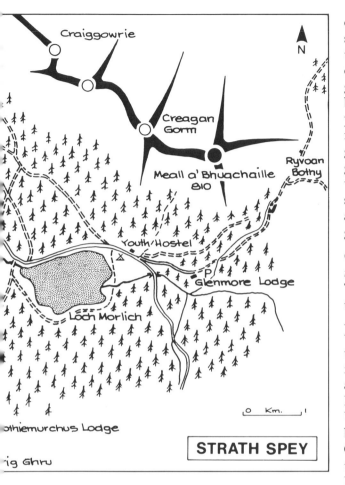

Craiggowrie

Creagan Gorm

Meall a' Bhuachaille 810

Ryvoan Bothy

Youth Hostel

Glenmore Lodge

Loch Morlich

othiemurchus Lodge

·ig Ghru

0 Km. 1

STRATH SPEY

outlook far up and down Speyside. From Meall a' Bhuachaille the path drops west to a 624m col and then climbs up to Creagan Gorm (kraikan 'gorom) or blue little rocky hill, at 732m. Beyond to the north-west rises the rough rocky 686m hill of Craiggowrie (Creag Gaibhre) or goat's rock. You can go downhill west from there to the Slugan or south towards Loch Morlich by a path to the cottages at Badaguish.

Geal Charn *(from An Geal-charn, the white hill)* (821m)

This hill rises from an extensive tract of high moorland east of Abernethy Forest, and looks well from the Grantown-Tomintoul road. The best approach is from the end of the public road at Dorback Lodge, by a track leading across Dorback Burn to Upper Dell, next following the bulldozed track to Allt nan Gamhainn, and then walking up the broad ridge west of Coire an Uillt Mhoir (4½ kilometres, 450m ascent). The views south across the vast Caiplich moors to Beinn a' Bhuird and Ben Avon are magnificent. Across a little plateau south-east of the summit lies Geal Charn Beag, a lower top close to The Castle rock at the head of the Ailnack gorge.

Geal Charn and further south the slightly lower Carn Bheadhair (karn'vair) at 803m both sweep up from the east end of the Abernethy pine forest, and carry snow patches unusually far into the summer for such low altitudes. From Abernethy a bulldozed track runs towards them up the Faesheallach Burn to an altitude of about 620m, north-west of Bile Buidhe. Stretching from Eag Mhor over Geal Charn, a fence continues south of the Castle and then goes east to Glen Avon.

Ben Rinnes *(from Beinn Rinneis, probably headland hill)* (840m)

Ben Rinnes dominates lower Speyside and from Ross-shire across the Moray Firth looks bigger than the Cairngorms. It is a grand and beautiful individually shaped conical hill, gradual on its Spey side, steep on the Glen Rinnes side. Being isolated, it commands a glorious view over the Laich of Moray and across the Moray Firth to

The Kincardine Hills seen across Loch an Eilein from Kennapole Hill

the hills of Ross, Sutherland and Caithness. The actual summit, the Scurran (from Gaelic sgoran) of Lochterlandoch, is a granite tor, and two other tors stand on the north-west side towards Aberlour. The easiest way to climb Ben Rinnes is to drive up the Dufftown-Tomintoul road and then from 290 356 up the side road to the north-west to where a bulldozed track leads off to the left. An easy climb then follows west up a track to the top via Round Hill and Roy's Hill (4 kilometres to the summit, 550m ascent). Another way goes south of Aberlour from the distillery near Milltown of Edinvillie, from which an old track goes uphill to about 470m; many years of peat digging to fire the whisky stills have removed a big patch of thick peat here.

FORESTS, MOORS AND LOWER HILLS

Rothiemurchus. Rothiemurchus is the gem of Spey forests, giving a magnificent contrast of high hills, lochs and rich natural woodland. One of the finest tracts of forest in Britain, it stretches from Loch an Eilein to Loch Morlich. Near Coylumbridge many birches grow, but the bulk of Rothiemurchus Forest consists of naturally-seeded pine, with many junipers underneath. Regeneration is excellent in the lower forest but poor in the higher parts where deer are abundant in winter.

Apart from Loch Morlich, Loch an Eilein is the most beautiful loch in Strath Spey, a sheltered sunny loch at 256m, nestling among high wooded slopes. It reaches only

The castle of Loch an Eilein

l9m in depth. Loch an Eilein ('ailin) or loch of the island was named after an islet bearing a 14th century ruined castle, where one of the last ospreys in Scotland nested before the old Scottish stock became extinct early this century. Where the road ends at the north end of the loch, there is a good view of the island. A nature trail goes round the loch. Ord Ban or fair round hill, rising west of the loch, is well worth the 170m of ascent by a footpath to the 428m summit for its grand views of Spey and hill. Its slopes are thickly clothed with birch, and under them lies a carpet of lush green vegetation due to the rich limestone. To the south-west of Loch an Eilein, a track runs round below Kennapole Hill, and at about 270m comes to Loch Gamhna (gawn) or loch of stirk, a beautiful little loch with water lilies.

On the other side of the Spey from Ord Ban rises the wooded 358m hill of Torr Alvie, which bears a tower commemorating the 5th and last Duke of Gordon. As the hill stands alone in the centre of the valley, it gives fine views both up and down Speyside. At its base lies Kinrara, home and burial place of Jean Maxwell the Duchess of Gordon, who helped to raise the Gordon Highlanders.

Glen More. East of Rothiemurchus stretches Glen More, from Gaelic Gleann Mor or big valley. Here also stood a great natural forest, but after the 1914-18 War it was one of the first areas to be bought by the Forestry Commission which replaced much of the natural woodland with densely planted pine and spruce. Later the

Commission turned this 'Queen's Forest' into the Glen More Forest Park. You will see an interesting contrast between the natural forest of Rothiemurchus and the mostly artificial forest of Glen More as you drive up the Glen More road and enter the Park at the cattle grid and fence just short of Loch Morlich. The Forestry Commission caters for visitors to the Park, including a visitor centre and waymarked walks through the woods.

Lying at about 320m in a great forested basin below Cairn Gorm, Loch Morlich ('more-lich') has one of the finest settings of any lake in Britain. The view over pine-clad ridges to the snowy corries of Cairn Gorm seems like a scene from subarctic Lapland, as does the view from the golden strand at the loch's east end looking far over the spacious sweep of Strath Spey to the distant rolling hills of the Monadh Liath. The loch is shallow - only 15m at its deepest - but covers 120 hectares, the biggest sheet of water in the Cairngorms massif. It supports a variety of habitats for wildlife, and the Forestry Commission have left some of the best of the old pines around the loch as well as patches of alder and some scrub. A Forestry Commission road comes to Loch Morlich from the north by the pass of An Slugan. The Slugan is part of an old right of way and now leads to the public road north of Loch Pityoulish. Just north of there you will see the fine old church of Kincardine with its narrow 'Leper's Window' where in the old days the diseased people stood outside and peered in during the church service.

The old Glenmore Lodge is now a youth hostel, and past it on the left stand the Forestry Commission's visitor centre and then the Reindeer Centre. About one kilometre from the camp site, up the road towards Ryvoan, lies the new Glenmore Lodge. In the late 1940s the Scottish Council for Physical Recreation set up their outdoor centre at the old lodge, starting courses in skiing, mountaineering, canoeing, sailing and other outdoor sports. To cater for the increase in the number of people taking these courses, the Council, now called the Scottish Sports Council, then built the larger new lodge. On the staff are some well known climbers in the forefront of rock and ice climbing and mountain rescue techniques in Scotland.

Lochan Uaine and Ryvoan. A gravel road leads from Glenmore Lodge through the Ryvoan Pass to Abernethy. The pass is narrow, with broken rocks and tree-studded screes on Creag Loisgte (kraik'loishk) or burnt rock on the west side, and on Creag nan Gall (kraikna'gal) or rock of the lowlanders on the east side. In the middle of the pass, at about 358m, lies An Lochan Uaine ('ooan) or the green lochan, one of the chief wonders of the Cairngorms. The water has an extraordinary pale greenish-blue colour, the old legend being that this resulted from the fairies washing their clothes in it; it looks so brilliantly translucent that you can easily see the fallen logs and stones on the bottom. The echo here sounds very fine, reflected back from the screes of Creag nan Gall. Beyond the lochan, the track climbs out of the scattered trees to the grand viewpoint on the moorland top at Ryvoan (Ruighe a' Bhothain, ree'vo-an) meaning the shiel of the bothy. Formerly a farm, Ryvoan is now an open bothy 4 kilometres from the Glen More camp site and at about 400m in altitude. About half a kilometre before you reach Ryvoan, another rough road forks right and leads for about 2 kilometres eastwards past Loch a' Gharbh-choire to Bynack Stable beside the River Nethy.

Abernethy Forest. North of Glen More, Abernethy Forest extends far as the largest tract of natural pine forest in Britain. Here you can drive for miles along public roads through the forest, and wander in pine woods so big that you can easily imagine yourself to be in Scandinavia or Russia. It is a magnificent place for wildlife, and is now owned by the Royal Society for the Protection of Birds. From Ryvoan the track leads 4 kilometres north to the beautiful old croft at Rynettin and then north to the public road at 012 162 one kilometre from Forest Lodge. From there one can go west by the road through the crofts of Tulloch. The higher crofts are empty and ruined, but this still looks a varied and pleasant landscape with patches of arable farmland, wood and scrub, offering fine views over Abernethy Forest. Abernethy Forest has several tracks offering walks through magnificent native pine forest. The path round the north side of Loch Garten also leads through pine forest by the lochside, giving views of the distant hills.

Nethy and Dorback to Tomintoul by Bridge of Brown. Some fine tracks lead east from the basin of Nethy to Tomintoul. In the old days wooden utensils which had been made in the forests of Strath Spey were carried over the hill to Tomintoul and on by the Steplar Road to the Cabrach and Aberdeenshire. The present road from Grantown to Tomintoul, which is joined by a branch from Nethy Bridge, goes by the picturesque little wooded gorge beside Bridge of Brown. It forms part of the military road from Crathie to Grantown that was built in 1754 by the Army to make it easier for them to enforce the subjugation of the Highlands. From this road, or from the public road to Dorback, a grand view opens out over the great expanse of the Nethy valley up Strath Nethy to Bynack More and Cairn Gorm, with a glimpse of Beinn Mheadhoin behind, and through the gap of Ryvoan Pass and beyond Glen More to the rocky gash into the Lairig Ghru at Creag a' Chalamain. Below Dorback Lodge the glacial deposits are of fine sand, which has formed small dunes in the midst of the heather moorland.

Nethy to Tomintoul by Glen Brown. Distance: from Dorback Lodge via Lynachork to Tomintoul 10 kilometres, ascent 200m. The direct track from the Braes of Abernethy to Tomintoul starts along the north side of Dorback Lodge. It passes through a grassy hollow by Fae and Letteraitten to Glen Brown ('brooin), 'Brown' being an absurd anglicisation. This route passes many deserted ruined crofts, and Glen Brown, although once well populated, is now almost empty. The track then strikes across another grassy col by Stronachavie to the gaunt ruin of Lynachork, where you wade the River Avon across to Tomintoul, or you can take another path from Stronachavie past Torran to the Bridge of Avon at the ivy-clad Kylnadrochit Lodge. Here, where the River Avon hurries swiftly over grey rocks and stones among birch, willow and trembling aspen, you can appreciate the old saying:

> The watter o Aan it rins sae clear
> Twad beguile a man o a hundred year

Looking across Strath Nethy from Meall a' Bhuachaille towards Geal Charn

Nearer Tomintoul the road passes a limestone quarry and goes round a hillside which is lush green from the fertility of the rock. Here, lime-loving hill plants such as viviparous bistort grow at the roadside.

Nethy to Avon by Ailnack. Distance: from Dorback Lodge to Avon bridge at Dalestie 12 kilometres, ascent 350m. This route from Dorback to Tomintoul was the recognised way in the old days for travellers going direct from Abernethy to Strath Don. Here you take the track which runs 5 kilometres up the Dorback Burn south-east of the lodge to end at the col leading to the Water of Ailnack. The route continues as an old path south of Carn Ruadh-bhreac, and crosses the Water of Ailnack at a ford at 132 124, lying just below the junction of streams to the west of Carn Ruabraich. The route then goes south of Carn an t-Sleibhe and Geal Charn (now a bulldozed track there), and drops to the Avon at 160 103 south of the bridge at Dalestie. Beyond, the old route continues 4 kilometres south to Inchrory and then east for 9 kilometres down Feith Bhait (fay'vatsh) to the Cock Bridge by Don, or east for 12 kilometres over the Eag to the Cock Bridge. Opposite Dalestie, another path climbs past Clach Bhan on to the moor towards the Water of Ailnack, by a route called the Pass of Alltan Nathrach.

An interesting walk takes you from Dorback Lodge for 7 kilometres to the Ca-du Ford and down the Water of Ailnack to Delnabo (total 12 kilometres, total ascent

The Cairngorms from the Grantown to Tomintoul road

from Dorback about 200m). Indeed, it makes a fascinating day to explore the whole course of the Water of Ailnack. This word comes from Ailneag ('alnak) or little stony one, a good name as it has two remarkable gorges or canyons, an upper one at The Castle and another above Delnabo by the River Avon. Near the upper end of the ravine on the west bank, The Castle rises as a striking pinnacle of rock whose summit can easily be reached from the neck connecting it to the steep hillside behind. It is always a surprise when you come upon this winding ravine through which the Water of Ailnack forces its way, as the surrounding countryside looks so peaty, gently undulating, and devoid of crags. Rocks on either side bar easy progress along the actual stream, but for climbers it makes an interesting trip to go down by the stream itself. After the upper canyon, which stretches for over one kilometre, the stream comes into open moorland again down to the Ca-du Ford. Below here it plunges again into another remarkable gorge which extends for 4 kilometres down to Delnabo (Dail nam Bo or haugh of the cows). A bulldozed track runs from Delnabo almost two thirds of the way to Ca-du, above the north bank of the Water of Ailnack.

Upstream from The Castle, the Water of Ailnack becomes Uisge Caiplich or the Water of Caiplich ('kaplich meaning place of horses). This district stretching from the Dorback hills to Glen Avon consists of vast expanses of peaty moors and rolling hills, with winding shallow glens stretching for miles. To some it may seem desolate and even dreary or boring. However, it is a place that gives a feeling of great space and grand wildness. Far beyond to the south stand the fantastic rocky warts of Ben Avon and the rolling slopes and fine corries of Beinn a' Bhuird. The low hills and high moors carry an interesting vegetation on the peaty flats and bare dry tops, and support a few dunlin, greenshank and other moorland birds. Navigation is difficult on a misty day.

The Hills of Cromdale. These form a distinct barrier between Spey and Avon, and are prominent in the view from near Dulnain Bridge and Grantown. The best viewpoint is the 628m Sgor Gaoithe (skor'gooee) or peak of wind, the shapely little top one kilometre above the road from Grantown to Bridge of Brown. Below it there is a magnificent roadside viewpoint where the road to Nethy Bridge branches off, looking above the great peat bogs towards Dorback Burn and the pine carpet of Abernethy to the Cairngorms and Monadh Liath; indeed, it is one of the best views from any road in Scotland.

To the north-east of Sgor Gaoithe the ridge of hills continues for 4½ kilometres at over 600m to the highest 722m top at Creagan a' Chaise, where the big cairn was erected in 1887 to commemorate Queen Victoria's jubilee. From here the broad back of the ridge stretches for 9 kilometres further north-east to the slightly separate northern end of the ridge at Creag an Tarmachain. The Hills of Cromdale have crisp walking on lichen and moss on the highest points but blanket peat on the flattish ground high up, and heathery well-drained moors lower down. To the west, the hills slope to the Haughs of Cromdale, a name with a tautology, as Crom-dhail means curved haugh. On the bottom edge of the hill, back in 1690, the Battle of Cromdale was fought between a force of Highlanders and the troops of King William who routed them. Nearby stands Clach nam Piobair or stone of the pipers, a boulder where pipers urged on the Highlanders.

Strath Avon. The name Tomintoul comes from Tom an t-Sabhail (tamin'towel) or hillock of the barn. One of the highest villages in Scotland, it stands at about 345m among open high moors and low rounded hills 13 kilometres from the base of Ben Avon, which is the nearest of the high Cairngorms. It makes a useful stopping place on several cross-country walks, and a base for exploring Glen Avon and the Water of Ailnack. The finest way out of Tomintoul goes by the road that runs down the east side of Strath Avon. For variety of river and hill scenery, the catchment of the River Avon cannot be bettered in Scotland. There is no dull stretch in the whole 70 kilometres of the river's course, from the arctic stony snowy wilderness of the Ben Macdui plateau, over the wild dark cliffs to Loch Avon, and down to the luxuriant sheltered beeches of Dalnasaugh where it flows deep and dark to enter the swift water of Spey. Strath Avon is one of the best parts, where groves of silver birches soften the valley side and where oystercatchers and sandpipers sweep over the water and call loudly by the shingles. The old church of Kirkmichael, near where green Glen Lochy comes in from the Hills of Cromdale, is a particularly lovely spot.

Dufftown and lower Spey. The hill of Little Conval near Dufftown has an interesting old fort on its top, and its higher neighbour Meikle (locally Muckle) or big Conval gives its name to the local distillery of Convalmore. Ben Aigan rises commandingly over the steep richly wooded banks of lower Spey. This part of the valley from Craigellachie up to Cromdale is one of the finest, though lesser-known parts of Spey, where the river winds among green haughs below steep slopes clad in birch and pine, rising further back to the extensive heather moors of Knockando (nok'andoe) and Tulchan. Near Archiestown there is a particularly interesting view right into the Slochd Mor of Beinn a' Bhuird.

Lower Moray and Nairn. These two counties contain a higher proportion of woodland than any others in Scotland, and a high proportion of wild moor and hill. You can walk for miles through vast tracts of Scots pine like a forest in northern Finland, rich in capercaillies, red squirrels, crossbills, crested tits, red wood ants and other boreal forest animals. The high moors give wonderful views far out over the low coast to the peaks across the Moray Firth from Ben Wyvis to the beautiful cone of Morven in Caithness.

There are many shallow glens, once populated by farmers and crofters but now sadly empty in most places. These moors and hills are rich in wildlife. It is a country of vast space, with gentle slopes rolling into the distance. Despite the low rainfall, the shallow gradients and thus poorer drainage have encouraged peat to build up thickly, and wet bogs cover some of the flatter ground. The contrast in climate and scenery between the lush, warm Laich (lowland) o Moray and the cold hill country of Braigh Moireibh (upland of Moray) comes as suddenly as anywhere in Scotland. Here is a good district for cross-country walks along old tracks, and in hard winters a fine place for ski touring. It is a complex tract of country, difficult to get to know, apparently featureless and uniform at first sight, but really all different and full of interest on closer acquaintance. In mist, dark or storm it can be quite a difficult place for navigation.

A good walk is down the fine wild stretch of Findhorn which starts at Ruthven south-east of Loch Moy, off the A9 Inverness-Aviemore road north of the hamlet of Tomatin (Tom Aitinn, tom'atin or hillock of juniper). The River Findhorn races past great shingle beds into a narrow, twisting, steep-sided valley. Once you are into Nairnshire, the steep glens which cut into the hills on either side show many gravel scars from erosion. Beyond Drynachan, the Findhorn valley becomes wooded, especially below Dulsie Bridge and Glen Ferness (distance from A9 road to Drynachan 12 kilometres, to Dulsie Bridge 20 kilometres).

The glens above Drynachan lead up to extensive plateaux rising to 600m where there is an unusual tundra-like vegetation rich in Cladonia, the 'reindeer moss' lichen. One of the biggest of these plateaux lies on the 659m Carn Glas-choire, 5 kilometres in walking west-south-west of the summit of the B9007 Forres-Duthil road, and also accessible (6 kilometres) by a bulldozed track from 914 281 up to the flat ground east of the top. Better still is the plateau on the remote Carn nan Tri-tighearnan or hill of the three lairds, north-east of Loch Moy. Distance: from 777 335 on the A9, up the east side of Loch Moy and then by a path, 10 kilometres. From Drynachan Lodge 4 kilometres.

The B9007 road from Nairn to Carrbridge runs into Inverness-shire at the fine steep gap of Beum a' Chlaidheimh (baima'chligh) or gash of the sword, which shows up well in the northward view from Rothiemurchus. East of here the hills have many small crags. These rocky hills stretch north to Lochindorb and east of the Forres road north of Grantown. Lochindorb itself, with its old ruined castle on an islet, lies hidden behind a low hill. Dava Moor near here stretches far out as a rolling wide heather tract dotted with clumps of juniper and pine, and with many lochans and flat peat bogs. One of the best hills, well worth climbing, is the Knock of Braemoray (455m) overlooking the vast Dunphail and Altyre moors by the River Divie. It rises one kilometre from the A940 just north of Dava and gives a very good view. An old road across the moors here, which makes a fine cross-country walk, goes 13 kilometres from the A940 at 020 465 beside the viaduct at Dunphail, east past the farm of Johnstripe, and over to 121 500. This crosses the rolling gentle slopes of former moorland above Dallas, beside the headwaters of the River Lossie, an area now mostly afforested. The old railway line, now disused, also offers a walking route. Another good way goes for 15 kilometres from the viaduct to 047 338, up the River Divie and over the top to the south by Badahad to the woods of Castle Grant.

On the lower ground, the banks of the River Findhorn from Dulsie Bridge down past Sluie to the Forres-Inverness road make one of the finest walks in lowland Scotland, through magnificent river and woodland scenery along the edge of historic Darnaway Forest (distance from Dulsie Bridge to Ferness bridge 9 kilometres, to A96 28 kilometres). To the south-east of Forres, the extensive pine woods of Altyre and Romach Loch in its steep defile are interesting features, as is the steep stony escarpment near Pluscarden. The tidal flats of Findhorn Bay are one of the best places for wading birds in east Scotland.

Speyside Way. This long-distance walking route goes from Spey Bay, where the River Spey runs into the Moray Firth, to Ballindalloch, then crosses the shoulder of Ben Rinnes into Glen Livet, and ends at Tomintoul. It partly follows the old railway, and partly old tracks, paths, and occasionally a section of public road. An extension runs along the Moray Firth coast to Cullen in Banffshire.

CLIMBING

Farletter Crag is a low-lying valley cliff 30m high at 826 031, south of the B970 road beside Loch Insh, with a number of routes varying from Severe to E6. There has been much recent climbing development on this crag, and there are now several routes in the high E-grades. A good inland crag stands at Huntly's Cave in a gorge 5 kilometres north of Grantown beside the A939 road to Forres, at 024 327. The cliff forms a very steep 10-15m outcrop with a line of overhangs. A number of routes have been made, and a second small crag lower down the glen on the other side gives a few good routes about 20m in height; all these will be described in the forthcoming SMC Guide *Highland Outcrops.* On Ben Rinnes, the largest Scurran or tor makes a short climb about Very Difficult in standard on rough granite.

On the coast between Burghead and Lossiemouth, an unusual stretch of Triassic sandstone cliff of a beautiful warm creamy-brown colour faces the Moray Firth. The rock is very steep, most routes being Severe or higher in standard. Although only 10-20m high, these cliffs give very good climbing. One of the best climbing areas there is at Cummingston at 130 692 east of Burghead. Just west of Elgin in the Quarry Wood beside the A96 road to Inverness, the Old Quarry at 188 628 is another accessible climbing ground, with 20-25m routes on quarried standstone. The SMC Guide *North-East Outcrops* describes the climbs on the Moray coast and Elgin in detail.

SKIING

When there is general snow cover, the forests, moors and hills offer a great variety of conditions for cross-country skiing. In Glenmore Forest and some areas else-where, dense plantations are impenetrable, so forest tracks offer the only routes; some at Glenmore are waymarked. The Moray-Nairn moors sometimes become a snowy landscape of vast space, and skis offer a good way to explore this unusual landscape.

FURTHER READING

W.Forsyth (1900) *In the Shadow of Cairngorm.* A good account of the district, its history and bygone life.

D.A.Woodburn (ed) *Glen More Forest Park.* Short articles on old way of life, geology, vegetation, wildlife, and forests and plantations, and useful bibliography of books on Strath Spey.

The following are of historical interest:

R.Anderson *Ben Aigan.* CCJ 2, 150.

C.G.Cash *The Rothiemurchus Forest fire.* CCJ 3, 96.

A.I.McConnochie *Loch an Eilein and its Castle.* CCJ 3, 104.

C.G.Cash *The Loch an Eilein ospreys.* CCJ 4, 125, and 5, 270.

C.G.Cash *Timber floating at Rothiemurchus.* CCJ 4, 301.

CHAPTER 2

Cairn Gorm and Ben Macdui

Cairn Gorm	1245m	005 041
Ben Macdui	1309m	989 989
Cairn Lochan	1215m	986 026
Creag an Leth-choin	1053m	969 033
Bynack More	1090m	042 063
A' Choinneach	1017m	032 048
Carn a' Mhaim	1037m	994 952
Derry Cairngorm	1155m	017 980
Beinn Mheadhoin	1182m	025 017
Creag Mhor	895m	058 048

All the above hills are Munros, except for Cairn Lochan and Creag an Leth-choin which are prominent tops, and Creag Mhor which is a Corbett.

Ben Macdui and Cairn Gorm form a rampart of high ground east of the Lairig Ghru, in the centre of the Cairngorms massif. At 1309m, Ben Macdui is the highest hill in the Cairngorms and only Ben Nevis rises higher in Britain. The plateau between Ben Macdui and Cairn Gorm is unique in Scotland as a large tract of varied subarctic terrain; nowhere else in Britain looks so like hills in Greenland or arctic Canada. Streams from both hills plunge in waterfalls into the great trench of Loch Avon, unsurpassed by any Scottish loch in its grandeur and wild, remote setting, and in this sense it is one of the wildest places in Europe outside Norway. Reaching about 240m high, the cliffs at Loch Avon make a magnificent climbing ground, and there are fine crags and corrie lochans on the north slopes of Cairn Gorm and the south-east and east sides of Ben Macdui. The hills around Cairn Gorm and Ben Macdui, such as Derry Cairngorm and Beinn Mheadhoin, also have magnificent wild landscapes. Although much lower than Ben Macdui, they are among the highest hills of Britain.

GEOLOGY, LANDFORMS AND WILDLIFE

The rock is virtually all granite. At Coire an Lochain a huge slab of granite retains its virgin pink colour because of the snow avalanches and water that pour down it every summer. There are many varieties of crag, varying from broken rocks disintegrating into scree in the Lairig Ghru to the sheer smooth wall of the Shelter Stone

ACCESS
Cairn Gorm rises above the Coire Cas chairlift and ski area where a public road from Coire Cas car park leads down through Glen More to Coylumbridge and Aviemore. Ben Macdui stands at the southern end of a high plateau stretching south from Cairn Gorm, and most people climbing it come via the car park at Coire Cas and the chairlift above it. The public road to Coire Cas has so eased access that most people going to Loch Avon and even Beinn Mheadhoin now do so via Cairn Gorm.

Derry Cairngorm, Carn a' Mhaim and the east corries of Ben Macdui are easiest to reach from Deeside, where a public road runs from Braemar to Linn of Dee and then around to lower Glen Lui. An enlarged new car park was opened in 1991 east of the Linn of Dee, on the north side of the river. Roadside parking at and beside the locked gate at the bottom of Glen Lui, where the gravel road leads to Derry Lodge, has been discouraged because cars have sometimes blocked access to the gate. A new footpath has been made from the new car park north-east through the plantation to join the road to Derry Lodge a short distance up from the locked gate.

PUBLIC TRANSPORT
As in Chapter 1. Also bus from Aberdeen to Braemar, post-bus from Braemar to Linn of Dee, and bus in summer from Pitlochry to Braemar.

ACCOMMODATION AND OTHER FACILITIES
For the Spey side of the hills, see Chapter 1. On the Dee side, there are hotels, bed and breakfast accommodation and a youth hostel at Braemar. The Cairngorm Club has a large hut at Muir of Inverey; members of other climbing clubs should apply via their club secretaries. A board at the top end of the car park at Coire Cas gives the latest forecast of weather for the upper part of Cairn Gorm, including wind direction and speed.

BOTHIES AND SHELTERS (see also Chapter 3)
Jean's Hut at 981 034 in Coire an Lochain was removed in 1986. The Shelter Stone at 003 016 lies at about 755m, above Loch Avon. Bob Scott's Bothy is at 042 931 near Derry Lodge. The Hutchison Memorial Hut at 023 998 lies at about 700m in Coire Etchachan south of the path. Jamie Murray's Cave at 023 055 on the west side of Garbh Allt, 2 kilometres north of The Saddle north of Loch Avon, makes a shelter for three under a boulder.

MAPS
Ordnance Survey 1:50,000 Sheets 36 and 43

Crag. In the early 1960s, a big rockfall on Carn Etchachan exposed a new face of fresh pink granite. Arctic-like braided streams, stone stripes and polygons are common on flat ground on the plateau, and mud flows occasionally occur on Cairn Lochan during the big summer thaw. With the biggest and most varied area of arctic-like terrain in Britain, the plateau and shoulders between Cairn Gorm and Ben Macdui are of great interest to naturalists. Many big snow patches lie higher and longer here than anywhere in Britain, so the special snow-patch vegetation is very rich. The great whaleback of Cairn Lochan is especially interesting for the extensive gravelly barrens of three-leaved rush on its summit, gradually merging lower down into an unusually large area with a continuous turf of alpine grassland along Feith Buidhe. Along the flat top of Miadan Creag an Leth-choin, on the gentle slopes east of Coire na Ciste and on A' Choinneach, woolly hair moss dominates the vegetation, mixed

Beinn Mheadhoin (left), Lochnagar and Carn Etchachan from the slopes of Cairn Lochan

with three-leaved rush and heaths. The many corrie cliffs have an interesting arctic-like vegetation ungrazed by sheep or deer, and a subarctic heath grows round the head of Loch Avon.

The wide mossy flushes and streams are a special feature at the higher altitudes, and in summer are attractive feeding places for insect-eating birds. Extensive boulder fields occur on Derry Cairngorm, Ben Macdui and over much of the ground from Lochan Buidhe towards Loch Etchachan. The ptarmigan is the commonest bird. Special features are that these hills are a good breeding haunt for snow bunting and dotterel, and one of the best places in Britain for insects of arctic origin. In some summers a snowy owl hunts the plateau. Domestic reindeer from the herd at Glen More often live on the plateau in summer, but the numerous red deer stags, hinds and calves which used to summer there have gone. There have long been many good trout in Loch Avon. Crows and seagulls now hunt the plateau, attracted by scraps of food from tourists.

ESTATES

The Aberdeenshire part is on Mar Lodge Estate, the Banffshire part and Strath Nethy belong to the Royal Society for the Protection of Birds, Creag an Leth-choin is on Rothiemurchus, and the north side of Cairn Gorm and its corries belong to Highlands and Islands Enterprise.

HISTORY

Johan Blaeu's *Atlas Novus* of 1654 shows 'Carn-gorum', and not far to the south-west also 'Corintrack' which is probably Coire an t-Sneachda. In her *Guide to the Beauties of Scotland* (3rd edition 1810) the Hon Mrs Murray Aust describes an ascent of Cairn Gorm in 1801. Further back in time comes the story of Fuaran a' Mharcuis or well of the marquis, the spring beside the track north-east of the summit of Cairn Gorm. It was named after the Marquis of Huntly who chased MacCalum Mor, Marquis of Argyle, westwards after the Battle of Glen Livet in 1594.

The first account of Ben Macdui appears in the *General View of Aberdeenshire* (1811) by the Rev Dr G.S.Keith who, in 1810, surveyed the altitudes of some Deeside hills using a barometer. Keith made the height of Ben Macdui to be 4300ft. In the 1800s many thought Ben Macdui was the highest hill of Scotland, but when Dr Keith sent his son with the barometer to Fort William, he reported that Ben Nevis was 50ft higher. The argument was not finally settled till the Ordnance Survey set up their trigonometrical station on Ben Macdui in 1847; the ruined remains of the surveyors' stone hut, which local people still call the Sappers' Bothy, still lie just east of the summit. As a result, Ben Macdui was recorded as 4296ft and Ben Nevis as 4406ft. The story is that John Hill Burton, an 'old adherent' of Ben Macdui, would 'fain have gone down on his knees and begged the surveyors not to depose his beloved mountain'.

The 19th century was the great period for lairds building memorials for themselves on Scottish hilltops, dominating the surrounding countryside. Fortunately, what would have been the worst of these excesses in Scotland was not carried out. This was the Earl of Fife's plan, described in 1819 in *The Caledonian Itinerary*, to build a sepulchral pyramid 100ft high on the summit of Ben Macdui, with a burial vault inside. On their pioneering explorations of natural history, Prof W.MacGillivray and other naturalists of the early 1800s climbed Ben Macdui. In October 1859 Queen Victoria went up to the top on a pony by Glen Derry, and later wrote 'Never shall I forget this day or the impression this very grand scene made upon me; truly sublime and impressive; such solitude'.

Dr Keith wrote of a story that grass growing on the hills became poisonous to horses. The local legend was that the grass was poisoned by a glutinous matter ejected by the Famh, a mythical monster which appeared only at the head of Loch Avon, only at daybreak and only on the highest verge of the hill. Another old local legend is that a giant spectre called Am Fear Liath Mor (m-fer-leea'more) or the big grey man, haunts Ben Macdui. When Prof N.J. Collie, the well known Victorian mountaineer, stood alone on the summit, he heard footsteps in the snow like somebody accompanying him, and was so scared that he ran fleeing from the top (CCJ 11, 214). Many others have had strange experiences there (Further Reading). Perhaps the best story is of one Aberdeen climber, on leave in the mid-1940s, who emptied his army revolver into one particularly menacing shape of mist!

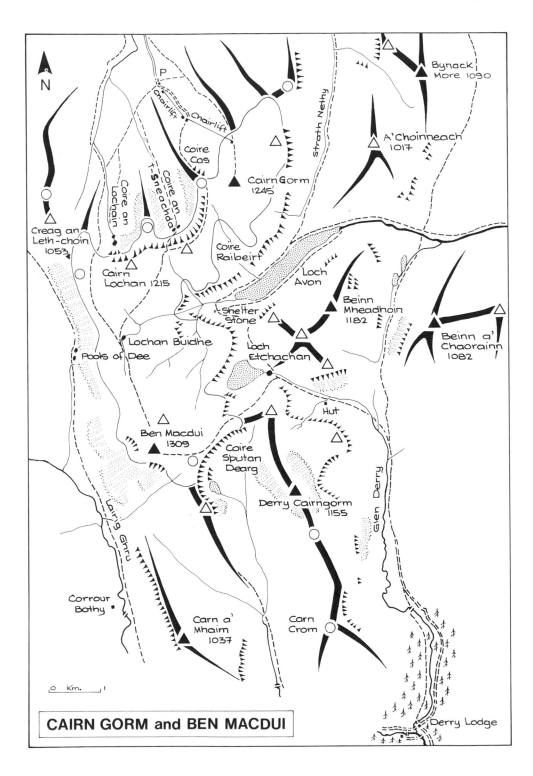

N

P

Chairlift   Chairlift

Coire
Cas

Strath Nethy

Bynack
More 1090

A'Choinneach
1017

Cairn Gorm
1245

Coire an
Lochain

Coire an
t-Sneachda

Creag an
Leth-choin
1053

Coire
Raibeirt

Loch
Avon

Beinn
Mheadhoin
1182

Cairn
Lochan 1215

Shelter
Stone

Beinn a'
Chaorainn
1082

Lochan Buidhe

Loch
Etchachan

Pools of Dee

Hut

Ben Macdui
1309

Coire
Sputan
Dearg

Glen Derry

Derry Cairngorm
1155

Lairig Ghru

Corrour
Bothy

Carn a'
Mhaim
1037

Carn
Crom

0   Km.   1

Derry Lodge

CAIRN GORM and BEN MACDUI

During the 1939-45 war, commandos and mountain troops trained in the Cairn-gorms, and their many stone bivouacs still stand north-east of Ben Macdui. In the early 1940s a British services plane crashed at the top of Allt a' Choire Mhoir north-west of the summit. Others crashed on Stob an t-Sluichd, in Coire na Lairige of Braeriach, and on lower hills.

VIEWS FROM THE SUMMITS

From the hill ridge of Cairn Gorm between the Ptarmigan Restaurant and Cairn Lochan, the view is one of the finest in all Scotland. The north slope of Cairn Gorm drops 900m to Strath Spey with no intervening ranges of foothills, so you have the effect of walking on a great uplifted terrace, on the roof of Scotland. Below, the pine forests of Glen More and Rothiemurchus spread like big green carpets towards the upper Spey and Creag Meagaidh, the Monadh Liath and the Morayshire moors. On fine days Loch Morlich turns into a mirror reflecting the pines on its north bank. Across the blue Moray Firth rises the cone of Morven in Caithness, and in clear weather you can see the hills of west Sutherland, Torridon, Kintail and Knoydart, up to 160 kilometres away.

In 1897-98, A.Copland, first chairman of the Cairngorm Club, surveyed the panorama of hills to be seen from Ben Macdui, and published it (CCJ 2, 73, 243, 314, 391; and 3, 119). Later, J.A.Parker checked and revised it, and in 1925 the Club built his indicator on the summit. The furthest hills on it are: to the south-south-east the Lammermuirs at 150 kilometres, and to the north Ben a-chielt of Caithness at 140 kilometres. On the clearest days, many further distant hills can be seen that are not shown on the indicator, including peaks in Knoydart, Torridon and north-west Sutherland.

THE HILLS

Cairn Gorm *(from Gaelic An Carn Gorm, the blue hill)* (1245m)
Cairn Gorm dominates Strath Spey and looks a beautiful peak from around Nethy Bridge and Dulnain Bridge. From Loch Morlich, it and its corries form one of the best views in Scotland. It has become well known as a ski ground and also for walking, rock climbing and other outdoor pursuits.

SKI DEVELOPMENTS
Since 1960-61 when a new road and chairlift were built, the easiest access to Cairn Gorm has been by Glen More. From east of Loch Morlich, a public road passes beyond the Glen More camp site and heads through the woods up into Coire Cas to a car park at 650m, with toilets, telephone and restaurant. From here a chairlift goes up to the middle station at about 760m. A chairlift leads from there to the top station and Ptarmigan Restaurant at about 1080m. Just above the forest edge on the road to Coire Cas, a spur road goes east to a car park at the foot of Coire na Ciste. A chairlift (winter only) and ski tows lead up this corrie to the basin and ski tow east of the Ptarmigan Restaurant. The ski facilities are run by the Cairngorm Chairlift Com-

pany, which operates the chairlifts from Coire Cas to the Ptarmigan Restaurant at all seasons. Construction work scarred some hillsides and led to soil erosion, but this has decreased due to better tracks, new drains and reseeding of bared ground. If you are not using the chairlift, do not wander about and thus damage the reseeded patches, but stay on the prepared tracks. A rough road zigzags from the car park to the Ptarmigan Restaurant.

WALKING ASCENTS TO CAIRN GORM

From Coire Cas. From the Ptarmigan Restaurant a short walk of less than one kilometre with a 150m ascent, along a path constructed with boulders and marked by posts, goes straight uphill to the summit of Cairn Gorm, at a cairn on an outcrop of granite. Walking routes from the car park are to take the winding road up to the Ptarmigan Restaurant, or to break off the lower part of that road beside the Fiacaill Tow and walk on to Fiacaill a' Choire Chais. This prominent broad stony ridge leads up the west side of the corrie to its top at 1141m and then one turns east to climb to the summit of Cairn Gorm.

By the path from Glen More. Distance: about 7 kilometres from the camp site, 920m ascent. The walker who wishes to avoid the ski slopes can go up the old path to Cairn Gorm. Although the road in the lower forest obliterated most of it there, you will still find it alongside the stream of Allt Mor, just after the road crosses the bridge halfway up the forest; it then climbs among some fine old pines. Then it crosses the first, now disused ski road on the hill beside the big bends, and slants uphill near the huge boulder of Clach Bharraig ('varig) to the ridge at An t-Aonach or the height. The path now leads straight up the long ridge of Sron an Aonaich or nose of the height, past the granite tor of Caisteal Dubh or black castle to the Ptarmigan Restaurant.

Descent by Cairn Lochan. Distance: 5 kilometres from Cairn Gorm to Creag an Leth-choin. A good route for descent is round to Cairn Lochan (from Gaelic Carn Lochain or lochan hill), and then to Creag an Leth-choin. You drop down the dome of Cairn Gorm west to Fiacaill a' Choire Chais at 1141m and then follow the path south, at first down to a col at 1099m and then gradually rising along the cliff edge of the wide Coire an t-Sneachda to the highest top at 1176m. Beyond, the path nears the cliff edge and drops down to the 1111m col at the top of the long green Coire Domhain (kor'daw-in) or deep corrie.

An easy climb follows over short turf and gravel to Cairn Lochan at 1215m, where the cairn stands close to the cliff edge (3 kilometres from Cairn Gorm, 180m ascent). Here you look down the steep crags of Coire an Lochain (korin'lochan) or corrie of the lochan, one of the most impressive corries of the Cairngorms. The granite of the Cairngorms weathers in horizontal and vertical lines, often producing an effect like huge masonry. This is particularly striking in Coire an Lochain, where some of the rocks look as if built in gigantic towers.

From Cairn Lochan, easy walking follows along the broad whaleback which stretches south-west for over one kilometre towards the Lairig Ghru. A cairn past the end of the flat part marks the junction of Inverness, Banff and Aberdeen counties;

Coire an Lochain

it is Carn nan Tri Crioch ('tree'kreech), or cairn of the three boundaries. From it you drop down the stony slope towards Creag an Leth-choin on to a wide green flat, which rises slightly on to stony ground to a cairn at 1083m at its south-west end; the name of this green is Miadan Creag an Leth-choin ('mee-adan or meadow). From the Miadan a path goes downhill to the north-north-east, beside the stream and then slanting across the steep grassy slope west of Coire an Lochain. If snow lies here, even in summer, avoid this path as the slope is steep and prone to avalanches. An easier and safer way off, which gives grand views across to Coire an Lochain, goes by a path down the wide ridge which starts at the north end of Miadan Creag an Leth-choin from the cairn on Fiacaill an Leth-choin. Alternatively one can go north-west towards Creag an Leth-choin and then downhill along Allt Creag an Leth-choin, eventually on a path. Both ways take you to the path leading to the Coire Cas car park, or to another path to Glen More by a footbridge over the Allt Mor just south of the trees. Distance: from Creag an Leth-choin to car park 4 kilometres, from Cairn Lochan via Fiacaill an Leth-choin to car park 5 kilometres.

Descent by Ryvoan.   An interesting way down goes by the long north ridge past Cnap Coire na Spreidhe at 1151m ('krap-korna'spray) or knob of the cattle corrie. You will find it delightful walking over the mossy and gravelly ground, and by skirting the cliffs you can look into the great dark gulf of Strath Nethy. A pleasant walk follows past a 1028m top and north of it down the long nose of Sron a' Cha-no, past a fenced tree plot to Lochan na Beinne and down the Allt Ban by a path on its north side to Glenmore Lodge, 8 kilometres from Cairn Gorm. An alternative route is to climb the 742m Stac na h-Iolaire and drop north down Mam Suim (mam'sooeem) and Creag nan Gall on the way to Ryvoan, 9 kilometres from Cairn Gorm, and then by An Lochan Uaine on the walk back. This goes past several crags and valleys, now almost dry, which were cut by great rivers flowing out when the big Glen More glacier was hemmed in here by Cairn Gorm and Meall a' Bhuachaille. Particularly striking among these are Stac na h-Iolaire or precipice of the eagle, and Eag a' Gharbh Choire.

WALKING IN CAIRN GORM'S CORRIES

The corries of Cairn Gorm are rough, bouldery and fairly unfrequented, despite their accessibility from the car park at Coire Cas. At the north end, Coire Laogh Mor (korlay'more) or big corrie of calves, is a small steep bowl fringed with broken rock. Coire na Ciste (korna'keesht) or corrie of the chest, a steep narrow corrie, holds the best ski run on Cairn Gorm. Coire Cas carries a conspicuous steep snow wreath at its top, which lasts far into the summer; its name is Cuidhe Crom (kooee'krom) or crooked wreath. Avalanches occur here and the snow often turns dangerously icy even in summer.

The beautiful Coire an t-Sneachda (korin'tray-achk or corrie of the snow) is well worth exploring. Take the track that leads west from the car park, and once round the corner, diverge left from it along an upper path slanting uphill to head into Coire an t-Sneachda. A great mound of glacial debris lies high in the east side of the corrie, and further up are small lochans. Here you stand among great boulder fields and scanty vegetation, looking up at a long and varied set of crags. From the upper lochan a former deer path now known as the Goat Track zigzags up to the 1111m col on the plateau above, east of Cairn Lochan. Although this route is easy, the path is very loose in places due to heavy use, and in winter conditions it can be dangerous.

Coire an Lochain is Cairn Gorm's most striking corrie, with a steep wall of dark cliffs, long-lying snow patches and small lochans far below. A very unusual feature is the great curtain of bare granite which slopes downhill from the base of the cliffs. From near Grantown, it glistens in the sun and in certain lights has a pink colour. Separating Coire an Lochain from Coire an t-Sneachda rises a long stony ridge climbing to the little peak of Fiacaill Coire an t-Sneachda. The rocky ridge above it is the Fiacaill Ridge. One of the few narrow rock aretes in the Cairngorms, it makes an interesting summer ascent involving easy scrambling, and can be difficult in winter.

On the south side of Cairn Gorm, Coire Domhain plunges, after its long green upper section, into a narrow stream-bed running steeply to Loch Avon.

The next corrie to the east is Coire Raibeirt (kor'rabert) or Robert's corrie. A very wide green corrie with many boggy flushes, it opens out on the south side of the ridge at the top of Coire Cas. To the east of Coire Raibeirt and beyond a rocky tor at 1082m lies a shallow, nameless green corrie drained by a Feith Buidhe, much tinier than the one out of Lochan Buidhe. Still further round the corner higher up and due

Coire an t-Sneachda

east of Cairn Gorm, a small sandy hollow faces east on the hillside. Snow often lies long here, as also in the hollow to the north nearer Cnap Coire na Spreidhe where a stream furrow running east into the Garbh Allt has the name Ciste Mhearad (keesht'mairad) or Margaret's coffin.

Ben Macdui *(hill of Macduff)* (1309m)
The Macduffs or Earls of Fife for long held the lands of Mar which include this hill. Ben Macdui lies so much in the centre of the Cairngorms that you do not see it well from most places further out, but at Inverey you will get a fine distant view of it. It is the most arctic-like place in these islands. Of all the hills in the Cairngorms, it also has the finest set of high lochs and lochans; and with the Sticil, Carn Etchachan, Coire Etchachan and Coire Sputan Dearg it easily excels with its grand precipices.

WALKING ASCENTS TO BEN MACDUI
From Coire Cas. Distance from the top of Cairn Gorm: 6½ kilometres, 275m ascent. Because the ski road and chairlift reach so high on the hill, most people now climb Ben Macdui from the north, and the easier access has led to some inexperienced and inadequately equipped tourists wandering over the plateau in summer. Routes as far as the col east of Cairn Lochan are described above. From that col at 1111m, at the edge of the cliffs of Coire an t-Sneachda, a narrow path slants slightly uphill to the south-south-west along the west side of Coire Domhain; it then passes over a low neck and runs horizontally south-west to Lochan Buidhe. The second-lowest

point on this high-level walk lies at 1125m beside this tiny lochan, called Lochan Feith Buidhe (fay'pooee) or lochan of Feith Buidhe by the older local folk. At just over 1120m it is the highest named tarn in Britain. Here the water flows into Banffshire, but only 100 metres to the west across flat turf the ground drains into the March Burn (from Gaelic Allt na Criche, burn of the boundary), at first passing through a stretch of wet boggy ground verging on being another lochan.

From Lochan Buidhe the path, marked by cairns, leads south up a gentle slope, then south-east for 90m of ascent more steeply up the gravelly and bouldery front of the North Top to 1250m, and finally south-south-west to the summit at 1309m.

A good return route is by a path from west of Lochan Buidhe, skirting the west shoulder of Cairn Lochan to Miadan Creag an Leth-choin, and then by a path down the north ridge from the Miadan to join the main Northern Corries path back to the car park. This also makes a fine ascent route from the car park (8 kilometres, 730m ascent to Ben Macdui summit), as does the slightly longer alternative by the path up Allt Creag an Leth-choin and so to Miadan Creag an Leth-choin. An advantage of these two routes is that the walker is soon out of sight of the car park and ski developments as soon as the first corner is passed, within 300 metres of the car park. Moreover there are magnificent views of Coire an t-Sneachda and Coire an Lochain (see also Cairn Gorm, Descent by Cairn Lochan, last paragraph).

Another route from the Coire Cas car park is by the steep Goat Track up the head of Coire an t-Sneachda to the 1111m col east of Cairn Lochan and then southwards past Lochan Buidhe, but the Goat Track is rather loose and unstable in places.

By Glen Derry. Distance: 12 kilometres, 880m climb. This excellent varied route offers a gradual ascent with a good path. Starting at 420m, the first 6½ kilometres up Glen Derry are the same as the Lairig an Laoigh route (Chapter 3). At 035 992 the Ben Macdui path forks left to the north-west, off the Lairig path, crosses the Coire Etchachan Burn by a footbridge, and heads into Coire Etchachan (kor'aitshachan) past the Hutchison Memorial Hut at about 700m. This corrie is a large bowl with steep craggy sides. On the south and west sides rise the rocks of Creagan a' Choire Etchachan, meaning the crags of Coire Etchachan, which are especially striking on the steep west wall. Further back from that wall, a nameless stony cone rises to 1108m behind the corrie.

After climbing steeply up the roaring burn, the path comes out suddenly beside Loch Etchachan at just over 922m, the highest big loch of this size in Britain. At its east end lies the beautiful grass and thrift-margined Loch Etchachan Beag or little loch Etchachan. The scene is arctic. Towards Ben Macdui, beyond a fine subarctic heath above the south shore of the loch, stretches a complex terrain of broken crags, bulging shoulders and vast boulder fields, with many hollows where snow lingers far into the summer. Usually the loch has some ice for more than half the year. To the north, a flat col leads through towards the gulf of Loch Avon, with Cairn Gorm rising beyond and the rocky Carn Etchachan sweeping up to the west of the col. Slanting up the slope on the south side of the loch, the path to Ben Macdui comes

Ben Macdui (right) and Carn a' Mhaim from the south

out beside a cliff top on the left. The cliff drops abruptly into Coire Sputan Dearg (kor spootan'jerrek) or the corrie with red spouts, so called from the red scree in the main gullies. From the big spout here, the view down Glen Luibeg is magnificent. After a further climb near the cliff edge, the path reaches the plateau and goes west to the ruined Sappers' Bothy and 200 metres further on to the summit cairn.

By Glen Luibeg. Distance: 9 kilometres, 880m climb. This is the shortest way from Derry Lodge. The first 3 kilometres are the same as for the Lairig Ghru. Then, about 300 metres before the Lairig path crosses the Luibeg Burn, your path slants up to the right. About 2 kilometres further up, the burn forks at 560m, the long ridge between the forks being the Sron Riach or really Riabhach (stron'ree-ach) or brindled nose. The path climbs steadily up short grass and heather to a tor and then becomes indistinct, but the way ahead is obvious over sparse vegetation, gravel and stones, with fine views over to Cairn Toul and Derry Cairngorm. At about 1100m you come suddenly to a cliff edge where there is an impressive view down to Lochan Uaine at about 955m. Here in Coire an Lochain Uaine snow lies in a couple of pockets far into the summer, beside the 300m of wet avalanche-prone slabs rising to the nameless pyramid peak above (the name Stob Coire Sputan Dearg was an invention for Munro's Tables). The best route now heads up the boulders by the cliff rim to the marvellous viewpoint of this peak at 1249m, but you can avoid the boulders by slanting left up a grassy slope to the plateau south-east of the ruined Sappers' Bothy.

By Allt Clach nan Taillear. To or from Corrour Bothy, a good route goes by the long broad ridge south of Allt Clach nan Taillear (4½ kilometres, 760m climb). When you are coming off Ben Macdui it is safest to descend to 996 984 before turning down the south bank of the stream. The direct route from the summit cairn to the lower part of Allt Clach nan Taillear ('talyer') has to cross Coire nan Taillear by a frieze of broken slabby rock which stretches along the plateau edge south of the summit and leads on to a very steep slope below. Huge cornices build up here and avalanches occur even in July.

By the Pools of Dee. The easiest route here leads up the March Burn to Lochan Buidhe and then south to Ben Macdui. From the summit of the Lairig Ghru at about 835m, you have 3 kilometres to go and a 480m ascent to Ben Macdui, first by a steep climb up loose scree and boulders for 240m. There are better ways up on either side; look for one of the deer tracks that slant uphill at an angle, as this makes an easier and safer ascent. Icy snow at a high angle lies in a snow bridge at the top of the March Burn far into the summer, but it can usually be bypassed on either side at that season. In winter it frequently becomes a dangerous route, often icy and at other times avalanche-prone, and the same goes for the entire west face from Creag an Leth-choin to the Allt Clach nan Taillear. The ridge south-west of the Ben Macdui cairn, bounding Coire nan Taillear on its west side, you will find a possible exception; as it is heavily boulder-strewn, winds often blow it clear of snow, but you should not depend on this.

From Loch Avon. Distance: 3½ kilometres 580m climb. Loch Avon (for routes to the loch, see two sections below) lies at the start of the finest way up Ben Macdui. You slant up by the side of the Garbh Uisge, a roaring cascading stream, which in places dashes over smooth beds of bare granite. For 250m of height it makes a steep but easy enough way as the slope is well broken by boulders and ledges of vegetation. On the steepest narrow part at about 900m you can easily scramble up and around the boulders, but in winter this place can be icy. Above this point is a gently rising basin with boulder fields and snow wreaths, where the Garbh Uisge divides in two. The main stream is Garbh Uisge Mor, which leads up through a magnificent piece of arctic terrain beside some high lochans. It rises in an upper basin called the Snowy Corrie where huge drifts last into the summer; the skyline facing you as you walk up the basin is the plateau east of the ruined Sappers' Bothy.

WALKING IN BEN MACDUI'S CORRIES

For the hillwalker the corries of Ben Macdui are magnificent to explore. Coire Etchachan, Garbh Uisge and the Snowy Corrie have already been described. A fine route is to go up Glen Luibeg to where the burn forks below the Sron Riach, and then climb by a path up the east bank of the eastern stream far up into the wilds of Coire Sputan Dearg. A sunny, sheltered corrie, it has a beautiful setting. On the way it is well worth climbing up the side stream to Lochan Uaine and then dropping north into Coire Sputan Dearg. From the north-east end of the cliffs in Coire Sputan Dearg a short easy walk leads up to the 1053m neck west of the conical, gravelly, 1108m point at 010 996, and then down to the path above Loch Etchachan. The 1108m point has often been called Creagan a' Choire Etchachan erroneously, as the Creagan really refers to the crags to the east in Coire Etchachan.

North of Ben Macdui on its west side, the Allt a' Choire Mhoir drains the uppermost gentle gravelly hollow towards the North Top, then runs through a green patch among boulder fields - often deeply snow covered in late summer – and then hurries steeply into the Lairig Ghru. Another bouldery but unnamed corrie lies south of Coire Mor, fringed with a frieze of broken remains of crags.

LOCH AVON AND THE SHELTER STONE

Loch Avon ('aan) lies at about 725m in a deep cliff-ringed trench between Cairn Gorm and Ben Macdui on their east sides. Anyone descending to it from either of these hills, especially in winter, should remember that this is one of the most inaccessible places in the Cairngorms, and that to escape one will either have to climb out again or else walk miles down the uninhabited Glen Avon. The loch stretches 2½ kilometres long, up to 300 metres wide, and only about 35m at its deepest, with several beautiful beaches of fine golden and white sands. To get the best view of it, you should approach from the lower end by the Lairig an Laoigh or The Saddle, and then go up the loch side. The long line of this grand sheet of water leads the eye up to the dark headwall of cliffs beyond the top of the loch, and to the streams that come foaming like white ribbons over the slabs and rocks. These all join into one stream running into the west end of the loch; it passes through a little green of turf and flowers, called Meur na Banaraiche or finger stream of the dairymaid.

Walking routes to Loch Avon. Leaving the Ben Macdui path at Loch Etchachan, you cross the flat ground north of the loch and then drop down a steep path for 150m in altitude to the Shelter Stone (2 kilometres). The first sudden view of blue Loch Avon is breathtaking, and the path then goes below the great craggy pyramid on the north spur of Carn Etchachan, down to the Shelter Stone. Distance; 11 kilometres and 500m climb from Derry Lodge. Another way from the Derry, which is 4 kilometres further but involves 180m less climbing, goes by the Lairig an Laoigh, breaking off by a path round the west side of the Dubh Lochan and then continuing by a path up the south side of Loch Avon.

From the north, a much-used way, now a path, approaches from Strath Nethy (10 kilometres from Bynack Stable east of Ryvoan to the Shelter Stone) by The Saddle at 807m, and then along the north side of the loch. From Cairn Gorm you can come down the Allt Coire Raibeirt by a path down the easier east side of the steeper part of the burn (3½ kilometres from Ptarmigan Restaurant to Shelter Stone), but take care as the steepest part of the path has eroded and is loose. The next burn to the west, the Allt Coire Domhain, offers another way down, again by a path on its east side, and this is easily reached from the Coire Cas car park by the path up the Fiacaill a' Choire Chais. Another way to Allt Coire Domhain from the Coire Cas car park is by the steep Goat Track up the head of Coire an t-Sneachda, but the Goat Track is rather loose and unstable. Both the routes by Allt Coire Raibeirt and Allt Coire Domhain are steep, and avalanches have occurred there in winter; at that season The Saddle is usually a safer, but much longer, way.

Carn Etchachan and the Shelter Stone Crag

The Feith Buidhe or yellow bog-stream, after meandering through a beautiful green basin on the high plateau, suddenly crashes over the steep rocks of Creag na Feithe Buidhe in a waterfall, but you can find an easy sporting route to the tops up here in late summer by zigzagging through the wet granite slabs. Finding a good way down is less easy, and this route should be avoided by hillwalkers in winter or early summer because it is so often heavily corniced with snow. When descending from Lochan Buidhe, you will find it much safer and easier to go south-east just before the stream steepens at the waterfall, next traverse a stony shelf to the north of a broken slabby cliff towards the Garbh Uisge Beag, and then drop easily into the main basin of the Garbh Uisge and so to Loch Avon by that stream. In misty summer weather, hillwalkers who have no experience of rock scrambling and little experience of navigating in complex terrain should avoid the routes from the Feith Buidhe round to the Garbh Uisge inclusive.

The Shelter Stone.   Clach Dhion or stone of the shelter lies at the head of Loch Avon on the south side. It is the largest of the many big boulders - a relic of some colossal past rock fall - lying below the Shelter Stone Crag. Clach Dhion fell on smaller blocks leaving a natural chamber underneath. The sides have been packed with stones and sods, so that the inside feels dry and fairly wind-tight. In winter the entrance often becomes snowed up and snow may remain in the shaded interior long after it has gone from outside the stone. Nearby stands a smaller shelter stone, also improved by draught sealing, which visitors sometimes use when Clach Dhion has no room

Beinn Mheadhoin from the top of Castle Gates Gully

left. In bad weather it may be hard to find Clach Dhion. If so, its characteristic shape and colour are a help. From below it looks roughly rectangular, but its west end rises 2 to 3m higher than the east end and carries a cairn. The lowest part of the side facing the loch has a pale appearance, in a zigzag pattern that reaches higher at the east end, with darker rock above. You must stoop when entering, but the roof slopes upwards and at the far side you can almost stand upright. At first it seems dark inside, but as your eye becomes used to the poorer light you can see the inside of the shelter. On the floor, 8-10 can sleep, but there is comfortable room for only 5-6 to sleep, cook meals and hold rucksacks.

A.I.McConnochie measured Clach Dhion as 44 x 21 x 22ft high, 'which, allowing 12 cubic ft to the ton, would make its weight nearly 1700 tons'. In August 1926, Dr W.Bulloch measured it as 43 x 20 x 22ft. A sample of Clach Dhion, later examined in London, weighed 2.58g per cc, which would give 1361 tons as the weight.

Clach Dhion was described in 1794 in The Statistical Account (12, 429) which referred to it as a retreat for freebooters holding 'eighteen armed men'. Later it became well known for visitors to the Cairngorms. One of the longest visits by a climbing party, lasting 10 days, was described in the Aberdeen Free Press in September 1886, in articles that contain historical and topographical information about the Cairngorms. In 1924 a visitors' book was placed inside Clach Dhion, and completed volumes lie in the Cairngorm Club's library in Aberdeen. Over the 14 years from 1931-43, an average of 525 people visited the Stone annually, and about one-fourth of them stayed at least one night. In 1933, which had a very fine summer, 523 visited in July, with 129 on one day alone, and 1018 came during the year. From 1931-43 the monthly averages were: 5 in January, 0.5 in February, 3 in March, 9 in April, 35 in May, 100 in June, 212 in July, 131 in August, 56 in September, 7 in October, 1 in November and 2 in December (see CCJ 11, 212; and especially 17, 212).

The Cairngorm Club originated at Clach Dhion. The first climbing club in Scotland, it was founded there on the morning after the night of Queen Victoria's Golden Jubilee, on 24 June 1887. In 1965 the Lord Lyon King of Arms of Scotland granted the Club a coat of arms with the motto Clac-dian (CCJ 17, 225). In fact, 'dian' means violent or vehement, the very opposite sense to 'dion' or shelter!

Creag an Leth-choin *(kraikan'laichin or rock of the half-dog or lurcher)* (1053m)
An old legend was that a deer chase ended here and in the fury of the hunt one of the dogs went over the cliff. One of the most spectacular hills in the Cairngorms, Creag an Leth-choin is the fine rocky peak dominating the east side of Lairig Ghru. A path, skirting along the east side of the furthest north rocks, goes up to about 1000m altitude on the north slope. Lower down, this path climbs from south of Creag a' Chalamain, after running in from the Glen More direction. The best route is to reach this path after climbing up through Rothiemurchus on the Lairig path (10 kilometres from Coylumbridge to summit, 820m of ascent). The easiest though dullest way goes from the Coire Cas car park by the path that runs up Allt Creag an Leth-choin and so westwards to the top. The southern of the two tops at 1053m carries a cairn right on the cliff edge in a wonderful setting looking along the huge trench of the Lairig Ghru. The northern top at 1026m overlooks Glen More.

Bynack More *(Beidhneag, 'beinik, meaning doubtful, originally was Beinn Beidhneag)* (1090m)
Distance: 5 kilometres from Bynack Stable east of Ryvoan, 640m climb. Bynack More rises high out of Strath Nethy and the flattish range of lower hills towards Tomintoul. A beautiful conical peak when seen from the north, it dominates Abernethy Forest. A good way up goes by the Lairig an Laoigh path to the long plateau 2 kilometres north of the summit. Leaving that path at 792m where it begins to drop down Coire Odhar, you walk along flat ground and then climb south up the prominent northern nose of Bynack More. For 300m in height it rises past some interesting rocky knobs. The prominent niche in the summit as seen from Strath Nethy is a grassy hollow between two lumps of rock. Here there opens out a fine view of the northern spurs of Ben Avon and Beinn a' Bhuird and of the great expanse of the Caiplich moors. Bynack Beg stretches out as a lower top 800 metres to the north-west of the summit, reaching about 970m altitude. The most interesting place on the hill is at Sabhalan Beithneag or Barns of Bynack, with lie south-east of the summit of Bynack More and 120m in height below it, but almost invisible from it. The Sabhalan are an extraordinary group of granite tors rising from the bare hillside, bigger and steeper than most other tors in the Cairngorms. Do not mistake them for the much smaller tors of Sabhalan Beaga Beithneag or Little Barns of Bynack on the south slope, which can

easily be seen from the summit. You can vary the return journey by descending to Strath Nethy by Allt a' Choire Dheirg, so called from its fine little corrie with reddish rocks and scree. The grassy haughs by Nethy-side are a pleasant way back to the Lairig track.

The hill mass continues south-west of Bynack More for 4 kilometres to The Saddle at 807m, a col that leads on to Cairn Gorm (summit of Cairn Gorm 1½ kilometres distant, 440m ascent). On the way to The Saddle, you pass over the 1017m A' Choinneach, meaning the moss, an interesting medium-level plateau where the walking is excellent on a carpet with much woolly hair moss.

Because of the ease of access from the public road and chairlift on Cairn Gorm, many people going to Bynack More and A' Choinneach come that way. Bynack More stands only 4 kilometres in distance from The Saddle south-east of Cairn Gorm, and The Saddle is 1½ kilometres from Cairn Gorm summit, or 2 kilometres from the Ptarmigan Restaurant via the eastern slopes of Cairn Gorm. The total ascent is 460m from The Saddle to Bynack More via A' Choinneach, plus 440m ascent back to Cairn Gorm summit or 340m to the Ptarmigan Restaurant by the eastern slopes.

Another two routes start from the car park at Coire na Ciste on Cairn Gorm, at 550m altitude. One heads for 2 kilometres eastwards past a small tree plantation to a 721m col, then down a rough hillside with glacial meltwater channels to Strath Nethy, and so up the north-west ridge of Bynack Beg to Bynack More (5½ kilometres, 750m ascent). The other goes up the east side of Coire na Ciste to the col one kilometre north-north-east of Cairn Gorm, then down to The Saddle, and so to Bynack More as described above (8½ kilometres, 1040m ascent).

Carn a' Mhaim (*karna'veim, hill of the pass*) (1037m)
Distance: 5½ kilometres from Derry Lodge, 630m ascent. You can easily climb this hill from the Lairig Ghru track one kilometre west of where it crosses the Luibeg Burn, but by far the best approach comes from the long north-north-west ridge that connects it to Ben Macdui, called Ceann Caol or thin end. The ridge is fringed with rocks and offers wonderful views across Glen Dee to The Devil's Point. The south top, so obvious from the Derry, stands slightly lower at 1014m; it rises above the green Coire na Poite (*korna'potsh*) or corrie of the pot, facing Glen Luibeg.

Derry Cairngorm (1155m)
Distance: 5 kilometres from Derry Lodge, 750m ascent. Local people used to call it simply Carn Gorm or blue hill, and later it became Cairn Gorm of Derry to distinguish it from the Cairn Gorm at Glen More. A beautiful high cone, from Inverey or Glen Lui it seems to tower above Ben Macdui. Climbing it is a good way to vary the return journey to Derry Lodge from Ben Macdui. The top consists of a boulder field, which you can skirt on the east side by cutting immediately above the highest rocks of Coire an Lochain Uaine. It is well worth diverging to look down into that beautiful corrie with its waterfall, sheltered lochan at about 755m, and sunny rocks, immortalised by William Smith's lovely poem. The rocky top north of the lochan has the name Sgor an Lochain Uaine. On the way south to the Derry, you pass the boulder

Bynack More from Beinn a' Chaorainn

strewn dome of Carn Gorm Beag or little Cairn Gorm at 1040m and then drop to the fine viewpoint of Carn Crom or curved hill at 890m. Just before climbing the last short rise up to Carn Crom, go left to the edge to get a grand view into Glen Derry. Below lies Coire na Saobhaidhe (korna'saivee) or corrie of the fox's den, a wild place with wet slabby rocks. Further down the Derry Burn winds sinuously through green flats dotted with ancient pines.

Beinn Mheadhoin *(in local speech Beinn Meadhon or middle hill, bain'main)* (1182m) Distance: 9 kilometres from Derry Lodge, 760m climb. Beinn Mheadhoin blocks the north end of Glen Derry, a great mass of a hill with a prominent tor on its summit. You get a grand view of it above the old pines if you climb the knoll immediately behind Derry Lodge. From upper Glen Derry, it rises in a spectacular, triangle-shaped broken crag to a fine point at 1082m. The easiest way up goes from Loch Etchachan, or from the 740m col beside the highest part of the Lairig an Laoigh path at the top of Glen Derry. Several great tors rise from the whaleback of Beinn Mheadhoin, called Sabhalan (barns) Beinn Mheadhoin.

The summit itself consists of a big tor with a cairn perched on top, but you can easily scramble up the north or shorter side for about 6m. You will enjoy fine views if you descend a little to the west to look down over Loch Avon. Be careful in mist as Beinn Mheadhoin has many crags and slabs around it. The north shoulder above the Dubh Lochan has a little point that looks striking from near Nethy Bridge.

Since the public road and chairlifts greatly eased access to Cairn Gorm, people often climb Beinn Mheadhoin from that side. A short route from Cairn Gorm is by the path down Allt Coire Raibeirt to Loch Avon, next up the path towards Loch Etchachan, and then diverging from it eastwards to the top of Beinn Mheadhoin (from Loch Avon 2½ kilometres distance and 460m ascent, and from the Ptarmigan Restaurant 6 kilometres via Cairn Gorm summit or via the eastern slopes of Cairn Gorm). From Loch Avon there is a 520m ascent back up to Cairn Gorm summit (420m ascent to Fiacaill a' Choire Chais and the same to the Ptarmigan Restaurant via the eastern slopes). An alternative route from the Coire Cas car park is by the Goat Track up the head of Coire an t-Sneachda and then down Allt Coire Domhain (9 kilometres, 930 m), but the Goat Track is rather loose and unstable.

Creag Mhor *(big rocky hill)* (895m)
This remote hill rises east of the pass of Lairig an Laoigh, south-east of Bynack More. It has a small plateau shared with the 848m hill of Dagrum (Da Dhruim, 'dagrum, meaning two ridges) to the north-east. Creag Mhor has rough granite tors, and both hills show big expanses of granite gravel and sand, indicating severe exposure combined with very infertile soils. Creag Mhor has a small granite tor on its summit. The easiest approach is from Glenmore Lodge by the Lairig an Laoigh path (see Chapter 3) as far as the crossing of the Glasath burn, and then walking uphill by a 200m climb to the summit (12 kilometres from Glenmore Lodge, 710m ascent).

CLIMBING

COIRE AN T-SNEACHDA
The accessible northern corries of Cairn Gorm were explored fairly early. In 1904 an SMC party led by Harold Raeburn climbed *Pygmy Ridge* of Coire an t-Sneachda, and in the 1930s the Moray Mountaineering Club were active in Coire an Lochain. In Coire an t-Sneachda, the main crag below the highest top on the plateau above is the dome-shaped *Aladdin Buttress,* leading to the pinnacle of Aladdin's Seat, which ends well down the wide gully of *Aladdin's Couloir* (Grade 1). On Aladdin Buttress, routes on the right part are on direct lines, the *Magic Crack* (100m, HVS) being the best. The top of Aladdin Buttress ends in the easy upper part of Aladdin's Couloir which leads out by conspicuous slopes of red grit stretching right to the plateau edge. However, a better finish goes up the separate 10m rock of Aladdin's Seat at the top of Aladdin Buttress, which forms the upper couloir's right edge and looks a spectacular pointed pinnacle from the plateau. Pygmy Ridge is the other separate and larger triangular mass of rock lying slightly further along from the top part of Aladdin's Couloir, making a delightful short climb (Moderate). To the right, nearer the col towards Cairn Lochan, stretches the long Fluted Buttress with its many straight ribs of rock, its tiny pinnacles called The Fingers up near the plateau edge, and its many gullies which give good ice and snow climbs in winter. Away to the west and hidden from Glen More stands the fine, steep, bulging Fiacaill Buttress, which has been climbed by several routes. Fiacaill Buttress is split by a steep shallow couloir, the *Fiacaill*

Couloir, which gives a good Grade II winter climb. The *Fiacaill Ridge* itself, on the very edge that separates the corrie from the nearby Coire an Lochain, makes an easy scramble in summer, and a Grade I route in winter conditions.

COIRE AN LOCHAIN

Here a compact set of high projecting buttresses rises above the reddish Great Slab. One of the best climbs in the Cairngorms is *Savage Slit* (Very Difficult) on the large western or No 4 Buttress. Well seen from the cliff top to the east, this remarkable crack goes straight up the east wall of the projecting buttress on beautiful rough granite. *Fall-out Corner* (VS) is an even more spectacular route up the exposed corner about 10m to the right of Savage Slit. The rock on No 3 Buttress gives an excellent 60m route, *The Demon* (E2), up the steep section in the middle of the buttress. Some of the other, easier routes in this corrie have patches of gravel, vegetation and shattered rock, but when gripped by winter frost and snow these north-facing crags at such a high altitude, finishing at nearly 1200m, give fine climbing. The obvious gully between No 2 Buttress and No 3 Buttress is *The Couloir* (Grade 1). In recent years this corrie has been the scene of great advances in winter climbing technique, epitomised by the (as yet unrepeated) ascent of *Ventricle* (HVS, Grade VI).

SMALLER CRAGS NEAR GLEN MORE

A practice ground with short pitches on dry granite lies on Creagan Dubh or black little rock, the slabby black outcrop near the foot of Coire na Ciste. A better place is on the short but steep crag to the south-east of Creag a' Chalamain. Creag an Leth-choin has several obvious ridges of dark granite up to nearly 100m high on reasonably sound dry rock, offering climbs about Moderate in standard, which give sporting ways of reaching the plateau from the Lairig Ghru. In winter, the gullies between the ridges can make ice climbs of 220-300m.

LOCH AVON BASIN

The finest climbing ground of Cairn Gorm and Ben Macdui, shared with both, lies on the big granite crags in a huge amphitheatre around Loch Avon. Next to Cairn Gorm are the slabby, easterly Stac an Fharaidh, then the Stag Rocks west of Coire Raibeirt, and then the steep wall of Hell's Lum Crag on the Cairn Gorm side of Feith Buidhe. On the Ben Macdui side east of Garbh Uisge is the spectacular steep wall of the Shelter Stone Crag, and further east beyond Castle Gates Gully the high, domed Carn Etchachan. Further round still, on Beinn Mheadhoin, is the slabby cliff of Stacan Dubha.

STAC AN FHARAIDH

Immediately south of Cairn Gorm you drop into a shallow corrie east of Coire Raibeirt, with a tor at one side. Below here, a grand wall of slabs with rough rock drops 150m to Loch Avon; it is Stac an Fharaidh (precipice of the ladder), standing to the west of The Saddle. The cliffs have an east and a west flank. Good routes on the left part of the east flank are *Whispers* (VS) up the left edge and *Bellows* (HVS) up cracks about 12m to the right. There is also good climbing using cracks up the slabs on the west flank.

THE STAG ROCKS

On the west side of Coire Raibeirt, these rocks present a long face of black rough granite above Loch Avon. The cliffs rise in two main sections separated by the scree-filled *Diagonal Gully*. On the left section, the 150m *Afterthought Arete* goes up the long sharp edge at the left end of the cliffs, to the right of a wide scree gully; although only Moderate in difficulty, it makes a fine climb. Further to the right, the imposing steep 180m wall of the Longbow Crag forms the northern part of Stag Rocks. A fine route on it is *Longbow Direct* (VS); starting at the pink water-worn fault left of the centre of the Longbow face, it leads up and over the 'Longbow' or roof in the middle of the face. Another good route is *The Sand-Pyper Direct* (VS), starting near the centre of the Longbow Crag.

HELL'S LUM CRAG

Between Coire Raibeirt and Feith Buidhe soars the smooth, polished, Hell's Lum Crag. Most routes run wet even in fairly dry weather, but the rock is clean and sound, and in winter the water turns the climbs into grand ice pitches. The tallest main part of the crag forms The Frontal Face, reaching 200m in height. The VS *Hellfire Corner* takes an excellent line up the main left-facing corners in the middle of the face. The VS *Clean Sweep* is another excellent route up the pink, leaning corner to the right. On the left part of the crag, the long dark slit of *Deep-Cut Chimney* (Very Difficult) offers a fine climb, giving spectacular scenery in its upper reaches where the chimney cuts far back into the cliff. Round the corner to the left, the great black recess going from top to bottom of the crag is *Hell's Lum*. Running water drenches this gully in summer, but in winter it becomes a fine ice climb until deep snow buries the ice pitches.

THE STICIL

The rock of An Sticil (the kiln-rafter or beam), later called the Shelter Stone Crag, a 240m north-facing wall of slabby granite, is undoubtedly one of the finest crags in Britain. Harold Raeburn climbed the prominent feature of *Raeburn's Buttress* on the Sticil's left flank as early as 1907, but then the crag remained unexplored for decades. Between Raeburn's Buttress and the huge sweep of central slabs, *Sticil Face* gives an excellent climb (Grade V) in winter. *The Citadel* (VS) goes right up the main face in a direct line, by the chimney at the right side of the central slabs. *The Needle* (E1) is a magnificent route going fairly directly to the top of the crag, while *Steeple*, just to the left of The Needle and between it and The Citadel, is an excellent direct line on clean rock of sustained severity on a stupendous face. Other grand routes which go up the forbidding smooth central slabs further left, in the very middle of the Sticil's dark north wall, are the remarkable E2 climb *The Pin*, and *Thor* (E5), and the E2 *Snipers*. These three very fine routes start from the grassy terrace which slants upwards and along the face from the foot of Raeburn's Buttress, and break the great slabs above to reach the grassy ledges on the upper traverse of the Sticil Face route. *Aphrodite* (E7) is a recent climb which takes a direct, uncompromising line up these slabs, and is probably the hardest climb of its type in Scotland. To the right of The Sticil, the Forefinger Pinnacle, one of the most remarkable rock features in the massif, giving short routes up to 30m varying from Moderate to Severe. The Sticil's left flank ends at Castle Gates Gully, an easy scree shoot leading to the plateau.

CARN ETCHACHAN
This great domed crag rises to the east of Castle Gates Gully. Although it is one of the biggest cliffs in the Cairngorms, with some excellent crack routes on sound rock, no climbs were done here till a sudden spate of new routes in the early 1950s. The lower part of the cliff is partly vegetated, and a grassy terrace leads across the face from the Loch Etchachan side, giving access to 90m of clean, steep upper rocks. Here are some fine routes on excellent granite, requiring jamming, laybacks and friction on steep cracks and ribs, *Boa* being particularly good up a superb crack. The excellent *Crevasse Route* (Mild Severe) with a window high up, is a popular climb up the first buttress along the terrace. To the right of

Kiwi Gully, Hell's Lum Crag

this upper face a couple of much longer routes form magnificent winter climbs, the best being *Route Major* (Grade IV) from the lowest rocks below Castle Gates Gully right to the summit cairn at 1113m. The nearby *Scorpion* (Very Difficult), starting slightly higher up Castle Gates Gully below the protruding rock mass of The Sentinel, gives a fine Grade V climb in winter.

STACAN DUBHA
On the Beinn Mheadhoin side of Loch Avon, an imposing set of steep bulging crags called Stacan Dubha or black precipices offers a few routes up to 140m. Although

Djibangi, Creagan a' Choire Etchachan

they look impressive at first sight, the climbs are not of high quality as many of the ribs are disconnected by broken rock.

COIRE SPUTAN DEARG

Sheltered from the prevailing wind, the crags here are sunny, yet it looks an alpine corrie with deep snow fields till midsummer and sound rough granite. The corrie has for long been a popular climbing ground. A fine route though short is *Crystal Ridge* (Difficult and Grade III) up the edge of a rough slab alongside a steep left wall. To its right rises the 120m steep Grey Man's Crag which forms the main face of rock in the corrie. On Grey Man's Crag, *Hanging Dyke* (Very Difficult) gives a particularly good ascent. Starting just to the right of the lowest rocks, it goes up a dyke where the rock has the superficial appearance of ancient dark brickwork. *Grey Slab* is another excellent route, up a prominent corner just to the left of Hanging Dyke, tending to lead leftwards. *Glissade Gully*, the leftmost of the three main spouts or scree gullies, usually gives good glissades until June. To the left of the middle spout, which is named *Narrow Gully*, *Snake Ridge* (Severe) provides a classic route with a hard middle section. To the right of Narrow Gully, three parallel buttresses of steep black granite soar to the plateau. The middle one called *The Black Tower* makes an excellent climb (Severe). *Flake Buttress* to its right rises into a fine pointed ridge; although steep, it is only Moderate and Grade II, and has good clean rock, making an interesting sporting route to the top.

The big bulging slabs in the south part of the corrie - The Red Slabs - offer several routes on very rough granite varying from Severe to VS and up to 120m high. Further south, starting at the side of Lochan Uaine, you can have a good long winter route up to the pyramid peak on the plateau edge 300m above; it lies mostly on steep snow, but has some broken rock except after deep snow when the whole face becomes a beautiful smooth slope of steep snow. It is liable to avalanche.

COIRE ETCHACHAN

On the broken buttresses of the Beinn Mheadhoin side of Coire Etchachan many ribs of broken rock offer scrambling, and in winter the gullies give sporting ways to the top.

The best cliff in Coire Etchachan is the grand 120m east-facing wall which forms part of the line of crags making up Creagan a' Choire Etchachan. On its left side, the dark, wide, recessed gully of *The Corridor* splits the cliff. The Bastion projects out as the fine convex bulge to its left, wider at the foot than at the tapering top. Outstanding here is the 90m climb *The Talisman* (Hard Severe) which goes up The Bastion's right edge, next to The Corridor. *Quartzvein Edge* (Moderate), at the left edge of The Bastion, is a popular climb. Many other fine and mostly harder routes have been done, the best being on the 110m high sweep of smooth slabs called The Crimson Slabs. These look particularly impressive from the path going up the higher part of the corrie, especially when the water trickling down parts of the slabs glistens in the sun. The two obvious crack corners piercing these slabs have both become classic VS routes, *Djibangi* on the left and *The Dagger* on the right. Djibangi is now the more popular, and also one of the best winter routes in the Cairngorms (Grade IV). Other grand lines up The Crimson Slabs are the excellent *Scabbard* (VS), the impressive *Stiletto* (El) up a thin crack to the left of The Dagger, and the delicate *King Crimson* (E3) which goes directly up the slabs to the left of Djibangi.

SKIING

Cairn Gorm's northern corries of Coire an t-Sneachda, Coire an Lochain and Allt Creag an Leth-choin (Lurcher's Gully) are popular as an accessible excellent area for ski touring.

In good conditions, Cairn Gorm and Ben Macdui make a superb ski tour, and the plateau corries often hold big snowfields far into June. The runs off Ben Macdui to the Lairig Ghru by Allt a' Choire Mhoir and Allt Clach nan Taillear are excellent ski-mountaineering routes, sometimes with cornice problems. The descent to Loch Etchachan and down Coire Etchachan makes a very good run. Various routes down to Loch Avon are all liable to avalanche.

Ski run down the Allt a' Choire Mhoir

Derry Cairngorm and Beinn Mheadhoin offer good ski-mountaineering with an interesting variety of terrain, and Carn a' Mhaim and Bynack More give straightforward ski touring, the former only when deep snow covers the rough bouldery slopes.

FURTHER READING

A.I.McConnochie. *The central Cairngorms.* CCJ 1, 309, 366.

W.Garden *The central Cairngorms* (Guide Book article). SMCJ 7,323.

G.Barlow *On the possibility of seeing the Cuillin from the Cairngorms.* SMCJ 26, 16.

A.Gray (1970) *The Big Grey Man of Ben Macdhui.* A detailed account.

CHAPTER 3

Lairig Ghru, Glen Feshie and Lairig an Laoigh

ACCESS
All three passes can be approached from Speyside or Deeside, and all three cross from Spey to Dee or vice versa. Parties with two cars often combine to leave the first car at one end and the second at the other, and then meet and exchange car keys in the middle. Lairig Ghru is most easily approached from Aviemore, Glen Feshie from Kincraig on Speyside, and Lairig an Laoigh from Glen More near Aviemore. The other ends of Lairig Ghru, Glen Feshie and Lairig an Laoigh all meet at the Linn of Dee. Public roads go to Tolvah and Achlean on the west and east sides of Glen Feshie, and to Glenmore Lodge and the Linn of Dee. Cars should be parked north of Achlean at 853 977, and east of the Linn of Dee on the north side of the river.

ACCOMMODATION
As in Chapters 1 and 8. Also Glen Feshie Hostel at Balachroick, 850 009; March Guest House, Lagganlia, 857 040; Insh House at the junction of the road up the west side of Glen Feshie with the B970, 836 038

BOTHIES AND SHELTERS
Lairig Ghru: Bob Scott's Bothy 042 931, Corrour 982 958, the tiny Garbh Coire Bothy 959 986 on south bank of stream 1½km west of Lairig path. The Sinclair Memorial Hut at 959 036 was demolished in autumn 1991. Glen Feshie: Ruighe Ealasaid at 003 869 (partly ruined), Eidart bothy 510m at 906 885, Ruigh-aiteachain 846 927, Inshriach 884 056. Lairig an Laoigh: Ryvoan 006 115, Bynack Stable 020 104 by Nethy side east of Ryvoan, Fords of Avon Refuge 042 031 on north bank of River Avon at 690m, Hutchison Memorial Hut 023 998.

MAPS
Ordnance Survey 1:50,000 Sheets 35, 36 and 43

Through the great rampart of the high Cairngorms go three of Scotland's finest hill passes. Once much used by Highland folk for cattle droving and other trade, which went on through Lairig Ghru up till the early years of this century, all three are now rights of way. Where you leave the public roads to get on to these tracks, locked gates bar the way for cars, but an open part at the side is wide enough for walkers, bicycles and ponies to pass.

Looking south through the Lairig Ghru from Creag an Leth-choin

GEOLOGY, LANDFORMS AND WILDLIFE

See the chapters covering the hill country through which these three passes run: Lairig Ghru, Chapters 1 and 8, Glen Feshie 5 and 7, Lairig an Laoigh 1, 2 and 8.

ESTATES AND LAND USE

The Aberdeenshire parts of all three routes are on Mar Lodge Estate. The Inverness-shire parts of Glen Feshie and Lairig Ghru lie on Glenfeshie and Rothiemurchus Estates respectively. The Royal Society for the Protection of Birds has the Abernethy end of Lairig an Laoigh. This is deer-forest country. Although all three routes pass through some fine natural forest, there are virtually no young trees outside fenced exclosures in Glen Feshie, Mar, and the upper parts of Rothiemurchus and Aber-nethy, because too many red deer eat them. The fenced areas show that seedlings thrive if deer are kept out.

HISTORY

Above the Lairig Ghru path in Glen Luibeg stands an ancient solitary pine high on Carn Crom, called Craobh an Oir (kree-an'or) or tree of the gold. An old legend tells how a Mackenzie of Dalmore buried a stolen crock of gold here, and later moved it to near the top of Cairn Geldie, north-east of Geldie Lodge. Beside the Lairig path in upper Glen Dee, half way between Corrour and Allt Clach nan Taillear, stands the group of weathered, ribbed stones called Clach nan Taillear ('talyer) or stone of the tailors. Here three tailors perished while sheltering in the snow one New Year's Eve. They had wagered that they would dance a reel on the same night in Rothiemurchus and Braemar. Having danced in Speyside, they set out through the Lairig, only to succumb on the way. General Wade surveyed the route for a road from the Linn of Dee to Kingussie through Glen Feshie, but never built it.

Beside the footbridge in Glen Derry 2½ kilometres north of Derry Lodge, at a place still called the Derry Dam, there once stood a sluice for floating cut trees down the glen. It was built in the early 1800s by Alexander Davidson, a noted Deeside character who turned to poaching after the timber floating, and whose racy life story appears in Michie's *Deeside Tales*. The Lairig an Laoigh path up Glen Derry passes below Derry Cairngorm and its hanging corrie of Coire an Lochain Uaine. It was at the side of the burn from the lochan that William Smith or Gow, often called Uilleam Rynuie, built the little shelter commemorated in his poem 'Allt an Lochain Uaine'. Smith, whose home lay at Rynuie on the Abernethy side of the Cairngorms, still has descendants in Strath Spey today. A famous deer stalker in the 1700s, Smith used to make poaching raids into Mar Forest with a gun presented to him by the laird of Rothiemurchus. His favourite resort was Lochan Uaine with its fine view down to the Derry, where he could be on guard against the Earl of Fife's 'foresters' or deer stalkers, the 'red foxes', as he called them, coming up the glen to catch him. The first verse is given below, along with a fairly direct translation by the present writer.

Aig Allt an Lochain Uaine,	*At the burn of the green lochan*
Gu'n robh mi uair a' tamh,	*I was staying a time,*
'S ged bha'n t-aite fuar	*And though the place was cold*
Bha'n fhardach fuathasach blath,	*The dwelling was wonderfully warm,*
Ged thigeadh gaoth 'o thuath orm	*Though wind from the north would come on me*
'Us cathadh luath o'n aird	*And fast drifting snow from the height*
Bhiodh Allt an Lochain Uaine	*The burn of the green lochan would be*
Le'fhuaim ga m'chuir gu pramh	*Putting me to slumber with its sound*

This poem, sung to the beautiful melody found in the collections called 'Gu ma slan a chi mi' or 'Good health be with you', was for several generations the most popular song in Braemar and Strath Spey. As the old language has gone, only a few local people now know it, but it should rank as the finest song of the Cairngorms.

LAIRIG GHRU

Name: Lairig Ghru (larig'groo), pass of Dhru or Druie, referring to the stream draining the north side of the pass. Distance: from Whitewell to the locked gate at the foot of Glen Lui 28 kilometres (see Chapter 2 for the Linn of Dee car park and path to the Derry road), from Coylumbridge 30 kilometres, total ascent 670m. You can shorten this by cycling 5 kilometres up the private road from the locked Lui gate to Derry Lodge or at the Rothiemurchus end on the gravel road to the Cairngorm Club footbridge.

The Lairig Ghru is the finest and best known pass in Scotland. From Strath Spey its huge dark cleft carves a deep 'V' between the great masses of Braeriach and Ben Macdui, and its red screes glow red in the evening sun. From Rothiemurchus the Lairig has an air of mystery, dark and somehow more challenging than the high tops around it. It takes you into the very heart of the Cairngorms and through a rich variety of hill and natural woodland scenery. The Lairig Ghru should remain the finest cross-country path in the country, and a grand challenge to the hillwalker. We must guard its priceless value.

The best approach is to start in Rothiemurchus and finish on Deeside; the climb up into the great 'V' of the Lairig by the pine forest offers one of the most magnificent walks of Scotland. From 915 106 near Coylumbridge a rough road goes up Rothiemurchus. You take the path that breaks off at 917 100 to the left of this road and leads to the Cairngorm Club footbridge. Another way is to drive up the public road from Inverdruie to Whitewell, walk down to Lochan Deo and then east along a gravel road to the footbridge erected by the Cairngorm Club in 1912 (CCJ 7, 235). The bridge stands not far below where the Allt Druidh from the Lairig Ghru joins the larger stream of Am Beanaidh from Gleann Einich. On the parapet it is miscalled the 'Allt na Beinne Mhoir' footbridge, from the old map error for Am Beanaidh (Beanaidh is pronounced 'bennie). A tablet on the parapet gives approximate distances and times:

	Hours	Miles
To Aviemore	1½	4
Coylum Bridge	¾	2
Lairig Ghru summit (2733 ft)	3	5½
Derry Lodge	6½	14
Linn of Dee	8	18
Braemar	10	24½

Beyond here you pass a beautiful grassy clearing, once cultivated as the croft of Allt Dhru, and then come into the forest to the junction of the four paths, often called Piccadilly. To your left a track leads to the old Medicine Well and over the River Luineag by a ford at 934 098 up from Aultnancaber (altna'gaper); ahead lies the way to Loch Morlich, with a spur road coming off it further on which leads up to the army's Rothiemurchus Lodge. Your path to the Lairig turns right and then climbs through small pines and heather high above Allt Druidh, with wonderful views back over Rothiemurchus. For 2½ kilometres the path crosses open peaty moorland. Almost 8 kilometres from Whitewell and the same distance from the west end of Loch Morlich, an alternative path comes in on the left from Glen More. Starting from the road from Glen More to Coire Cas at 985 074, it crosses the Allt Mor by a footbridge and leads south-west through a rocky gap south-east of Creag a' Chalamain, now called the Chalamain Gap but formerly Eag Coire a' Chomhlaich. In the narrow defile of the gap the path disappears among a jumble of huge boulders which give difficult and slow going. Once through the gap, the path descends slightly to join the main Lairig path.

Looking towards The Devil's Point, Cairn Toul and Braeriach at the southern approach to the Lairig Ghru

Beyond the point where the path comes in from Chalamain Gap the pass begins to narrow. From here on the screes and crags of Creag an Leth-choin hem in the pass on the east, and those of Sron na Lairige on the west. Violent winds often funnel through this narrow part of the pass even when the rest of the Lairig is fairly calm. The path rises up the long narrow trough along increasingly stony ground, until near the summit at about 835m the floor of the pass becomes rough with boulders, which local people no longer clear from the path as they did annually last century. Nevertheless, a good Highland pony can still go through the Lairig Ghru; the other two passes are easy for horses. You will find the summit a very good place for ptarmigan, which nest there regularly; this is the only one of the three passes where you can depend on seeing them. Just past the summit, the March Burn plunges down from the plateau, only to disappear underground below the boulder fields. However, the water comes out on the Dee side of the summit as a series of one large and three smaller beautiful pools in hollows of the boulder field. Their old name was Lochan Dubh na Lairige or black lochans of the Lairig, which anglicisation has turned into the erroneous name the Pools of Dee.

The path soon comes to easier ground and drops gradually into Glen Dee, giving magnificent views up to An Garbh Choire and the soaring peak of Cairn Toul. After 3 kilometres downhill, the rough path goes on the level. It crosses Allt Clach nan Taillear (9 kilometres from the Derry) and shortly afterwards comes to the group of

In the upper part of Glen Feshie near Carnachuin

curiously ribbed stones called Clach nan Taillear on the east side of the path. Above, the slope of Carn a' Mhaim has been rent by furrows gouged out by debris slides in torrential rains; Charles Robertson at Corrour witnessed one such torrent in 1901.

To the south of here a footbridge crosses the River Dee over to Corrour Bothy below The Devil's Point. The views are very fine; above on the east side, the slabby rock faces of Carn a' Mhaim lead north to the enormous screes of Ben Macdui. As you go south, the views of The Devil's Point and then the grand opening of wild Glen Geusachan, with its green floor hemmed in by rocky hillsides, look especially impressive. Here the Lairig path divides. The right branch goes 9 kilometres down the east side of the narrowing Glen Dee to the White Bridge and then another 5 kilometres to the Linn of Dee. Before reaching the White Bridge you pass the Chest of Dee (Gaelic Ciste Dhe; keesht'yay), a place of beautiful wide dark pools and rapids set among square-topped masses of rock.

The more interesting left branch climbs gently to 610m to curve round Sron Carn a' Mhaim, and then heads east for Derry Lodge. Near here you pass the lonely peaty waters of Lochan Feith nan Sgor (lochan of bog of the rocky hills, fainna'skor), and then gradually drop into Glen Luibeg. Now comes a grand viewpoint down to the first pine trees which are always a welcome sight, to Lochnagar far beyond, and north up to the fine cliffs of Coire Sputan Dearg on Ben Macdui. You can usually cross easily where the path reaches the Luibeg Burn, but in high water should go

400 metres upstream to a bridge built by the Cairngorm Club. The first copse of trees below here is Preas nam Meirleach (praiss na'myarlach) or copse of the robbers. After the ford, the path crosses the Sands of Lui, a stretch of gravel washed down by floods in 1829 and 1956, and then comes through the beautiful winding Glen Luibeg with its scattered old pines down to beside the cottage at Luibeg, at about 420m near the Derry. From here the path goes east to the Derry Burn at a footbridge, and so reaches the road at Derry Lodge (for continuation to the Linn of Dee, see Chapter 2 under Access, and Chapter 8 under Glen Lui).

GLEN FESHIE

Name: Gleann Feithisidh (glin'faishee) or glen of boggy haugh. Distance: from Linn of Dee to Ruighe Ealasaid 7 kilometres, to beside Geldie Lodge 12, to county boundary 16, to Eidart bothy 18, to Ruigh-aiteachain 26½, to Carnachuin 28 kilometres and another 4 and 6 kilometres to public roads at Achlean and Tolvah respectively; total ascent 180m. From the Linn of Dee at 370m, a gravel road beyond a locked gate goes west through pine woods and then along the open Glen Dee with its old ruined farms to the White Bridge at nearly 410m. Now you turn south-west up the Geldie, getting fine spacious views up to Beinn Bhrotain and Beinn a' Ghlo. The road passes a plantation enclosing the ruin of Ruigh nan Clach (rooee na'glach) or shiel of the stones. You continue to west of where the Bynack Burn meets the Geldie Burn below the partly-ruined stable at Ruighe Ealasaid (rooee'yalasitsh) or Elizabeth's shiel. From here the rough road turns west to beside the site of the former Geldie Lodge. On the way you cross Allt Dhaidh Beag and Mor, two fast burns coming off Beinn Bhrotain; these names are map errors for Daimhidh ('davee), from damh meaning a stag. At about 520m altitude and 300 metres before the road crosses the Geldie, the path to Glen Feshie continues westwards along the north bank of the stream.

Glen Geldie is unique in Scotland for a special character of extraordinary remoteness, loneliness and wildness combined with high arctic-like hills nearby; a wide treeless glen runs up for miles of very gentle slopes on either side to the massive stony high tops and green tundras of Beinn Bhrotain and Monadh Mor in the north and An Sgarsoch and Carn an Fhidhleir in the south. Other places in our region have this spacious character, but nowhere is it as strong as in the Geldie. In deep winter snow this character is enhanced by the pervading whiteness of the smooth slopes, unrelieved by any of the black wind-scoured ridges so common in the steeper Cairngorms. Through this flat landscape the path to Glen Feshie climbs imperceptibly to the summit at about 560m, at the watershed between Spey and Dee where only a low bank of moorland separates the two. Standing at this spot, you can easily imagine how the east-flowing upper River Feshie once ran into Geldie and Dee, and how a very little gravel dumped by glaciers could easily block it and move it in that great bend – locally called the Turn o the Feshie – far round into Glen Feshie and the Spey. Below here you can cross the fast River Eidart ('aitshart) by a footbridge 300 metres upstream from the Feshie, which was built in 1957 by the Scottish Rights of

Way Society. To the north, the Eidart runs for about 1½ kilometres in a miniature rocky canyon. A small bothy stands 300 metres further down the Feshie side from the River Eidart, beside the main path.

At the rocky little gorge of Allt na Leuma (altna'lyaim) or burn of the leap, which is the stream whose upper fork has the name of Allt Coire Bhlair, you come to a vehicle track down Glen Feshie. The scenery becomes striking as the glen narrows almost to a canyon and bends sharply at the Caigeann, between steep hills with many broken crags, foaming waterfalls, screes, and in places fine clumps of old birches and pines. Lower down, where the glen curves north, it opens out into wide grassy flats where the river wanders among great shingle beds and you pass through lovely glades of ancient pines and junipers. Unfortunately the fine old walking path through the woods has been obliterated by a bulldozed track.

Beside the bothy at Ruigh-aiteachain (rooee'aitshachan), you can see the ruins of The Huts where Landseer once painted a fresco above the fireplace, still visible until about 1930. A road bridge over the Feshie is at Carnachuin, from which a private road continues to the locked gate near Tolvah (from Toll a' Bhathaidh (tole'vaa) or hole of the drowning). About 1½ kilometres down the public road from the locked gate the old right of way goes off to the right at a point south of Ballintean. It continues as a pleasant path near the river, ending at the west side of Feshiebridge. A nearer public road comes to Achlean on the east side, and you can cross the Feshie to reach it by a footbridge 600 metres south of Stronetoper. At 847 976, north of Stronetoper, an old drove road and right of way runs west across the Allt Chomhraig for 11 kilometres to Drumguish. At the foot of the glen, Feshiebridge is a charming spot where the river winds darkly through a deep pool overhung by trees and spanned by a fine old bridge.

LAIRIG AN LAOIGH

Name: Lairig Laoigh (larig'looee) or pass of Lui, distinguishing it from Lairig Ghru or Druie pass. Distance: from locked gate at the foot of Glen Lui at 366m to Derry Lodge 5 kilometres (see Chapter 2 for Linn of Dee car park and path to the Derry road), to the forking of the path in upper Derry 11, to Fords of Avon Refuge hut 15, to Bynack Stable at Strath Nethy 24, to Glenmore Lodge 28½ kilometres and to public road at 012 162 west of Forest Lodge 31 kilometres; total ascent from the foot of Glen Lui 490m.

Though not quite so grand as the Lairig Ghru, the Lairig an Laoigh is a very fine walk taking you through the magnificent pine woods of the Derry and Abernethy and into a wild tract of country at the head of Glen Avon and the Caiplich. A good approach starts from Derry Lodge at about 420m. Crossing the Derry by the footbridge just past the lodge, you come on the old path which here leads through one of the finest pieces of ancient pine forest in Scotland. On the left rise the high knolls of Na Toman Dearg, now fenced to allow regeneration of the pines. About 1½ kilometres up, the path bends left away from the stream; beyond, hidden from

The Caledonian pine wood in Glen Derry at the southern approach to the Lairig an Laoigh

the path, lies a stretch of beautiful falls and smooth shelving rocks. The path now climbs a mound giving a grand view of upper Glen Derry, and crosses a footbridge at about 500m to the east side, immediately below the site of the old Derry Dam. You can also reach this spot by a track bulldozed up the east side of the Derry woods from Derry Lodge, but it is far less attractive than the old path.

From above the footbridge at the dam site, the bulldozed track now carries on north along the previous line of the old path, giving fine views over the green, pine-studded flats to the stony corries of Derry Cairngorm. The bulldozed track ends 2 kilometres north of the dam site below the screes of Craig Derry, but the path continues through a fertile meadow to the Glas Allt Mor (glasalt'more) or big green burn. Beyond here at nearly 600m altitude it diverges, left to Coire Etchachan, right to the Lairig an Laoigh slanting up to the pass at about 740m between Beinn Mheadhoin and Beinn a' Chaorainn. At the top of the pass, a grand prospect opens north down Allt an t-Seallaidh (altan'jawlie) or burn of the view, to the Dubh Lochan and beyond to Glen Avon. You cross the Avon at about 690m at Ath nam Fiann (Ath meaning ford). The Fords of Avon Refuge hut stands near here on the north bank.

Ahead, the path runs on the level past the waters of Lochan a' Bhainne or lochan of the milk, and then climbs gently to over 770m on the east shoulder of Bynack More. It then drops slightly into the wide green peaty basin of Coire Odhar, crossing the little stream of Uisge Dubh Poll a' Choin or black water of the dog's pool. A number of people have died in this area by wandering in winter storm north-east down this stream or down the burn of Glasath further south, instead of keeping uphill round Bynack More. The gentle walking downhill by these streams takes you on to the vast windswept moor of the Caiplich, miles from any house. Indeed, if you are to walk the Lairig an Laoigh in winter and do not know it well, it is safer for this reason to start at the north end and finish at the Derry, as you then come to this deceptive part while you feel strong at the beginning of the day. On the last section from Avon south to Derry Lodge, the route looks obvious as you merely have to stay in a fairly straight line along the bottom of the valley, hemmed in between the hills.

On the north side of Coire Odhar you climb again gently to 792m over the north shoulder of Bynack More, before beginning the long descent to the footbridge over the River Nethy at about 442m, beside Bynack Stable. A more interesting alternative for a summer walk, and a safer detour on a bad winter day, is to go from Ath nam Fiann up to Loch Avon, climb to 807m at The Saddle, and then walk by a path down the Garbh Allt to Strath Nethy, below the great broken cliffs of Cairn Gorm and A' Choinneach.

The quickest and very fine way down from Bynack Stable in Strath Nethy leads along the rough road to the Ryvoan Pass south of Loch a' Gharbh-choire. You then drop past lovely Lochan Uaine into the pines towards Glenmore Lodge (Chapter 1). Another way runs from Ryvoan north past Rynettin, a beautiful place overlooking Abernethy pine forest, and to Forest Lodge, one kilometre west of which you come to the public road to Nethy Bridge. The old Lairig an Laoigh path breaks off to the right, just before the path reaches the footbridge near Bynack Stable. Lower down it goes through fine old pines along the east side of the Nethy to Forest Lodge, and from the pine-edge onwards has been replaced by a gravel vehicle track.

SKIING

All three passes have been crossed on ski, but obviously the Glen Feshie route at its much lower altitude requires more general snow cover. The Lairig Ghru can be a tough journey on skis, as the snow there often lies very deep and powdery. However, after a long hard winter it can be much faster than in summer; in April 1951 the writer crossed in only four hours from Aviemore to Luibeg without any hurrying, on perfect hard-packed snow that covered every boulder, stream and hollow under a uniform, smooth sheet. The Lairig Ghru is often hard going on skis because many boulders are still projecting through, and severe southerly gales often funnel through the northern section from the summit to Rothiemurchus.

FURTHER READING - HISTORICAL

R.Anderson *Glen Feshie*. CCJ 1,348.
H.Macmillan *The Lairig Ghru*. CCJ 2, 297.

CHAPTER 4

Braeriach and Cairn Toul

Braeriach	1296m	953 999
Cairn Toul	1293m	963 972
Sgor an Lochain Uaine	1258m	954 977
The Devil's Point	1004m	976 951
Beinn Bhrotain	1157m	954 923
Carn Cloich-mhuilinn	942m	968 907
Monadh Mor	1113m	939 942

The Lairig Ghru divides the four 1200m hills of the Cairngorms into two parts. Cairn Gorm and Ben Macdui stand to the east, whereas to the west of the Lairig and Glen Dee rises Braeriach, facing Aviemore, and to the south of it Cairn Toul of Mar. For variety of hill and corrie scenery these two hills and their surroundings are equalled in the Cairngorms massif only by Cairn Gorm and Ben Macdui. For wildness, remoteness and freedom from the recent effects of man, they are clearly unmatched. This is the only large part of the Cairngorms which has escaped the bulldozer and the scars of new vehicle tracks, although these have penetrated the fringes at Gleann Einich and Glen Dee. It is therefore now one of the most precious parts.

The hills listed above are all Munros, except Sgor an Lochain Uaine and Carn Cloich-mhuilinn which are prominent tops.

GEOLOGY, LANDFORMS AND WILDLIFE

The rock is nearly all granite. Gleann Einich, An Garbh Choire and Glen Geusachan were worn away as long glaciated trenches, with many small hillocks of glacial debris. The same kind of material dams up several lochs. The long-lying snow patch in Garbh Choire Mor is Scotland's most permanent snow, having melted only twice this century, in 1933 and 1959. Unusually extensive boulder screes cover Cairn Toul's summit and the Coire Bhrochain side of Braeriach. Beinn Bhrotain is notable in having a big expanse of sandy gravel, almost devoid of vegetation, just east of its summit. Glen Geusachan shows many signs of recent and past catastrophic erosion from debris flows, which tore huge furrows down the steep slopes on either side, due to heavy rain storms funnelling off expanses of bare slabby rock higher up.

ACCESS, PUBLIC TRANSPORT AND ACCOMMODATION
As in Chapter 3.

BOTHIES AND SHELTERS
As in Chapter 3. The tiny, cramped Garbh Coire Bothy stands on the south bank of Allt a' Gharbh Choire below the waterfall from Lochan Uaine, and holds 4-6 people. In Garbh Choire Dhaidh is a built-up cave under a large boulder with a cairn on top, just above the pools along the course of Dee at 946 987; it holds two people.

MAPS
Ordnance Survey 1:50,000 Sheets 36 and 43

The cliffs of Cairn Toul and Braeriach at An Garbh Choire are good places for uncommon arctic-alpine plants. Extensive areas of arctic-like barrens with three-leaved rush are on the Braeriach plateau, and big stretches of alpine grassland on the south flanks of Cairn Toul and Monadh Mor. Dotterel and snow buntings breed on these hills. Red deer graze most of the ground in summer, but nearly all of them leave for glens much lower down in winter. Spawning salmon go up the Geusachan Burn and up the Dee past Corrour, and the char, a northern relict fish, lives in Loch Einich.

ESTATES

The Aberdeenshire part is on Mar Lodge. The Inverness-shire part draining to Gleann Einich is on Rothiemurchus, and that draining to Glen Feshie lies on Glenfeshie estate.

HISTORY

Blaeu's *Atlas* in 1654 names only 'Bini vroden' in this group of hills. In 1810, Dr G.S.Keith climbed Braeriach and Cairn Toul, and made one of the earliest recorded Scottish climbs, the ascent of the Dee waterfall in Garbh Choire Dhaidh. He wrote 'It was in flood at the time, from the melting of the snow and the late rains; and what was remarkable, an arch of snow covered the narrow glen from which it tumbled over the rocks. Here our landlord and our guide ascended the mountain by an easier, though more circuitous course; but I was determined not to lose sight of the river. We approached so near to the cataract as to know that there was no other lake or stream; and then we had to climb among huge rocks, varying from one to ten tons, and to catch hold of the stones or fragments that projected, while we ascended in an angle of 70 or 80 degrees.'

In earlier centuries, many folk from Rothiemurchus summered at shielings in upper Gleann Einich. They grazed their black cattle on the fertile grass of the wide Coire Odhar south of the loch, where streams foam over the broken rocks from the Moine Mhor above. Here was born an earlier Grant of Rothiemurchus, John of Coire Odhar, who left money to build Coylumbridge and a house at the head of Loch Einich 'which should always have meal in it'.

During the 1800s, a wooden sluice gate at Loch Einich produced a rush of water for floating timber lower down in Rothiemurchus.

In her *Memoirs of a Highland Lady*, Elizabeth Grant described how the man who went up to open the sluice gates once perished in the snow, and how a young shepherd also died in a snowstorm on Braeriach. Carrie Nethersole-Thompson of Whitewell told the present writer in 1974, how some cattle belonging to her grandfather fell to their deaths over the cliffs of Coire Bhrochain on Braeriach in bad weather after straying from Gleann Einich. Doubtless it was the jawbone of one of them that Seton Gordon found about 1927 below the cliffs (*The Highlands of Scotland*, p139).

Last century, people from Mar grazed their cattle at Glen Geusachan and up the Coire Odhar of Glen Dee, but in the late 1800s the area was kept clear for deer. The zigzag paths of Coire Dhondail and on Cairn Toul's Coire Odhar date from the deer stalking heyday of last century. So does Corrour Bothy, built in 1877 to house a deer watcher in summer; the last watcher, Frank Scott, left in 1920. Subsequently Corrour (kor'ower) became an open bothy. Already in 1928, when a party from the Rucksack Club at University College in Dundee left a visitors' book, hundreds were visiting annually. From June 1928 to April 1931, 1100 came, and from then till July 1933, 1000; over half stayed one night or more. Two thirds came in June and July, and only 60 between October and March during all five years. Later, some vandals tore off the woodwork for firewood until, by 1949, snow sprayed through the roof during hail storms. In 1950 the Cairngorm Club restored the bothy.

THE HILLS

Braeriach *(from Am Braigh Riabhach (brigh'reeach) or the brindled upland)* (1296m)
Braeriach, second highest hill of the Cairngorms and third in Britain, is a crescent-shaped massive bulk of a hill with bulging convex shoulders, many corries and a large summit plateau. From Aviemore it rises high above Rothiemurchus, but unlike Cairn Gorm lies mysteriously further back, behind an approach that hides under the hills of lower Gleann Einich. The three symmetrical northern corries carved out of its north face are a grand sight from Strath Spey. Other corries overlook Loch Einich, and on the south face towards Deeside lies the magnificent set of corries, shared with Cairn Toul, making up the huge amphitheatre around the glen of the Garbh Choire. Braeriach is so big and varied that no one can know it well who has not wandered into every corrie and explored its plateau and flanks without hurry.

WALKING ASCENTS TO BRAERIACH
From Glen Dee. See below under Cairn Toul.

From Gleann Einich by Coire an Lochain. Distance: from Whitewell to the summit 12 kilometres, total ascent 1000m. At Inverdruie, just past the road to Loch an Eilein, a public road slants right, going past Blackpark and ending at a car park beside Whitewell. Less than one kilometre to the south, beside Lochan Deo, you come to

Cairn Toul and Braeriach from Carn a' Mhaim

the private road to Gleann Einich at a locked gate. From here a rough track goes up the glen to Loch Einich.

Gleann Einich should be spelled Gleann Eanaich (glin'ennich) or glen of marsh. It is one of the grandest of Cairngorms glens, narrow and clothed with beautiful natural pine woodland in the lower part, then open moorland, and finally ending at Loch Einich where it becomes hemmed in by crags. Among the upper trees the old road slid away in landslides, so a new road was bulldozed uphill. At the point where the road leaves the last trees, the entry to the glen narrows between Cadha Mor on the west and the stony Carn Eilrig (karn'ailrik) or hill of deer-trap on the east. This narrow pass is Caigeann Beanaidh or rough pass of Beanaidh; here the road bends sharply at Windy Corner, where the wind often strengthens as you turn into the open glen to the south. On the hillside above, the solitary stunted pine of Craobh Thillidh, or tree of the return, still stands, now very ancient. In the old days in spring, cattle were driven through the forest as far as this tree and then found their own way to the shielings at Loch Einich, to which the people came a few days later. Below Craobh Thillidh, among the stunted outpost pines, the river of Am Beanaidh roars down over boulders. Above Craobh Thillidh you come into a long stretch of wide open glen, cross Am Beanaidh at a bridge, and 7 kilometres from Whitewell reach the burn of Beanaidh Bheag at about 470m. It is worth crossing Am

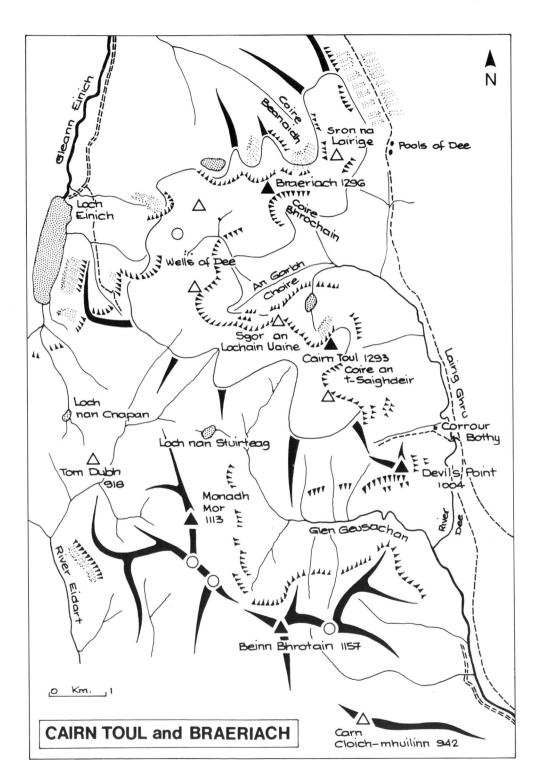

CAIRN TOUL and BRAERIACH

Beanaidh here and climbing the knolls beyond to see the hidden loch to the west. Its name is Loch (locally Lochan) Mhic Ghille-chaoil (lochan mig eelie'chooil) or lochan of the thin young man's son, who was said to have died here in a fight with Lochaber cattle thieves; a rusty dirk was found at the lochside in the early 1900s.

The easiest way to Braeriach from here goes just past Allt Easan na Bruaich, the next stream up the road, and then uphill to 930 010 where a path zigzags up to 1070m on the shoulder west of Loch Coire an Lochain. Distance; from Beanaidh Bheag direct to the summit 5 kilometres. However, you will find it well worth diverging to see the loch at about 995m; Loch Coire an Lochain is one of the highest in the Cairngorms. From it you can climb up either side of the corrie, the ridge between it and Coire Ruadh to the east giving particularly grand views. The final ascent to Braeriach goes along the top of Coire Ruadh.

From Loch Einich. Distance: 6½ kilometres, 780m ascent. A good, though longer route than by Coire an Lochain is to walk or cycle the last 3 kilometres of road beyond the Beanaidh Bheag to Loch Einich, 9 kilometres from the locked gate. The loch stretches 2 kilometres long, up to half a kilometre wide and just over 45m deep, and lies at 496m in a hauntingly lonely place amid wild scenery with vast broken crags. It has now been tapped by a pipe to give water for the rapidly growing villages of Strath Spey. Although less dramatic and varied than Loch Avon, Loch Einich gives a stronger feeling of mystery and of the puniness of man, perhaps because the more straight, open and wide U-shape of the glen shows the full sweep of these great hillsides.

The route from Loch Einich to Braeriach climbs by Coire Dhondail (kor'gowntal). About 400 metres before the road end, a stalkers' path slants uphill into the corrie. A deep recess surrounded with rocks, Coire Dhondail lies between Braeriach and the rocky spur of Creag an Loch. This spur runs northwards on the east side of the loch, and offers a fine way up to the plateau giving marvellous views and a little scrambling. In Coire Dhondail the path zigzags over the steep vegetation on the upper part of the corrie up to 1010m on the flat ground above. Avoid this place in winter, because of its cornices, icy snow and avalanches; at that time a safer and easier route goes up the broad slope north of the cliffs of Coire Bogha-cloiche. At the top of Coire Dhondail you come out on a wide terrace of turf and gravel at about 1000m. An easy climb follows from this terrace to the Wells of Dee or to the 1265m point at Carn na Criche at the south end of Braeriach's high plateau. For the rest of the route to the summit of Braeriach, see Cairn Toul to Braeriach (below).

It is easy to contour from the terrace above Coire Dhondail along the 5 kilometres to Cairn Toul, or to go south-east to Monadh Mor. All these south-west slopes of Cairn Toul and Braeriach are gentle, rolling down over crisp turf and heath to the Moine Mhor or great moss. About one kilometre towards Cairn Toul, going south-east along the terrace, you come to a stream draining a hollow due south of Carn na Criche, where a big snow wreath lingers far into the summer. The hollow has the grand old name of Clais Feith Inbhir Feithisidh or hollow of bog stream of mouth of the boggy haugh. This burn runs into the Allt Luineag - formerly often locally called

The corniced summit of Braeriach above Coire Bhrochain

Allt Luinneach - from the next hollow of Clais Luineag or Luinneach which lies to the east nearer Sgor an Lochain Uaine.

If you are returning to Gleann Einich from Braeriach you can drop down on either side of Loch Coire an Lochain. Alternatively you can go to 963 002 on the col towards Sron na Lairige and then east down the zigzags of the Duke's Path into Coire na Lairige (or Coire Ruadh as it was known to the old Mar stalkers) just south of the Pools of Dee (14 kilometres by this route from Derry Lodge). An interesting way back is to carry on over the 1184m Sron na Lairige (stronna'larik) or nose of the Lairig, and then go down its long north nose to the Lairig Ghru, a route which avoids the rough walking on the Lairig path (12½ kilometres to Whitewell). From Sron na Lairige the strong walker may prefer to visit the remote Lochan Odhar among its peat hags and then climb the beautiful cone of Carn Eilrig for a magnificent last view before dropping into Rothiemurchus.

From Glen Feshie.   An interesting route to Braeriach starts at the public road end at Achlean on the east side of the Feshie, and goes up the path over Carn Ban Mor to join the end of the bulldozed track at Allt Sgairnich on the Moine Mhor (for that part of the route see Chapter 5). From there one can walk round the south side of Loch nan Cnapan and then head north-east to Carn na Criche at the south end of the Braeriach plateau (distance from Achlean 13 kilometres, 1070m ascent).

The edge of An Garbh Choire between Braeriach and Cairn Toul

From the Cairn Gorm ski road.   Because of the ease of access, this has become one of the commonest ways to Braeriach. The shortest route is from the car park at 985 074 on the east side of the road below the forest's upper edge. From here a path leads south to a footbridge over the Allt Mor, then steeply uphill to the reindeer fence and along the edge of the steep bank above the Allt Mor to cross Caochan Dubh a' Chadha and continue through the rocky gap south-east of Creag a' Chalamain to meet the Lairig Ghru footpath. Here a path diverges to the right, southwards on to Sron na Lairige, and the route then goes round the top of Coire Bhrochain to Braeriach summit (10½ kilometres from the car park, 1000m ascent). An even shorter route is from the end of the private road to the army's Rothiemurchus Lodge south-west of Loch Morlich (8 kilometres, 920m ascent).

WALKING IN BRAERIACH'S CORRIES
The long, shallow Coire Gorm (kor'gorom) or green corrie goes down the middle of the Aviemore side of Sron na Lairige. A grassy open corrie, it often holds snow till midsummer. The easternmost of Braeriach's set of three northern corries, Coire Beanaidh (kor'bennie) now contains hardly any rock as its cliffs have long crumbled into great screes. The middle Coire Ruadh (kor'rooa) or red corrie has a beautifully symmetrical circular shape with broken rocks; a grand feature is the pair of narrow stony ridges on either side leading to the rounded top of Braeriach behind. The western Coire an Lochain looks finest, with its very high lochan that carries ice into

June or July, and its crescent of broken crags and late snow patches offering sporting easy lines to the plateau. Above Loch Einich, Coire Bogha-cloiche or stone-arch corrie has a frieze of broken cliff at its top. Coire Clach lies between it and the fine Coire Dhondail already mentioned, being no more than a shallow indentation in the bulging west slopes of Braeriach.

The most magnificent corrie of the Cairngorms is the vast super-corrie of An Garbh Choire (n'gara-chor) or the rough corrie. In late summer you can descend laboriously into it from Braeriach by the boulder slopes west of Coire Bhrochain. From the west, another good route drops from the low col west of Sgor an Lochain Uaine, where a wide shoot of boulders runs north down into the corrie. By far the most impressive route leads up Allt a' Gharbh Choire from the Lairig Ghru path. In this lower glen of the Garbh Choire, Cairn Toul's Coire an Lochain Uaine soars on the left, with the waterfall from its green lochan plunging over slabby rocks. Opposite on the right hangs Coire Bhrochain under the top of Braeriach.

Once past these two corries, you look into An Garbh Choire itself which forms a large complex sloping bowl between Sgor an Lochain Uaine and Braeriach. In the south, a striking face of dark precipice west of Sgor an Lochain Uaine is gashed by the dark furrow of Chokestone Gully. Further west lies Garbh Choire Mor ('gara-chor'more) or big rough corrie, with fine 100m cliffs rearing up out of great snow fields. It almost became a couple of corries; the outer is the whole wide stretch of Garbh Choire Mor, but within it, higher up and in the westernmost corner, a smaller recess holds Scotland's longest-lasting snow field. In this most alpine of Cairngorm corries you can often see small crevasses, bergschrunds, avalanches, enormous cornices, and rock which hides under snow for so much of the year that the grey-green lichens of Garbh Choire Mor have failed to colonise the virgin granite. A 30m vertical depth of snow occurs in some springs and some of the lower pitches of the rock climbs are buried till late summer. A group from University College in Dundee has done research on this snow field (SMCJ 28,273). Photographs taken by the writer in late April 1951, after the snowiest winter in the Cairngorms since the early 1940s, show that the snow almost buried the rock climbs south of Sphinx Ridge.

Northwards, a projecting broad nose separates Garbh Choire Mor from Garbh Choire Dhaidh, which is a map error for Dhe, pronounced Yay, meaning rough corrie of the Dee. When snowfree, this nose gives an easy way to the plateau, without rock climbing. It is fine to explore Garbh Choire Dhaidh. Although less snowy than Garbh Choire Mor, nevertheless it still looks a very snowy place at midsummer, and used to be called Fuar Garbh Choire, meaning cold rough corrie. A grand steep wall of granite rises north of the Dee waterfall, with smaller cliffs further north again. As Garbh Choire Dhaidh has more of a gently-sloping floor than Garbh Choire Mor, it is much more grassy. The waterfall plunges not in one great leap, but in a series of cascades down innumerable steps of pink granite, polished smooth by the force of the water and by frequent snow avalanches. Below, the stream runs through a tiny meadow of crisp herbage watered by spray. It then rumbles underground below boulders, and at the foot of the gentle basin opens into wide pools almost like tiny

Cairn Toul from Braeriach

tarns, shortly before rushing more steeply into An Garbh Choire below. Long after rain the black cliffs stream with water. The poet Hogg's lines are appropriate:

> The grisly cliffs which guard
> The infant rills of Highland Dee.

Coire Bhrochain (kor'vrochan), a hanging corrie lying under the summit of Braeriach, is one of the finest corries in the Cairngorms, a wild boulder-strewn but sunny corrie with some of the biggest cliffs in the massif. Its name might literally mean corrie of the porridge, but the meaning was given to the writer by native Gaelic speakers as the corrie where everything is in little bits, referring to the vast screes which cover the corrie floor more completely than in other corries in the massif.

Cairn Toul *(from Carn an t-Sabhail (karn'towel) or hill of the barn)* (1293 m)
Cairn Toul is by far the sharpest of the high Cairngorms. Although flat-looking and square-shaped when viewed from the west, it rises as a beautiful conical peak when seen from Braemar and Glen Dee, falling steeply for 680m to Glen Dee and with a hanging corrie nestling just below the summit. On its south-west flanks it slopes gradually into vast open green corries with screes and foaming burns towards the plateau of the Moine Mhor and the huge trench of Glen Geusachan, finest glen in the Cairngorms. The outlying hills of The Devil's Point, Monadh Mor and Beinn Bhrotain, which almost encircle Glen Geusachan, excel in wildness, variety and remoteness.

WALKING ASCENTS TO CAIRN TOUL
From Derry Lodge. Distance 11 kilometres, 1020m of ascent. The route from the Derry to opposite Corrour comes in by the Lairig Ghru path (Chapter 3). You now cross to Corrour Bothy at about 560m by the footbridge over the Dee, 7½ kilometres from Derry Lodge. Corrour Bothy was named after the wide Coire Odhar or dun corrie, which stretches behind the bothy from The Devil's Point round to Cairn Toul. A stalkers' path goes up the corrie from the bothy. Although steep, the last part is easily climbed by the path's well-made zigzags, but in winter it often has a bulging snow drift or cornice which occasionally avalanches. In icy snow or avalanche-prone snow, the ridge at the north end of the corrie makes a safer route, the scree slopes nearer The Devil's Point being sometimes also safer. One of the most delightful spots in the Cairngorms is where the Coire Odhar path comes on to the 915m flat sandy neck of An Diollaid or the saddle, connecting The Devil's Point to Cairn Toul. The burn of Allt a' Choire Odhair, icy cold and refreshing, hurries on among beautiful mosses. Behind lies the steep gulf of the Lairig Ghru; ahead, wide grassy slopes like a subarctic tundra stretch towards Monadh Mor.

From An Diollaid the way to Cairn Toul lies north along the edge of the corrie to a 1213m top overlooking the wild Coire an t-Saighdeir (korin'deitsher) or corrie of the soldier. Still following the cliff edge, you drop slightly to 1167m, and then comes the final rise over boulders to the top of Cairn Toul. From the summit two ridges, each with a cairn at its top, run towards Glen Dee below, enclosing the high hanging corrie of Coire an t-Sabhail. You can make a pleasant descent from the summit by dropping west to the col above Lochan Uaine, and then going down the green boulder-strewn valley of Clais an t-Sabhail (klashin'towel) or hollow of the barn, into Glen Geusachan.

From Glen More. Cairn Toul is often climbed from the Cairn Gorm ski road or from the army's Rothiemurchus Lodge (for total distances and heights from there to Cairn Toul, see under Braeriach above, and add the distances and heights under Cairn Toul to Braeriach below).

From Glen Feshie. For Cairn Toul the route from Achlean to Loch nan Cnapan is the same as for Braeriach (see above). The route from Loch nan Cnapan then lies east across flattish ground for 2½ kilometres towards Loch nan Stuirteag, and then north-east to Cairn Toul (from Achlean 12½ kilometres, 1070m ascent).

WALKING IN CAIRN TOUL'S CORRIES
Coire an t-Saighdeir is a wild corrie of boulder fields, broken rock and snow, lying south of the sharp peak of Cairn Toul. An easy way out in late summer goes by the Slichit, a wide gravelly shoot in the centre of the corrie, which leads through the cliffs to the 1167m col above. To the north, Coire an t-Sabhail is the fine hanging corrie immediately under the top of Cairn Toul. Although a continuous mass of boulders covers the corrie, nevertheless in deep winter snow it can offer a quick way off Cairn Toul. In suitable conditions it makes a fine glissade or trot from the top down this corrie and the snow covered burn below for about 680m of altitude to the water of Dee in 13 to 20 minutes, one of the longer glissades of Scotland (see SMCJ 15, 225).

Sgor an Lochain Uaine

Be careful at the very top, which is steep and often corniced, but the ridges on either side of Coire an t-Sabhail merely involve easy scrambling on steep boulders.

Lochan Uaine or green lochan in Coire an Lochain Uaine is one of the gems of the Cairngorms, lying at about 910m on a rocky shelf high on the north slopes of Cairn Toul. A small burn tumbles over the rocky lip of the corrie down to Allt a' Gharbh Choire 260m below. Steep slopes of rock, scree and grass sweep for over 300m above the lochan up to Cairn Toul and to the even more imposing sharp peak of Sgor an Lochain Uaine further west. The ridge running from the loch to the Sgor forms one of the few such aretes in the Cairngorms, and makes a fine way up which involves easy scrambling up steep boulders, narrowing to a crest near the top.

The Devil's Point (1004m)
From An Diollaid above Coire Odhar (see above), a short detour of 700 metres (100m in ascent) takes you to the summit cairn on The Devil's Point. This perch gives a magnificent aerial view down steep broken cliffs into Glen Dee and Glen Geusachan, with the Geusachan Burn winding far below through beautiful green flats. The Gaelic name of The Devil's Point was Bod an Deamhain (potin'john as in English John). Most books and references skate over this subject by noting The Devil's Point as a 'euphemistic' or 'literal' translation. It is time to be accurate and say that Bod an Deamhain means penis of the demon.

CAIRN TOUL TO BRAERIACH
This is the finest high-level hill walk in Britain. Distance 6 kilometres, total ascent 320m. After leaving Cairn Toul you drop about 150m in altitude west to the 1140m col along the edge of Coire an Lochain Uaine and climb again a short way to Sgor an Lochain Uaine or peak of the green lochan, sometimes called The Angel's Peak. This fine hill, 1258m in altitude, lies one kilometre west-north-west of Cairn Toul. From Sgor an Lochain Uaine you descend west along the cliff edge to the lowest point of the whole round, at about 1130m on the col between Cairn Toul and Braeriach, where you have a magnificent view down to Garbh Choire Mor and its snow fields. An easy slope leads up from the col, along the cliff edge where the biggest cornices in the Cairngorms build up in winter. You can keep following the steep edge all the way to Braeriach, or diverge on to the plateau, where the small cairn of Carn na Criche or cairn of the march stands near the highest point (1265m) of a great stretch of stones and gravel. To the north of here on the watershed rises Einich Cairn at 1237m, west of which you will get fine views of the Sgoran Dubh cliffs.

In the centre of the plateau, the infant Dee flows through banks of gravel after rising in a spring at the foot of a bank of grass and moss, which is crowned by a small cairn of white quartz stones. Here at 1220m a powerful stream gushes forth, to be reinforced further down by other springs; these are Fuaran Dhe (fooaran'yay) or Wells of Dee. 'No other river in the country has such a source, at such an elevation, and the whole scene is unique in British hills. This summit plateau of Braeriach in its bigness and bareness exceeds anything in the Cairngorms or in these islands' (Alexander, first edition of this Guide). Although not so variable as the Ben Macdui plateau, without its huge boulder fields and snow fields, nevertheless here there stretches a far bigger expanse of gravelly flat tundra. You also become aware of a feeling of vast space and of the attractive quality that some people notice about deserts. After flowing for 700 metres across the plateau, the infant Dee crashes over the rocky face of Garbh Choire Dhaidh and cascades for 150m to the bed of the corrie below. A large snow bridge lasts far into the summer at the top of the fall; below, the stream thunders on down to Glen Dee. Many think that the Spey is the fastest-flowing Scottish river, but the Dee far exceeds it, dropping from 1200m to the sea in only 137 kilometres.

About 300 metres north-east of where the Dee falls over, the cliffs, which have been almost continuous right round An Garbh Choire from Cairn Toul, come to an end. Here a wide bouldery slope faces south between Garbh Choire Dhaidh and Coire Bhrochain. It offers an easy though laborious way down in late summer, but in winter often carries a big cornice well below the top of the slope; if so, you can usually descend the ridge immediately bounding the west side of Coire Bhrochain. An easy 80m rise takes you over stony gravel from the plateau to the edge of Coire Bhrochain, and for the last 200 metres you walk along the top of its magnificent cliffs to the cairn of Braeriach. Immediately below that cairn the cliffs drop 230m past the prominent Black Pinnacle.

If returning to Deeside you descend to the col between Braeriach and Sron na Lairige. From here the Duke's Path zigzags down the steep grass of Coire na Lairige - called Coire Ruadh by the old folk of Mar - to the Lairig Ghru below. Avoid this route after deep snow, as a cornice often builds out here and avalanches sometimes occur. In deep snow the east ridge of Coire Bhrochain between it and Coire na Lairige makes a much safer descent, although rough and laborious because of boulders.

Beinn Bhrotain *(hill of the mastiff)* (1157m)
Monadh Mor *(from Am Monadh Mor, the big hill)* (1113m)
These are best climbed as a pair. Beinn Bhrotain (bain'vrotan) stretches far as a vast complex granite hill with many bulging shoulders, dominating Glen Dee and Glen Geldie. The easiest approach is to walk or cycle from the Linn of Dee for 5 kilometres up to the White Bridge in Glen Dee. From here a bulldozed track goes 5 kilometres up the west side of the Dee ending at Caochan Roibidh (kochan'roppie), a burn south of Glen Geusachan. Distance: from the track end at 480m to Beinn Bhrotain 3½ kilometres, ascent 690m.

Another way is to walk or cycle up Glen Geldie; you can then climb from the nearest point on the road there (see Glen Feshie in Chapter 3), past the Duke's Chair for 5½ kilometres to the summit. Looking prominent from the White Bridge is the nearer stony cone of Carn Cloich-mhuilinn (a map error for Carn nan Clach-mhuilinn, karna-glach'voolin, meaning hill of the millstones). It rises to 942m; you can easily climb this shapely top on the way up above the Duke's Chair. The upper corrie of Allt Garbh, south-east of the summit of Beinn Bhrotain, has the name Coire an t-Sneachda (koran'drechk) or corrie of the snow; here on the west slope of the burn a huge drift lasts far into the summer, often corniced on its east edge.

The Devil's Point and Ben Macdui from the south

Corrour bothy, with Ben Macdui beyond

At the col between Beinn Bhrotain and Monadh Mor

If you go one kilometre north-west of Beinn Bhrotain and 150m lower, you come to the col at 975m between the two hills, at a pass locally called Cadha nam Fiann (kana'vyung) . Here you look north down the wild Coire Cath nam Fionn (should be Cadha, not Cath), into which you can easily descend from here, and south down Allt Dhaidh Mor. Ahead, the slope rises to a beautiful green shoulder at 1093m called Leac Ghorm or green slope. From here you enjoy a delightful stroll on springy mossy turf to the 1113m cairn on Monadh Mor (monna 'more), which stands 2 kilometres from the col towards Beinn Bhrotain. To the west of the cairn, gentle slopes fall to the huge grassy and peaty plateau of the Moine Mhor. The east slopes are at first gentle but soon become steep and rocky. Moreover, 200 metres east of the summit, the high Coire Creagach (kor'kraikach) or rocky corrie falls off steeply with shelves of broken rocks and a steep snow field; the snow lasts long into the summer and stands out well even from as far as the Blue Hill at Aberdeen. For the easiest and most interesting way off Monadh Mor down to Glen Geusachan you should descend for 2 kilometres north to about 865m at Loch nan Stuirteag (lochna'styoortik) or loch of the black-headed gulls, a beautiful loch in a green basin lying 5 kilometres from where the Geusachan Burn enters the Dee at 496m.

The name Glen Geusachan comes from Gleann Giubhsachain (glin 'gyoosachan) or glen of little pine wood, and many roots of pines still stick out of the bare peat. Not a single tree now survives in the glen floor, but some small trees grow on the lower cliffs of The Devil's Point and Beinn Bhrotain, where they are out of the reach of red deer. Here is the most beautiful of the high hill glens in all the area described in this guide. Wild broken crags rise all around, running into screes and huge slabs of wet smooth granite. Streams foam down over the rocks, in places through hidden miniature upper corries that are almost invisible from the glen floor. In several places, enormous piles of boulders and gravel show where heavy torrents and debris flows have torn up the hillsides. Yet the floor of the glen forms a marvellous contrast, as the Geusachan Burn meanders peacefully through a fertile grassy flat over shingles and peaty pools.

If you are heading for the Derry, 6½ kilometres away, a good place for crossing lies about 700 metres north of the confluence of Geusachan and Dee, where the Dee flows in a thin sheet over slabs of pink granite. In higher water, a nearby place is better where you can jump across on big boulders, but you need to be sure-footed as the water surges strongly between the boulders; in flood, go to the Corrour footbridge. South of where the Geusachan enters the Dee lies a lovely quiet deep pool at a bend, called Poll an Eisg (pole an'aishk) or pool of the fish. One of the finest stretches of Glen Dee lies between here and Caochan Roibidh, where a great slabby crag of Beinn Bhrotain, shining with water, rears up above a moorland studded with lochans and pools.

Monadh Mor may be climbed from Achlean in Glen Feshie. The route as far as the end of the bulldozed track at Allt Sgairnich is the same as for Braeriach (see above). From there walk south of Loch nan Cnapan, past Tom Dubh, and on to the summit plateau of Monadh Mor (from Achlean 10½ kilometres, 960m ascent).

CLIMBING

The main feature of Braeriach and Cairn Toul for climbing routes centres on the very long and varied crags around the glen of the Garbh Choire, which in the Cairngorms massif are equalled only by that other grand set around Loch Avon. The Garbh Choire looks markedly different, however, as the cliffs lie at a higher altitude and also carry far more blown snow than the Loch Avon cliffs. The winter potential of the Garbh Choire cliffs is therefore very good. They are so snowy and icy that they give fine alpine-like winter routes on the long days and in the good weather of April and even May, when most other crags in the massif have thawed and become largely free of snow.

On Cairn Toul, the north-east ridge of Sgor an Lochain Uaine gives an easy scramble in summer and a Grade I winter climb from the shore of Lochan Uaine to the summit cairn of the Sgor. When combined with an ascent of Allt an Lochain Uaine which turns into great cascades of ice in winter (Grade II), the two routes together form an interesting winter ascent of 500m.

GARBH CHOIRE MOR
West of Sgor an Lochain Uaine a long line of rock extends round to Garbh Choire Mor and climbers call this subsidiary corrie the Corrie of the Chokestone Gully. The

wet *Chokestone Gully*, an impressive north-facing dark line which cleaves the cliffs for 150m, makes a fine Grade III climb in winter. The nearby long gully to its left is *The Shroud*, a good winter climb (Grade III).

The high inner recess of Garbh Choire Mor has buttresses of steep granite tinged greenish with lichens. In winter and even in spring the cliff-top carries a fringe of enormous cornices which make exit to the plateau a difficult problem, and cornices up to 11 metres thick have been recorded. The most remarkable feature in the corrie is Britain's longest-lying snow bed; after a hard winter the steep slab at the bottom of the cliff becomes completely buried with snow up to 30m deep. The cliff at this point is called *Sphinx Ridge* (Very Difficult, Grade II/III). It tapers to a fine crest above the gully to the north, and from this crest you look up to the rocky knob of the Sphinx which projects above. To the right of the obvious open gully - Great Gully - at the south end of the inner upper recess of Garbh Choire Mor rises the fine climb of *She-Devil's Buttress* (Very Difficult, 120m). Immediately to the right of She-Devil's Buttress, the 90m VS route of *Vulcan* goes up a prominent groove. To the right of the Sphinx, the prominent *Pinnacles Buttress* (Difficult) soars above the easy *Pinnacle Gully* on its left and *Phoenix Gully* (a classic winter route) on its right. The next buttress to the right, *Tower of Babel* (HVS), is one of the harder climbs of the massif.

GARBH CHOIRE DHAIDH

The Dee Waterfall makes an interesting route when icy in winter (Grade II). A beautiful 140m wall of cliffs extends on the north side of the waterfall. *The Great Rift* (Very Difficult) is the long dark chimney up the middle of the crag, making a grand climb up continuous granite which provides magnificent viewpoints across a belt of steep, ribbed slabs over to the Dee Waterfall. It is one of the best chimney climbs in the Cairngorms. One of the best and popular climbs of the Cairngorms, the *St Andrews Climb* (Severe), lies up the ridge just to the right of The Great Rift. As The Great Rift stays wet long after rain, it becomes heavily iced-up in winter and makes a fine Grade IV climb.

COIRE BHROCHAIN

This grand cirque carries a wild semicircle of big cliffs in a sheltered and sunny position. It holds a variety of interesting routes mainly of medium difficulty on clean granite. The cliffs consist of three main parts, a West Buttress which is separated by the wide West Gully from the Central Buttress below the cairn of Braeriach, and then the East Buttress made up of a set of distinctive small buttresses. High in the middle of Central Buttress, the prominent Black Pinnacle rears up below the summit of Braeriach. A popular climb is *Braeriach Direct* (Severe), which goes for 230m from the lowest rocks below the Black Pinnacle to the plateau just east of the Braeriach cairn. The nearby climb of *Bhrochain Slabs* (200m, Very Difficult), lying just to the west of the Black Pinnacle, gives a pleasant ascent on clean, rough slabs. There are several routes up the Black Pinnacle itself, starting from the broad Slab Terrace which you can easily walk up or down and which slants leftwards up from the east part of the corrie floor. The Black Pinnacle really forms a buttress which is slabby below and tapers to a point protruding above a neck that lies behind it and not far down from

At the top of Sphinx Ridge below the corniced rim of An Garbh Choire

the plateau edge. The Pinnacle's *Ordinary Route* (Moderate) goes from the highest part of Slab Terrace up the loose first pitch of Central Buttress Gully straight above (the gully separating the Black Pinnacle from the bulging Braeriach Pinnacle to the east). *The Direct Route* (Difficult) makes a better climb on a fairly direct line from the foot of the Black Pinnacle to its top. To the east of the Black Pinnacle, the projecting convex buttress of Braeriach Pinnacle takes you out at the plateau east of and slightly below the cairn of Braeriach; its final knob rises level with the plateau behind. The *Original Route* (Difficult) goes up the high part of the buttress from near the foot straight to the top. A more defined line is the exposed 100m *West Wall Route* (Mild Severe), on or near the left edge of the buttress on excellent steep rock.

OTHER CRAGS

The cliffs of The Devil's Point, although impressive, extensive and very high (up to 350m), generally lack definition and are mostly broken. The crags offer sporting ascents in winter and easy scrambling in summer on the way to the tops. The Devil's Cave, lying fairly low down in the middle of the slabs on the Glen Geusachan side, is an interesting place to visit, reached by heathery ledges from the west.

On Sron na Lairige, the 135m *Lairig Ridge* (Difficult) offers a sporting route on sound rock by the most obvious long ridge in the northern half of the line of broken rocks facing into the Lairig Ghru.

The ascent of Braeriach up Coire Gorm, looking towards Sgoran Dubh Mor

SKIING

The traverse of Braeriach and Cairn Toul is one of the best ski-mountaineering routes in Scotland. The northern slopes of Braeriach, the southern slopes of Cairn Toul, and the slopes of both hills towards the Moine Mhor offer excellent descents. Of particular note are Coire Gorm on the north side of Sron na Lairige, the slope west of Coire an Lochain, from the south side of Cairn Toul down towards The Devil's Point, from Cairn Toul into Glen Geusachan, and from the south-west end of the Braeriach plateau to the Moine Mhor. Beinn Bhrotain and Monadh Mor are also very good hills for ski-mountaineering, offering a great variety of terrain and some superb corries.

FURTHER READING

A.I.McConnochie *The western Cairngorms.* CCJ 2. 38.

D.McDougall *Loch Mhic Ghille-Chaoile: a tradition of the Cairngorms.* CCJ 2,294.

W.A.Smith *The western Cairngorms* (Guide Book article). SMCJ 7, 254.

CHAPTER 5

Sgoran Dubh and Carn Ban Mor

Sgor Gaoith	1118m	902 989
Sgoran Dubh Mor	1111m	906 003
Geal-charn	920m	884 014
Carn Ban Mor	1052m	893 972
Meall Dubhag	998m	881 955
Mullach Clach a' Bhlair	1019m	883 927

ACCESS, PUBLIC TRANSPORT, ACCOMMODATION AND BOTHIES
As in Chapter 1, and Chapter 3 (Glen Feshie). Public roads go to Whitewell at 916 085
below Gleann Einich, and up the east side of Glen Feshie from Feshiebridge to Achlean
(leave cars on the flat ridge at 853 977, north of the house).

MAPS
Ordnance Survey 1:50,000 Sheets 36 and 43

Rising from Glen Feshie, this 15 kilometre-long line of tops, connected by a high
plateau, forms a great rampart along the west end of Am Monadh Ruadh or the
Cairngorms. From between Loch Alvie and Kingussie you can see this particularly
well; the wall of steep lower hillsides, some with broken rocks, rears out of pine
forests and up to broad summits, in places cut by wild narrow side glens. Up there
on the top, a tableland of springy turf rolls on for miles. The deep craggy glens of
Einich and Eidart away to the east almost cut off these hills, but in the middle they
are connected to the loftier Braeriach, Cairn Toul and Monadh Mor by a flattish
broad belt of high peaty country named on the map Moine Mhor (from A' Mhoine
Mhor or the great moss), a grand subarctic wilderness with a habitat unique in
Scotland. It makes an easy trip from Glen Feshie to traverse all these tops in series,
as they all form mere bumps in a high-level whaleback ridge including Sgor Gaoith
and Mullach Clach a' Bhlair which are both Munros. A good way to appreciate the
full grandeur of the group is to come in from Gleann Einich and see the contrast
between the wild crags of Sgoran Dubh on that side and the smooth western slopes.
On the west side of the group, you will find the great rocky trench of Coire Garbhlach
above Glenfeshie Lodge especially worth visiting.

GEOLOGY, LANDFORMS AND WILDLIFE

Most of the rock is granite, including the great wall of cliffs west of Loch Einich. However, the floor of Glen Feshie itself lies over part of the huge Central Highland granulite formation of schist. This also makes up the south-west and south parts of the hill groups, for example at Coire Garbhlach (which also has some granite on its north side) and at Coire Mharconaich. The schist occurs again under the Moine Mhor through to Coire Odhar, in the Eidart glen and at Mullach Clach a' Bhlair. Coire Garbhlach has a remarkable, long, cliff-sided glacial trench, and the River Feshie is an unusual braided stream with great shingle beds. The Moine Mhor is notable for its extensive high peat bogs, and for the innumerable subarctic-like tiny hummocks caused by alternating frost and thaw on better drained ground.

On Creag Fhiaclach stands the best example of a natural upper woodland line still left in Scotland. All this ground is deer forest; in winter the deer crowd into Glen Feshie which they overgraze, but in summer they range far out across the Moine Mhor. Dotterel and dunlin nest on the tops and on the Moine Mhor. Many uncommon willows and other rare arctic-alpine plants grow on the fertile lime-rich rocks around the head of Coire Odhar above Loch Einich and at Coire Garbhlach.

ESTATES

The ground draining into Gleann Einich lies on Rothiemurchus, and that draining into the River Feshie on Glenfeshie Estate, except that the Scottish Natural Heritage agency owns Invereshie and Inshriach with a boundary from Creag Fhiaclach through Creag Dhubh and Carn Ban Mor to Creag Ghiuthsachan.

HISTORY

Clach Mhic Cailein, the Argyll Stone on Creag Dhubh, was named after the Earl of Argyll who passed here when fleeing home from the battle of Glen Livet in 1594, where he had been defeated by the Earl of Huntly. At Muileann Dubh near Feshie-bridge, later translated to its present name Blackmill, one of the party was said to have composed the popular Highland song and dance tune of *'Muileann Dubh'*. Ciste Mhearad or Margaret's coffin on Carn Ban Mor was called after a Margaret, who, jilted by Mackintosh of Moy, cursed sterility on his family and died there on her mad wanderings.

In his *Tour of Scotland* in 1774, Pennant was the first to mention any of these hills, writing of 'Sgorgave in Rothiemurchus', presumably meaning Sgor Gaoith. Later, Colonel Thornton in his *Sporting Tour*, published in 1804 (account in CCJ 2, 55), climbed Sgoran Dubh. High up, he 'deposited our champaign, lime, shrub, porter etc in one of the large snow-drifts, beneath an arch from which ran a charming spring' (probably Fuaran Diotach) ... It is impossible to describe the astonishment of the whole party when they perceived themselves on the brink of that frightful precipice, which separated them from the lake below ... Let the reader imagine a

Gleann Einich and Sgoran Dubh Mor

mountain at least eighteen thousand feet above him (probably Braeriach) and a steep precipice of thirteen thousand feet below'. Imagine the SMC Climbers' Guide he might have written! His lunch also far surpassed the modest sandwich of today's climber. 'The chief dish consisted of two brace and a half of ptarmigans and a moorcock, a quarter of a pound of butter, some slices of Yorkshire ham and reindeer's tongue with some sweet herbs .... These with a due proportion of water made each of us a plate of very strong soup, which was relished with a keenness of appetite that none but those that have been at Glen Ennoch can experience. We now drank in a bumper of champaign ... and with the addition of a tumbler of sherbet and a cordial, were enabled to pack up our apparatus and proceed.'

THE HILLS

Sgor Gaoith *(skor'gooee, peak of wind)* (1118m)
Sgoran Dubh Mor *(skoran doo'more, big black peaklet)* (1111m)
Sgor Gaoith is the highest point on the long hill ridge east of Glen Feshie, and Sgoran Dubh Mor is a top to the north. The eastern sides of Sgor Gaoith and Sgoran Dubh Mor fall in a spectacular line of crags dropping to remote Loch Einich. This is an interesting approach (see below). However, it is a long walk and there are no easy routes up the steep slopes above the loch.

Sgorr Gaoith from Sgoran Dubh Mor

The shortest and usual routes of ascent are from Glen Feshie. One way is to take the public road to Achlean, then go up the Allt Fhearnagan path to Carn Ban Mor (see below) and finally walk 2 kilometres north-north-east to Sgor Gaoith. A good and shorter route is to drive up the public road from Feshiebridge to 852 012 at the bridge over the Allt Ruadh. From here, a forest track leads east through a plantation and then through natural pine wood to 869 010. Beyond, a path climbs through pine trees up the north side of the beautiful glen of the Allt Ruadh. After crossing the small side burn of Allt Coire nam Bo, the path continues to a stile over an outer deer fence. Shortly after, the path crosses Allt Coire na Cloiche and turns south up the hillside. After that, the ground is rather boggy but soon becomes harder and easier as the path rises out of the corrie and on to the west slope of Meall Tionail. The path ends at the next big burn, the Allt a' Chrom-alltan. The best route from there is to cross the burn and climb east to the top of Sgor Gaoith (7 kilometres from the public road, 830m) where the small summit cairn is perched on the edge of the precipitous 600m drop to Loch Einich. Although these big crags are mostly broken, some of the buttresses consist of steep rock. On one of the buttresses under Sgor Gaoith stands the sharp pinnacle of A' Chailleach, or the old woman, her counterpart being a rocky pillar named Am Bodach, or the old man, near the top of the Creag an Loch spur of Braeriach opposite. From Sgor Gaoith you drop about 50m to a col and then climb the grassy slope leading to the big cairn of Sgoran Dubh Mor.

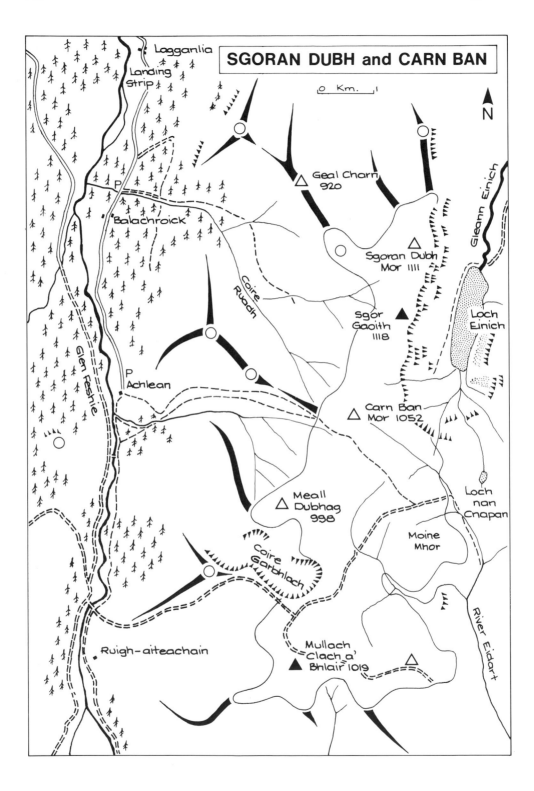

SGORAN DUBH and CARN BAN

A slightly shorter route to Sgor Gaoith, but without the full advantage of the path, is to leave the path where it crosses the Allt Coire na Cloiche and then head east-south-east up Coire na Cloiche to reach the broad ridge stretching from Geal-charn via the subsidiary 976m Meall Buidhe to Sgor Gaoith.

An interesting though long approach comes from Gleann Einich (for the route up the glen, see Chapter 3 under Braeriach). From Loch Einich, go up the west side of the loch by Ross's Path which climbs to 710m below the high corrie of A' Phocaid or the pocket. Distance: from the road end near Loch Einich to Sgor Gaoith 5 kilometres, 620m ascent. Broken rocks ring the top of A' Phocaid and the wider Coire Odhar (kor'ower) to the east, but you can pass fairly easily between them on to the plateau, to where Fuaran Diotach or dinner well flows from a beautiful spring in a grassy hollow. A gentle walk follows from there along to Sgor Gaoith.

Geal-charn ('gyal-charn) or white hill is the shapely top which stands out prominently in the view from Strath Spey, being the furthest west high hill of. the Cairngorms massif. Below Geal-charn, Creag Mhigeachaidh (kraik'vegechie) shows a fine rugged face of broken rocks and pine trees towards Glen Feshie. Here, in 1896 and 1900, avalanches swept hundreds of trees and masses of rock and boulders into the valley below (CCJ 3, 192).

From Sgoran Dubh Mor, the broad northern ridge makes an easy descent offering splendid views over to Braeriach on the right and down into Strath Spey on the left. On the way you pass the fine rocky 996m point of Sgoran Dubh Beag at the cliff edge, and further downhill a path leads to a col at 760m, just west of Coire Creagach and remote Lochan Beanaidh. On the gentle rise from that col to the flat 848m top of Creag Dhubh stand two small tors. The first is Clach Choutsaich or Coutts' Stone, the second being Clach Mhic Cailein or Argyll Stone, which looks prominent from the strath below. From Creag Dhubh the easiest way down lies over Cadha Mor (ka'more) and north to Whitewell.

An interesting way down from Sgoran Dubh is by the path down the east side of Allt a' Mharcaidh, from the col between Meall Buidhe and Geal-charn. The Allt a' Mharcaidh flows down a lovely glen which is wide and treeless higher up but lower down becomes narrow, steep and finely wooded with old pines. This glen (locally called Glen Markie) leads down to the swamp of Lochan Gorm on the valley flats beside the big pine woods of Inshriach.

Carn Ban Mor *(karn ban'more, big fair hill)* (1052m)
The easiest approach is to take the public road from Feshiebridge up the east side of Glen Feshie to Achlean (ach'lain). Distance to top: 5 kilometres, ascent 720m. From Achlean a vehicle track goes a short way uphill, changing to the Foxhunters' Path up the north side of Allt Fhearnagan (alt'yarnagan) or burn of alders. The path continues up Coire Fhearnagan to 1030m on the plateau just south of the summit. The hollow at the source of this burn, Ciste Mhearad, holds snow late in the year. Not far to the north of the path here, the hill slopes north into the wide Coire Ruadh and down to the Allt Ruadh, which gives another route of ascent or descent (see above).

Looking down Coire Garbhlach to Glen Feshie

Meall Dubhag *(from Meall Dubh-agaidh, lump of black cleft)* (998m)
This hill forms a mere bump rising from a big flat plateau, about 2 kilometres
south-west of Carn Ban Mor. The easiest approach is from Achlean by the path up
Allt Fhearnagan to its high point just south of Carn Ban Mor, and then south-west
over the plateau. A shorter route is to strike south-east from the old pine wood and
beautiful waterfalls at Badan Mosach and then go up the ridge on the west side of
Coire Gorm (4 kilometres, 670m).

Mullach Clach a' Bhlair (1019m)
The easiest approach is from Carnachuin on the west side of Glen Feshie. South of
Carnachuin, a vehicle track crosses the river at a bridge and then goes east up Coire
Caol to reach the ridge above, where there are grand views into Coire Garbhlach.
The track continues to 970m on the plateau, where it forks. The right fork leads close
to the summit of Mullach Clach a' Bhlair. The name refers to Clach a' Bhlair, a nearby
rock outcrop. At this point you stand 6 kilometres from Carnachuin by the bulldozed
track, ascent 670m. From the summit a long nose runs south-west to the rocky point
of Druim nam Bo at 918m, then beyond it to the tarn of Lochan nam Bo in a tiny
recess, and further still to end at Creag na Gaibhre. Creag na Gaibhre is a spectacular
viewpoint above an Alpine-like face of shattered rocks, screes and small trees,

dropping 300m to the flats of Feshie below. A zigzag path leads from the 737m top behind it north-west to Ruigh-aiteachain.

An alternative route to Mullach Clach a' Bhlair is from the public road end at Achlean on the east side of Glen Feshie. A footpath runs south along the east side of the River Feshie south of Achleum. One can head south-east across the moor by a small path, cross the Allt Garbhlach, and climb above the plantation of Coille an Torr to reach the ridge at Meall nan Sleac and shortly after join the route described above at the edge of Coire Garbhlach.

Coire Garbhlach

Beyond Mullach Clach a' Bhlair the bulldozed track from Coire Garbhlach goes 3 kilometres east. It ends at a point half a kilometre south-east of the nameless 971m plateau bump that rises east of the 958m col of Diollaid Coire Eindart or saddle of Coire Eindart. Here you stand near the cliffs of remote Coire Mharconaich, and look over the River Eidart to the great green bulges of Monadh Mor. Unfortunately, vehicles have roamed over these dry plateaux off the prepared gravel tracks, causing marks that take years to heal.

Another branch of the track goes north around the head of Coire Garbhlach and then north-east almost to the Allt Sgairnich ('skarnich) just west of Loch nan Cnapan. The 918m Tom Dubh or dark hillock rises between the Allt Luineag and Allt Sgairnich, about 4 kilometres from Carn Ban Mor by the track. In a secluded little basin north of Tom Dubh lies Loch nan Cnapan (lochna'krapan) or loch of the knolls, which sends its water north to the cascades of Coire Odhar and Loch Einich, but most of the burns on the Moine Mhor drain into the Eidart. Although bulldozed tracks have badly spoiled the feeling of wilderness on the Moine Mhor, the eastern parts of this great moss around Loch nan Cnapan and Allt Luineag are still wonderful places with unscarred green hollows of turf and moss, sparkling clear burns, and stony ridges. Green slopes rise gently to the snows and higher hills to the east.

For a more varied way to climb these hills, you can walk up Glen Feshie and take the path to the hut just west of where the River Eidart enters the Feshie. From there a path goes north-east, not far from the edge of a miniature rocky canyon with waterfalls, in which the River Eidart flows for 1½ kilometres. Above this the river runs through open shingle and grassy banks where the path goes up the east side. In the upper part of the glen on its west side rises a fine line of broken crags which finish at the north end of the east ridge of Coire Mharconaich. Further up still, the stream divides into branches which plunge steeply down rugged little ravines from the Moine Mhor above; this fork lies 6 kilometres from the Eidart hut and 15 kilometres from Ruigh-aiteachain via the Eidart. These steeper slopes hem in the grassy hollow and broken rocks of Coire Mharconaich (kor'varkonich). The main part of the corrie doubles back south-west in an inner recess, bounded on the east by a ridge which gives a fine walking route up to the plateau and Diollaid Coire Eindart.

WALKING IN THE CORRIES
The magnificent Coire Garbhlach is well worth seeing on the way down from these tops. As the crags are broken in many places, in the late summer you can scramble fairly easily down the screes near where the waterfall comes over from the Moine Mhor. At the subsidiary Fionnar Choire or cool corrie, which lies high on the north side of Coire Garbhlach and due south of Meall Dubhag, you can descend slopes of steep grass without rock. One of the main attractions of being right inside Coire Garbhlach is that much of the wide upper corrie is hidden from Glen Feshie by the narrow and curving entrance. This corrie looks unique for the Cairngorms, as it is not a typical corrie basin but a 2½ kilometre-long, narrow, V-shaped glen, with cliffs rising on either side and at its top, and with the bottom of the corrie leading steeply

downhill beside a roaring stream. It has some steep rock buttresses which support a rich alpine vegetation. If you merely wish to see the corrie and not go into it, the route by the bulldozed track along the south ridge gives a series of fine views into the corrie. The local pronunciation (kor'galach) suggests Coire Gabhalach or forked corrie.

CLIMBING

On Sgoran Dubh the SMC were early pioneers with several routes in March 1902. The rocky face runs for 3 kilometres and up to 370m high, with cliffs of dark, rough granite. The crags consist mainly of broken rock. The buttresses from north to south are Number 1 under Sgoran Dubh Beag, 2 and 3 under Sgoran Dubh Mor, 4 below Sgor Gaoith, and Number 5 further south including the pinnacle of A' Chailleach. The hollow between Numbers 1 and 2 is Coire Sgoran Dubh Beag, that between 2 and 3 being Coire Olc or evil corrie, later given the English name of Fan Corrie. The corrie between buttresses 3 and 4 is Coire Meadhon or middle corrie, and that between 4 and 5 is Coire na Cailliche, corrie of the Cailleach or old woman, referring to the rocky pinnacle. The gully of Sput Seilich or willow spout divides Number 1 Buttress into two parts, and makes a long, fairly easy, Grade I winter climb. Number 5 Buttress or *Pinnacle Ridge* (Moderate) offers an interesting easy way to the plateau up the right edge of the buttress, passing close by the remarkable pinnacle of A' Chailleach. Pinnacle Ridge gives a total vertical ascent of 370m (Grade II). These crags look well in winter snow, and there has recently been an increase in winter climbing on the Loch Einich face of Sgoran Dubh.

SKIING

In good snow cover, the series of hills from Sgoran Dubh to Mullach Clach a' Bhlair makes an excellent cross-country route, with superb descents off Sgoran Dubh into Allt a' Mharcaidh and off Carn Ban Mor into Coire Ruadh or Coire Fhearnagan. The Moine Mhor itself is a magnificent wilderness in snow, where an accomplished skier can normally travel considerably faster than a walker in summer.

FURTHER READING

R.Anderson *Glen Feshie.* CCJ 1, 348.

H.T.Munro *Loch Eunach, Sgoran Dubh, and the western Cairngorms.* SMCJ 2, 296.

W.A.Smith *The western Cairngorms* (Guide Book article). SMCJ 7, 254.

CHAPTER 6

Monadh Minigaig and Gaick

Carn na Caim	941m	677 822
A' Bhuidheanach Bheag	936m	660 776
Meall Chuaich	951m	717 879
Maol Creag an Loch	876m	735 807
An Dun	827m	716 802
Leathad an Taobhain	912m	822 858
Carn Dearg Mor	857m	824 912
Meallach Mhor	769m	777 909

The first three above are Munros and the rest Corbetts.

ACCESS
The main access to all this hill country is from the A9 road and nearby railway from Perth to Inverness. The easiest way to the north end is to leave the A9 at Kingussie, cross the River Spey and go to Tromie Bridge. The best ways from the south end are from Blair Atholl up Glen Bruar and from Calvine. The east Drumochter hills at the west end of the area are best approached from the A9 road near the summit of the Pass of Drumochter.

PUBLIC TRANSPORT
Rail: Trains from Perth to Inverness stop at Blair Atholl, Dalwhinnie, Newtonmore and Kingussie.

Bus: Perth to Inverness, stopping at main settlements.

ACCOMMODATION
Hotels and bed and breakfast accommodation are at Blair Atholl, Dalwhinnie, Newtonmore and Kingussie. Kingussie has a caravan site and youth hostel.

MAPS
Ordnance Survey 1:50,000 Sheets 35, 42 and 43

The Pass of Drumochter (drum'oochter) separates the more distinctive and higher hills on its west side, which used to be called Druim Uachdair or ridge of upper ground, from the smoother high ground to the east. This chapter describes the eastern hill country stretching across to Bruar and Feshie, part of the range whose old name was Monadh Minigaig. The name Minigaig ('meeniga- ik) probably comes from Mine-ghaig or smooth Gaick, in contrast to the nearby Garbh-ghaig or rough Gaick to the west. An old document gave the 'wild Month and hills of Mynygegg'.

Monadh Minigaig begins just east of Dalwhinnie and Drumochter, where a crescent of rounded hills, flat on top, rises to above 900m. Many walkers visit them as they are so near the road. Apart from this inhabited corner, the huge district stretching east from here to Glen Bruar, and north-east to Glen Feshie and Glen Tromie, extends far as a vast remote wild tract. The boundary between Perth and Inverness runs along an enormous medium-level plateau, with many rounded undulating bumps rising above 750m but none above 914m or 3000ft. Innumerable streams meander down gentle peaty slopes and hollows into lonely glens, with many peaty lochans and pools high up. There are also areas of spectacular country where the plateaux suddenly end in wild steep slopes, often with broken rocks, hidden corries and foaming burns. The ground around Gaick Lodge and south-wards to Sronphadruig Lodge has this wild character, and also some very fine lochs down in the glen bottoms. The three important cross-country routes offer more interest to hillwalkers than many of the rounded hills themselves. However, the other less spectacular glens and tops are worth wandering into, unhurriedly. Here you will still find wild country and peace, although bulldozed tracks scar some of the remote glens and hills. In winter mist, storm and snow, Monadh Minigaig is one of the more difficult high-level cross-country routes in the Highlands.

GEOLOGY, LANDFORMS AND WILDLIFE

A vast extent of the Central Highlands granulites or schists dominates the area. The smooth plateau far around shows how uniform a level this part of the Highlands reaches; from the tops you tend to see not low valleys but mostly other rolling whalebacks and plateaux rising to about the same height as the level you stand at. The deep trenches at Gaick are a good example of erosion by glaciers, and glacially-dumped gravel holds up the 31m deep Loch an Duin at its north end. The largest of the Gaick lochs, Loch an t-Seilich (lochan'tshailich) or loch of the willow, extends for 2 kilometres long, 30m deep in its original state, and 100 hectares in area.

This is an infertile high peaty country, much of which has little variety of wildlife. However the mossy tundras and peat bogs on the Dalwhinnie hills are exciting places for naturalists, with interesting vegetation and soil features, and outstanding habitats for montane wading birds. A similar vegetation grows on the bare hilltops further east around Gaick. The main plants on the area as a whole are the mixture of cotton grass, heather and deer grass so common on wet peaty ground in the Highlands, but lime-rich patches on a few crags away from grazing sheep support a much greater variety of plants. Fine old birch woods grow by Loch an t-Seilich of Gaick and down Glen Tromie, but otherwise the deer and sheep have put an end to most trees and scrub. Dotterel nest on the high tops and dunlin in the peat mosses. Ptarmigan are common, golden eagles and peregrine falcons hunt over the tops, and a few greenshanks nest in the lonely treeless glens.

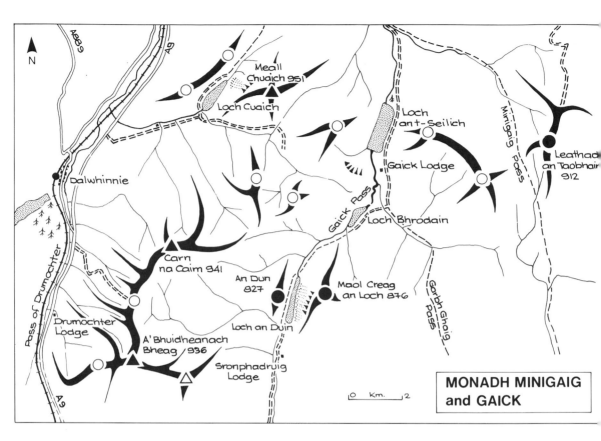

MONADH MINIGAIG and GAICK

ESTATES

Apart from the separate estate on the Dalnacardoch-Sronphadruig drainage, the Perthshire part all belongs to Atholl Estate at Blair Castle. Glenfeshie Estate owns the ground north-east of the Inverness-shire part of the Minigaig path. Gaick and Glen Tromie form one estate, and the land lying west to Dalwhinnie is on Phones. Deer and sheep are the main land use, with grouse shooting on the lower slopes.

HISTORY

Loch Bhrodainn of Gaick had an old legend that Brodan, the hound of Celtic myth, chased the White Stag of Ben Alder into the loch, where both sank for ever. Gaick is well known for the story of Call Ghaig or the Loss of Gaick (SMCJ 14, 181). In early January 1800, Capt John MacPherson of Ballachroan – known as the 'Black Officer' – and four companions had gone up to Gaick to shoot and were spending the night in a hut, when an avalanche from the steep hill above overwhelmed and killed them. MacPherson was a vicious recruiting officer, so folk looked on his end as a kind of judgement. Standing on the south side of the path immediately south of Gaick Lodge, a rough block with a Gaelic inscription commemorates the Loss.

The bare flats beside Gaick Lodge, looking south to Sron Bhuirich and A'Chaoirnich

The Pass of Drumochter lies on the route of the great Highland road which General Wade built from Perthshire to Fort Augustus to help his army control the Highlanders. The work finished in September 1729, and was celebrated with a feast – four oxen roasted whole and four kegs of brandy – held beside Dalnacardoch. The pass used to be called Strath Downaig on the north side and Strath Dubhaig on the south side. Until Wade built the Drumochter road to connect more easily with his Corrieyairack road to Fort Augustus, the Minigaig road over the Mounth to the east was far more important for travellers. Many used it for driving hill cattle (CCJ 7, 4) and indeed a few still did so until the end of the last century. A 16th-century document (MacFarlane's *Geographical Collections* 2, 598) mentions 'a way from the yate of Blair in Athoil to Ruffen in Badenoch maid be David Cuming Earle of Athoil for carts to pass with wyne, and the way is called Rad na pheny, or way of Wagon Wheels'. W.C.Smith (CCJ 7, 4) thought that this referred to the Minigaig but the present writer has heard the old road from Bac na Creige over Sron a' Chleirich – that is the Garbh-ghaig route – still called Comyn's or Cumming's Road by folk in Atholl, and this is well confirmed by Kerr's detailed study (see Further Reading). In Gaelic it was Rathad nan Cuimeineach.

The Gaick area was used for one of Scotland's early hydro-electric schemes. The engineers took south-flowing water from the Edendon Water through a tunnel to Loch an Duin, and raised Loch an t-Seilich 3m by a dam built in 1940 at its north end. From here, a 7-kilometre tunnel goes under the hills to Loch Cuaich and then east of Dalwhinnie by an aqueduct to Loch Ericht.

THE HILLS

A' Bhuidheanach Bheag *(the little yellow place)* (936m)
Carn na Caim *(karna'keim, hill of the curve)* (941m)
These two Munros make up part of the high crescent of hills along the east side of Drumochter Pass between Dalnaspidal and Dalwhinnie. The convex side faces Dalwhinnie, whereas the concave side encloses the wild Cama Choire or curved corrie above the headwater of the Edendon. All these tops are merely slight rises from a great high plateau, and thus not easy to find in mist. Although looking massive and rather dull from Drumochter as compared with the sharper more individual hills west of the pass, from their summits they give grand spacious views as you have come right to the centre of Scotland here.

Near Dalnaspidal the 928m Glas Mheall Mor or big green lump rises 5 kilometres away and 500m in altitude to the north-east, topped by a big cairn. From here you go 2 kilometres west-north-west to A' Bhuidheanach Bheag, where a large quartz cairn stands beside a fence running along the county boundary. (The original name for this was not Bheag but Mhor, the old name A' Bhuidheanach Bheag referring to the lower peaty bump at 672 772). Now you can diverge easily to Meall a' Chaorainn or lump of the rowan tree, which rises as a mere bump 1½ kilometres to the west at 916m. The main watershed carries on from A' Bhuidheanach Bheag along the fence north to a peaty col where a fine steep ravine runs into Allt Coire Chuirn. You can easily follow the fence far out north to Carn na Caim. Here, 6 kilometres from A' Bhuidheanach Bheag, the fence divides, the left branch going towards Dalwhinnie.

There is a much easier way of reaching this fine plateau by a track bulldozed almost to the plateau edge, starting from south of the Wade Bridge on the A9 just south of Dalwhinnie; its scar now shows for miles. A finer but much longer way to reach these hills comes from the Gaick Pass by Cama Choire.

Meall Chuaich *(lump at the Cuaich or cup)* (951m)
Meall Chuaich sweeps up from Loch Cuaich below it. This Munro stands out as an isolated rounded top which gives a very fine view up and down Strath Spey and up Loch Ericht to the Ben Alder hills. From the A9 north of Dalwhinnie, take the private road just south of the cottages of Cuaich and up to the loch at about 400m, and then walk south of the loch and up the west nose of the hill. Distance: from A9 to loch 5 kilometres, loch to top 3 kilometres, total ascent 600m.

Another approach (5½ kilometres) comes up the tree-lined Allt na Fearna from Bhran Cottage in Glen Tromie, and a third (6 kilometres) from Gaick Lodge by the zigzag path that climbs steeply up Sgor Dearg to the west on to a wide plateau, from which you drop to a 614m col and then follow the fence to the top.

Meall Chuaich and Carn na Caim

Maol Creag an Loch *(hill of crag of the loch)* (876m)
An Dun *(the hill)* (827m)
These two hills rise steeply on the east and west sides of Loch an Duin in the Gaick Pass, and give spectacular views down to the loch and along the pass. From Dalnacardoch on the A9 a private road runs north to Sronphadruig Lodge (see the Gaick Pass, below). Maol Creag an Loch stands 3 kilometres to the north-east, first of all east uphill to a col at 571m, then north up a ridge above the rocky face of Craig an Loch, and along the flattish summit plateau (550m ascent from Dalnacardoch).

About one kilometre beyond Sronphadruig Lodge, the road from Dalnacardoch ends at a small dam. The summit of An Dun stands about one kilometre to the north (11 kilometres from Dalnacardoch, 500m ascent). The hill has a remarkable shape, like some enormous old fortress, and its Gaelic name means a fortress as well as simply a heap or hill. It gives fine views into the wild Cama Choire to the west. Beyond rises another big plateau, edged by Vinegar Hill (one of the most absurd map names, anglicised from A' Mhin-choiseachd or the easy walking).

Leathad an Taobhain *(slope of the rafter)* (902m)
Carn Dearg Mor *(big red hill)* (857m)
Leathad an Taobhain stands on the watershed between Feshie, Tromie and Atholl, overlooking a remote tract of plateaux, peat bogs and easy-angled glens. Carn Dearg Mor to the north of it rises behind Glenfeshie Lodge. The two hills are easily reached

from the private road up Glen Tromie, but the shortest distance from a public road is from Achlean in Glen Feshie. From there the route goes south for just over one kilometre, next across a bridge over the River Feshie, and then south past Glenfeshie Lodge and up the bulldozed track to 847m on the top of Meall an Uillt Chreagaich. An easy walk follows to the 912m highest point east of the 902m top marked Leathad an Taobhain on the map (14 kilometres, 680m ascent), where a fine view opens out into the upper wide Glen Feshie and Glen Geldie. After returning almost to Lochan an t-Sluic, one can then take another bulldozed track north-west on to Carn Dearg Mor, follow a footpath up to 770m, and then have easy walking to the summit (6 kilometres and 380m ascent from Leathad an Taobhain).

Meallach Mhor (*big lumpy place*) (769m)
Meallach Mhor rises above the middle part of Glen Tromie and above Gleann Chomhraig. The best way to reach it is from Glen Tromie. The road up the glen is a right of way, and a bicycle can be taken for 10 kilometres from Tromie Bridge past Bhran Cottage to the foot of the hill. An easy walk then follows to the top (12 kilometres from Tromie Bridge, 520m ascent).

THE MOUNTH ROADS

The Pass of Drumochter. Here, rail and road cross the Mounth at the lowest point between Loch Laggan and the Cairn o' Mount at Banchory. With steep hills on either side, often sporting snow plumes of spindrift in winter, and the long open glens leading up to the summit, Drumochter Pass makes an impressive gateway to the wilder Highlands lying to the north. It is the highest railway pass in the Highlands, reaching about 450m, the nearby road going to about 460m.

The Gaick Pass. The word Gaick comes from Gaig ('ga-ik, meaning at a cleft), a good name for this, one of the most unusual valley trenches in the Highlands. It is an old right of way from Dalnacardoch of Atholl through to Badenoch. In 1774 the Government built the lodge at Dalnacardoch as a public rest-house, as you will see from the Latin inscription near the door. Distance: from Dalnacardoch to Sronphadruig 9 kilometres, to county boundary 11, to Gaick Lodge 18, to Bhran Cottage 25, to Glentromie Lodge 31½, to Killiehuntly 34, to Tromie Bridge 35 kilometres, total ascent 180m. From Dalnacardoch a rough private road goes up the Edendon Water to Sronphadruig Lodge (stron'fatrik) or hill nose of Patrick. Above the lodge, the glen of Edendon turns west into Cama Choire, but the path to Gaick goes north along the west side of Loch an Duin which lies in a narrow trench at about 485m between An Dun and the rocky face of Craig an Loch. A short distance north-east of the north end of Loch an Duin, the path becomes a bulldozed track which goes gently downhill towards Gaick Lodge, along the flattish grassy floor of a widening glen hemmed in by bold steep hills. Below Loch Bhrodainn ('vrottan) you cross the Allt Gharbh Ghaig, a burn which flows down from a wild glen to the south-east, and then come to Gaick Lodge. A private road goes from here down to the foot of Glen Tromie.

The view from Gaick Lodge looking back to the south towards Sron Bhuirich (stron'voorich) or nose of the roaring, is very impressive, as the foreground and hills have an unusual quality of openness and steep slopes. Stalkers' paths zigzag steeply up Sgor Dearg and the slope east of the lodge to the plateaux on either side. The Gaick hills are notable for their avalanches, which sometimes have even crossed the road along Loch an t-Seilich. In several cases, deer crossing steep slopes have started avalanches that killed them, or sheltering in the valley bottom have been over-whelmed by snow slides from above. The reason for the many avalanches is that drifting snow blows from the huge plateaux all around and piles up to great depths when it suddenly comes into the shelter of Gaick's steep slopes.

The Minigaig Road. This old track goes from Blair Atholl to Glen Tromie and Kingussie. Although now seldom visited, this interesting right of way over the Mounth takes you into some fine wild country. Distance: from Old Blair north of Blair Castle by the west side of Glen Banvie to Bruar Lodge 11 kilometres, to the stream fork at the top of Glen Bruar 16, to county boundary 21, to Glen Tromie road at Allt Bhran bridge 29, to Bhran Cottage 31, to Killiehuntly 40, to Tromie Bridge 41 kilometres, total ascent 680m.

From Old Blair you can now walk by a road up the west side of Glen Banvie and over a low ridge to Glen Bruar, but this way adds 2 kilometres extra to the journey. The old Minigaig Road goes up the east side of Glen Banvie by the road to Allt an t-Seapail (pronunciation and meaning is chapel), past the cairn of Carn Mhic Shimidh where a fight once occurred between the Murrays and Simon Lovat. You continue by an old path along Druim Dubh to Bruar Lodge. Great numbers of red deer stags live in Glen Banvie which forms part of the West Hand beat of Atholl, and the vegetation in the lower glen is grazed heavily by their concentrations in winter here, more so than at most places in the region described in this book. An alternative way to Bruar Lodge, one kilometre shorter, leaves the A9 at Calvine (kal'veen) and takes the road that winds north over Creag Bhagailteach. East of Calvine, try to see the fine series of three falls at Falls of Bruar (brooar or bridge-stream). The Duke of Atholl originally planted the woods here in response to Robert Burns's verse *'The Humble Petition of Bruar Water'*.

Beyond Bruar Lodge lies a small artificial loch where the glen narrows below steeper craggy slopes. The rough road ends at about 530m, above which the main stream divides. Two paths come in here, the Minigaig being the right-hand one. It climbs 230m to the flat top of Uchd a' Chlarsair or brow of the harper. In the next 3 kilometres you pass two little dips and then a long easy rise, marked with quartz cairns, to the summit at about 830m. It interesting to see how this path was cleverly made over hard ground through a great rolling district of soft moorland and peat.

At the summit you stand high over this hill country, and an easy stroll takes you the short distance north-east to the tops of Leathad an Taobhain. Just north of here, at the summit of Meall an Uillt Chreagaich, a bulldozed track runs north on the line of an old stalking footpath to Lochan an t-Sluic and Carnachuin in Glen Feshie. Distance: from county boundary to Carnachuin by this way 11½ kilometres.

From the summit, the Minigaig path drops down the grassy slopes east of Coire Bhran (kor'vran). It becomes a bulldozed track at the upper weir on Allt Bhran, and

The Gaick Pass from An Dun

after another 1½ kilometres enters Glen Tromie (Gaelic *tromaidh,* or elder tree). Here you join the private road from Gaick Lodge which runs down through fine groves of birch, alder and juniper under the rocky slopes of Croidh-la to the public road at Tromie Bridge. The original Minigaig route crosses the River Tromie at Dailriach (footbridge) one kilometre below Bhran Cottage and next climbs north-north-east. The path, now indistinct and not shown on current OS maps, passes just west of the cairn named Carn Pheigith and then east of Sron na Gaoithe. At this point it joins a path that is marked on current maps, and eventually becomes a vehicle track leading down west of Beinn Bhuidhe to Ruthven Barracks near Kingussie. Built in 1719 to check the Jacobites, the barracks were burned by Bonnie Prince Charlie in 1746.

The Garbh-ghaig Pass or Comyn's Road.   This old right of way lies mainly east of the Gaick Pass, with most of the Minigaig route further east still. The Garbh-ghaig route now follows a vehicle track from Old Blair up the west side of Glen Banvie to Ruichlachrie, then crosses to Cuilltemhuc on the west side of Bruar Water. From there it climbs north-west, indistinct and now largely obliterated by a bulldozed vehicle track, over Carn a' Chullaich to the old shielings of Ruighe a' Chire at the junction of Allt a' Chire Mhoir and Allt a' Chire Bhig.

Another old right of way to this point starts on the A9 west of Blair Atholl and is a shorter and easier route. Distance: from Clunes ('klooniss) Lodge at 783 672 on the A9 to the county boundary at Bac na Creige 14 kilometres, to Gaick Lodge

20 kilometres, total ascent 700m but only 450m if starting from Gaick Lodge. From Clunes Lodge a private road runs up Allt a' Chrombaidh. You cross a low ridge north-west to Ruighe a' Chire. The track is faint in places, but becomes clear on Sron a' Chleirich (stronna'chleerich) or hill nose of the priest. Beyond, it runs along the plateau, crosses the head of Feith na Mad, and rises gently to the county boundary at Bac na Creige (bachna'craik) or bank of the rocky hill. Here, at about 770m, you drop into Gaick. The Atholl side has shallow corries and gently sloping hillsides, but the Allt Gharbh Ghaig shows a sudden contrast, a wild glen with broken crags, steep slopes and foaming burns. At the bottom of the glen of the Allt Gharbh Ghaig the path becomes a vehicle track down to Gaick Lodge and Glen Tromie. From Glen Tromie the Garbh-ghaig route follows the line of the Minigaig Road past Carn Pheigith and east of Sron na Gaoithe to Ruthven and Kingussie.

An interesting alternative walk starts from the A9 at Dail na Mine (dalna'meen), further west than Clunes. Here you take the private road to the north past the ruined Glas Choire Lodge set on its green hillside to a hydro-electric dam on Allt Glas Choire ('glas chorrie) near where the Allt Dearg comes in. A bulldozed track goes from Druim Ruidh Chail to the top of Bachd Ban, from which a gentle stroll takes you up the broad ridge to the county boundary at Bac na Creige, 11 kilometres from Dail na Mine. You can avoid part of the climb by slanting further west through the col at Carr na Moine at about 660m, after a 430m ascent from Dail na Mine, to pick up the more westerly of the two paths down the Allt Gharbh Ghaig.

Before you reach Glas Choire Lodge, a road branches off to the east and goes to the stream to the west of the Allt a' Chire Mhoir. From here you can pick up the Comyn's Road on Sron a' Chleirich summit, but this route is 2 kilometres longer than the way going from Dail na Mine by Bachd Ban.

SKIING

This snowy area is very good for cross-country skiing, including ski-mountaineering on some of the steeper slopes around Gaick. The east Drumochter hills are well known for their downhill skiing potential. All the hills described above are good for skiing, and the Gaick Pass and Minigaig offer good cross-country routes in general snow cover. However, as the altitudes are lower than in the Cairngorms, the snow does not last so well into the spring.

FURTHER READING

A.I.McConnochie *The three Gaicks*. CCJ 9,71.

'H.W.' *Gaick Forest* (Guide Book article) SMCJ 8, 177.

H.Alexander *Gaick*. SMCJ 14, 178.

J.Kerr (1977) *Old Grampian highways*. Trans. Gaelic Soc. Inverness 49, 53-86. On Comyn's Road and Minigaig.

CHAPTER 7

Beinn a' Ghlo and Glen Tilt

Beinn a' Ghlo	1129m	970 732
Braigh Coire Chruinn-bhalgain	1070m	944 724
Carn Liath	975m	936 698
Carn a' Chlamhain	963m	916 758
Beinn Dearg	1008m	853 778
An Sgarsoch	1006m	933 837
Carn an Fhidhleir	994m	905 842
Beinn Bhreac	912m	868 821
Beinn Mheadhonach	901m	880 758
Ben Vuirich	903m	987 700
Ben Vrackie	841m	951 632

This chapter describes the vast area of hills from Glen Bruar in the west to Ben Vrackie near Pitlochry, and includes Carn an Fhidhleir and An Sgarsoch on the south of Glen Geldie.

Outcrops of limestone, diorite and other rich rocks make this a more fertile country than the Cairngorms massif. The hills are mostly rounded and green, well covered with a grassy vegetation which includes much moss and heath. As the lower slopes tend to be very gradual, peat has built up thickly there. These gentle slopes running for miles impart to these wide glens an air of enormous space. Far from being featureless, this gives the district part of its peculiar fascination. A working definition of a remote, roadless area involves ground more than a few miles from a public road. By this criterion, here we have one of the best roadless areas in Scotland. Along Glen Tilt the hillsides are greener and steeper than in the rest of Atholl, and the valley narrower with broken rocks in places.

GEOLOGY, LANDFORMS AND WILDLIFE

One of the main geological faults in the region passes along the line of Glen Tilt, then across by the Clais Fhearnaig near Glen Lui and along the cleft of the upper Gairn between Creag an Dail Mhor and Bheag. Most of the area lies over Central Highland schists with some quartzite, but granite occurs at Beinn Dearg and Beinn a' Ghlo, a large mass of the richer diorite around Carn a' Chlamhain, and lime-rich rocks along Glen Tilt and near Loch Loch including much limestone. The Water of Tarf once ran into Deeside near Bynack, but due to the glaciation a low ridge of glacial deposit turned the water in a very sharp bend into Tilt.

Comments on wildlife apply as in Chapter 6. However, Glen Tilt and Glen Loch, being much more fertile than most glens in Atholl and Gaick, are interesting places for arctic-alpine and lime-loving plants, including that rare alpine the yellow oxytropis.

ESTATES

Atholl Estates at Blair Castle own the Perthshire part (except for Glen Fender and the Loch Valigan ground to the south of Beinn a' Ghlo which are owned by Lude Estate, and the separate estate of Glenfernate). Mar Lodge Estate has the Aberdeenshire side. These are all deer forests, some with hill sheep, and some with grouse shooting on the lower ground.

HISTORY

According to an old legend, the Braemar men once tried to cut a trench through the flat ground at the watershed of Tilt and Bynack so as to divert the uppermost branch of Tilt into Dee, but were routed by the men of Atholl; some mounds by Tilt are said to be the graves of the Atholl men who died in the fight. Atholl has long been a famous deer forest, and at the base of Beinn a' Ghlo below Forest Lodge there are the remains of wolf pits. James V in 1529 and Mary Queen of Scots in 1564 attended deer drives there. In 1844, Queen Victoria and the Prince Consort saw a deer drive near Forest Lodge, and went through Glen Tilt to Deeside in 1861. The Duke of Atholl tried to close the glen in the 1840s but lost this important right of way case. *The Ballad of Glen Tilt*, reprinted in CCJ 3, 185 (see also CCJ 6, 310) told how Prof J.H.Balfour and a party of botanists went there:

> Twas a' to poo
>   Some gerse that grew
> On Ben Muich Dhu,
>   That ne'er a coo
> Would care to pit her moo' till'

On their way south they were challenged by the angry Duke:

> The Duke at this put up his birse,
> He vowed in English and in Erse,
>   That Saxon fit
>   Su'd never get
>   Ae single bit
> Throughout his yet,
> Among the Hielan hills, man.
> Balfour he had a mind as weel
>   As ony duke could hae, man,
> Quo' he, 'There's ne'er a kilted chiel
>   Shall drive us back this day, man.
> It's Justice and it's public richt,
> We'll pass Glen Tilt afore the nicht,
> For dukes shall we
> Care ae bawbee?
> The road's as free
> To you and me
> As to his Grace himself, man

Between White Bridge and the Linn of Dee stand the ancient ruins of the Dubrach ('doobrach) on the south side. After the 1745 Jacobite rising, some English soldiers were stationed here, and one of them, Sergeant Davies, was murdered in 1749 on a hillside up the Allt Cristie. Five years later, two local men were put on trial at the High Court in Edinburgh. The chief witness for the prosecution told how the English soldier's ghost had appeared and told him the murderers' names. When the defence advocate asked what language the ghost of the English sergeant used, and the witness said 'as good Gaelic as myself', the case collapsed in a burst of laughter. The full story was told in a book edited by Sir Walter Scott and published in 1831 for the Bannatyne Club, *Trial of Duncan Terig alias Clerk, etc.* The last tenant of Dubrach, old Peter Grant or 'Aal Dubrach', lived to 110 years; he died in 1824, the last of the Braemar Jacobite fighters for Bonnie Prince Charlie. In 1822, at the age of 108, he went to Edinburgh to meet George IV, descendant of the Hanoverian 'Wee Bit German Lairdie'. Taking him by the hand, the King said 'You are my oldest friend' to which Aal Dubrach instantly replied 'Na na, yer Majesty, I am yer aaldest enemy'. Hundreds attended the funeral of this great Deeside character, headed by pipers playing the tune *Wha wadna fecht for Chairlie*.

Beinn a' Ghlo from Ben Vrackie

THE HILLS

Beinn a' Ghlo *(hill of the mist)* (1129m)
Braigh Coire Chruinn-bhalgain *(upland of corrie of round blisters)* (1070m)
Carn Liath *(grey hill)* (975m)
It used to be Beinn a' Ghlo nan Eag (of the clefts), as told in Grant's *Legends of the Braes o' Mar*, and is pronounced bainnie'glo. Apart from Lochnagar which projects really as an offshoot to the north of the main watershed, Beinn a' Ghlo looks the finest hill in the whole range of the Mounth from Drumochter to Aberdeen. Much steeper and stonier than the other hills of Tilt or Geldie, it is also a far more complex hill, with many tops and corries. An old stalkers' legend was that it held 19 corries, in any of which a rifle could be fired without being heard in another. From the Cairngorms, its domed summit, flanked by subsidiary symmetrical tops on either side and seen across vast empty glens and lower hills, makes Beinn a' Ghlo one of the most beautiful and mysterious hills of Scotland.

To climb it you will probably go to Blair Atholl whose name comes from the very old Blar Ath Fhotla or plain of new Ireland. going back to the time when the Celtic rulers of Scotland were Irish. North of Blair Castle and its fine old larches and other trees stands the church at Old Blair, where Claverhouse, Viscount of Dundee, was buried after the Battle of Killiecrankie.

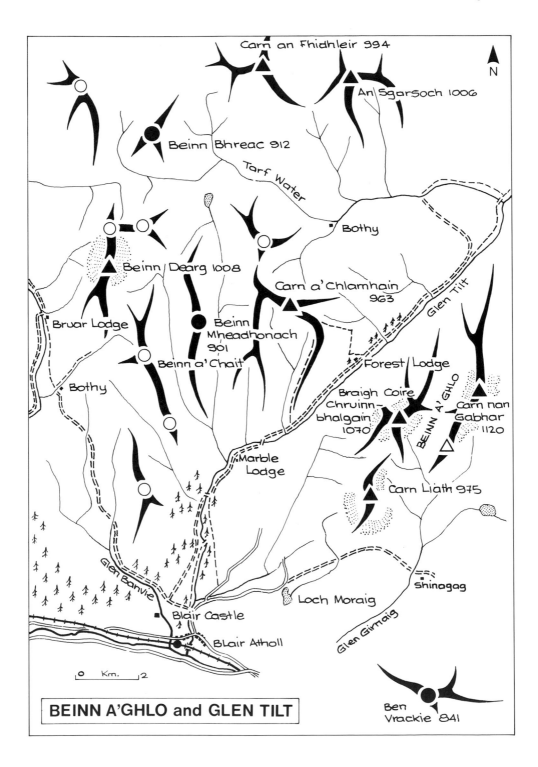

Carn an Fhidhleir 994

An Sgarsoch 1006

N

Beinn Bhreac 912

Tarf Water

Bothy

Beinn Dearg 1008

Carn a'Chlamhain 963

Glen Tilt

Bruar Lodge

Beinn Mheadhonach 901

Forest Lodge

Beinn a'Chait

Braigh Coire Chruinn-bhalgain 1070

BEINN A'GHLO

Carn nan Gabhar 1120

Bothy

Marble Lodge

Carn Liath 975

Glen Banvie

Shinagag

Loch Moraig

Blair Castle

Glen Girnaig

Blair Atholl

0   Km.   2

BEINN A'GHLO and GLEN TILT

Ben Vrackie 841

From Blair Atholl, the usual way to Beinn a' Ghlo goes up the south side of Glen Fender by a public road which ends beside Loch Moraig, and then by a track leading to Glen Girnaig, to about 440m altitude. You then climb north fairly steeply up heather and later mossy heath and screes to Carn Liath ('lee-a) at 975m, the conical top so prominent from Blair Atholl. You can also take a vehicle track from Monzie up the north side of the burn to about 560m, one kilometre due west of the summit. Distance: from Old Bridge of Tilt to Carn Liath 8 kilometres, ascent 820m. The next hill ahead, 3 kilometres to the north-north-east and beyond a col at about 760m, is Braigh Coire Chruinn-bhalgain. The route to the summit from this top, which stands out almost as a separate hill from Beinn a' Ghlo, lies east down a grassy slope to the 847m col at Bealach an Fhiodha, from where streams fall south to Glen Girnaig and north to Tilt. From the bealach you can go south-east for 800 metres to reach the subsidiary 1061m top of Airgiod Bheinn or silver hill; it forms the end of a long flattish shoulder running down from the summit of Beinn a' Ghlo 1.7 kilometres away to the north-east. The summit at 1129m is Càrn nan Gabhar or hill of the goats, where you stand 6 kilometres in distance from Carn Liath by the quickest route (by-passing Airgiod Bheinn), with an ascent of 550m. Thus the total distance from Old Bridge of Tilt to Carn nan Gabhar is 14 kilometres, ascent 1370m; same way back 400m of ascent.

The view from the summit cairn is fine, but grows even more striking if you go down to the east a little way, to look down the wild rocky east face to Loch Loch about 680m below and across to the line of crags on Creag an Loch above the east side of the loch. A good way off Beinn a' Ghlo starts by dropping 2½ kilometres down its north shoulder, then turns west to cross the footbridge over the Tilt just below where the Allt Fheannach comes in, and so down Glen Tilt. Remember that the River Tilt runs fast in flood, and that another bridge stands lower down the glen at Dail an Eas, just up from Forest Lodge.

An interesting route to Beinn a' Ghlo comes in from the east by Gleann Fearnach, a name incorrectly put on the map instead of Fearnaid ('fernit) meaning alder water. From the A924 road one kilometre north-west of Enochdhu, a private roads runs for 7½ kilometres up to Daldhu, and continues beyond to Fealar Lodge reaching 660m on the way. A fine, rich, green glen with many small outcrops of broken rock, Gleann Fearnach was home to a big farming community last century, but since then the people have all gone by emigration. From Daldhu at about 380m a bulldozed track leads north-west up Glen Loch to within 2 kilometres of Loch Loch, and a path carries on to the loch which lies at 450m, 5½ kilometres from Daldhu. Gleann Fearnach and this low pass over by Loch Loch to Glen Tilt once used to be a popular route for Highlanders driving their cattle to market in the south. Loch Loch lies among meadows in a deep trench with broken crags on either side. A good way to Beinn a' Ghlo goes straight up the wild face of Coire Cas-eagallach, or steep fearful corrie, west of the loch, where you can have some easy rock scrambling on the way up (2 kilometres Loch Loch to summit, 680m ascent).

Braigh Choire Chruinn-bhalgain and Carn Liath from the west across Glen Tilt

Carn a' Chlamhain *(hill of the buzzard)* (963m)
This is not Chlamain as misspelled on the map. This remote secluded hill lies about
2 kilometres north-west of Forest Lodge in Glen Tilt, on a plateau behind a steep
glen front. The easiest way up goes by the long ridge that rises east of the Allt
Craoinidh, starting from the Tilt road above Marble Lodge. From a point just east of
the bridge over the Allt Craoinidh one climbs directly north-east up the (initially)
steep hillside, and then by a path or the nearby vehicle track leading up the ridge.
Higher up the ridge becomes much less steep and eventually reaches a little plateau
south-east of the summit. There is a spectacular view at the plateau edge where you
look down a long steep face to the Tilt below. The summit of Carn a' Chlamhain
rises to the west, across this plateau. Distance from road above Marble Lodge: 4½
kilometres, ascent 700m.

Another good route starts at 935 743 above Forest Lodge, by a path that zigzags
steeply up to a cairn at 934 754, and then turns west to the top (3½ kilometres, 670m
climb). The summit also lies only 3½ kilometres south-south-west of the remote
bothy which stands above where Feith Uaine Mhor or big green stream enters Tarf
Water. An interesting route for descending Carn a' Chlamhain is to walk west for 3
kilometres and then south down the wild, narrow Gleann Mhairc or horse glen.
Queen Victoria was one of the early tourists to visit Carn a' Chlamhain, descending
by Sron a' Chro.

Beinn Dearg *(red hill)* (l008m)

Beinn Dearg (bain'jerek) takes its name from the reddish-tinged granite boulders on its upper slopes. It stands less than 3 kilometres north-east of Bruar Lodge (for route to lodge see Chapter 6, page 139). However, the easiest access is from Old Blair near Blair Atholl, by the private road which runs up the east side of Glen Banvie and then up Allt an t-Seapail to a bothy at Allt Sheicheachan (8½ kilometres from Old Blair). From there a vehicle track leads up the north side of Allt Sheicheachan and one continues by a path to 800m on the south side of Beinn Dearg, from where easy stony slopes lead north to the summit (14 kilometres from Old Blair, 840m ascent). For another way back you can walk south-south-east over the peaty moorland to Beinn a' Chait and Elrig, then take the road down Allt Slanaidh and so to lower Glen Tilt. A third way is to drop east into Gleann Diridh before you reach Beinn a' Chait. This glen becomes deep and narrow, with the burn running eventually into a little ravine. Further on it joins the Allt Mhairc beside a few small crags, beyond which some delightful grassy patches among birches lead down towards Glen Tilt.

An Sgarsoch *(meaning uncertain)* (1006m)
Carn an Fhidhleir *(karn'eelir, hill of the fiddler)* (994m)

These two remote hills look down over the vast peaty moors of Geldie, Feshie and Tarf. The easiest access is by cycling up to Geldie Lodge (Chapter 3). Distance: from Geldie Lodge to the summit of An Sgarsoch 4 kilometres, ascent 490m. A bulldozed track runs well up An Sgarsoch's north side to about 935 862. Longer ways are to come in from Glen Feshie, or to walk or cycle up Glen Tilt past Forest Lodge. From upper Glen Tilt a bulldozed track leads east of An Sligearnach or the place abounding in shells. It goes on the line of a former fine old path to a ford and hut by the Tarf Water at 520m. An Sgarsoch rises to the north-west, 5½ kilometres away by its east shoulder. On both its Geldie and Tilt sides it spreads out as a hill of broad ridges and wide open corries carpeted with short grass, moss and berry plants. In earlier centuries a market for cattle and horses, called Feill Sgarsaich, was held on the summit (see SMCJ 14, 104, and Further Reading).

An easy descent on the west side of An Sgarsoch takes you to a col at 710m. Beyond rises Carn an Fhidhleir's summit where the counties of Perth, Inverness and Aberdeen meet and where you will enjoy a fine view of the upper Tarf and the upper Feshie with its hundreds of small peaty pools. Distance: 4 kilometres from An Sgarsoch, ascent 270m. A quick way back goes north-north-east to the peaty stretch at the Geldie-Feshie watershed and then east down the north side of Geldie by the path. A bulldozed track runs from 925 856 east-north-east down to Geldie Lodge. If you are returning to Blair Atholl, a grand route is to descend into the magnificent wild area at the head of the Tarf, past the remote Loch Mhairc. From here you can go to Braigh Sron Ghorm and back over Carn a' Chlamhain to Marble Lodge by the Tilt, or over Beinn Dearg further west.

Ben Vrackie (841m)

The name of this graceful peak comes from Gaelic breac or speckled. A track from Moulin above Pitlochry goes north towards Loch a' Choire at about 520m, and a path continues to the top. Distance: from Moulin to summit 4 kilometres, ascent 690m. Ben Vrackie commands a magnificent view up the Tummel and across to the Moor of Rannoch. A fine way for walking back from Ben Vrackie is to drop west to the magnificent wooded gorge at Killiecrankie and the birches of Loch Faskally. The surrounding area is full of variety, a countryside broken up by many lumpy hills and small crags.

Beinn Bhreac *(speckled hill)* (912m)
One of the most remote and finest roadless areas in Scotland lies in the headwaters of Bruar, Tarf and Feshie. Here stands the rounded Beinn Bhreac above the source of Tarf Water. The easiest access is from Bruar Lodge (for route to the lodge from the A9 see Chapter 6). About one kilometre north of the lodge, a path strikes north-east up Allt Beinn Losgairnich to 720m. The route continues beyond the watershed on the east side of the next burn, picking up an indistinct path for over one kilometre. The way ahead to Beinn Bhreac is then obvious.

Beinn Mheadhonach *(middle hill)* (901m)
This aptly-named hill rises boldly between the two deep glens of the Allt Diridh and Allt Mhairc north of Blair Atholl. The easiest approach is from the public road end above Fenderbridge, by the Glen Tilt right of way (see below for detail) as far up as Gilbert's Bridge. You then cross the bridge and take a path up the west side of the Tilt to a bridge over Allt Mhairc. From the other side of the bridge a path runs north-north-west to above where the Allt Diridh runs into the Allt Mhairc. The southern slope of Beinn Mheadhonach rises ahead to an exposed plateau summit (9½ kilometres, 760m ascent). An alternative route to Gilbert's Bridge is from the public road at Old Blair by a private road up the west side of the Tilt.

Ben Vuirich (903m)
The name comes from Beinn Bhuirich or hill of the roaring. This hill is most easily approached from 012 638 on the A924 road in Glen Brerachan north-east of Pitlochry. From there a track heads northwards up the Glen of Tarvie Burn to 490m. Gentle slopes then lead north-west to Druim Mor and to the summit plateau of Ben Vuirich beyond to the north. At the top a fine view opens out to Loch Loch, Beinn a' Ghlo and Gleann Fearnach.

THE MOUNTH ROADS

Glen Tilt. One of the most popular of the Mounth crossings, Glen Tilt takes you over the lowest point between the Cairn o' Mount at Banchory and the Gaick Pass in the west. The best way starts at Blair Atholl and finishes at the Linn of Dee. Distance: from Old Bridge of Tilt at about 150m to Marble Lodge 6½ kilometres, to Forest Lodge 11, to Tarf Water 19, to county boundary 23, Bynack Lodge 26, the White Bridge 30, and to the Linn of Dee 35 kilometres; ascent 380m, but only 160m if you start at the Linn of Dee.

From Blair Atholl, the right of way up the glen goes up the east side past the Old Bridge of Tilt, and crosses the side stream of Fender at Fenderbridge. On the north side of the Fender you fork right at the road junction, and at the end of the public road at 884 672 then fork left below Kincraigie. The private track descends to the river near Croftmore, and continues to Marble Lodge. This part is a piece of lovely Highland scenery with a mixture of native and planted conifers, and groves of alders and gnarled ancient birches further up. At Marble Lodge you cross to the west bank of the Tilt. Now the glen becomes a more open, wilder, and remarkably long straight trench for miles between the steep slopes of Beinn a' Ghlo on the east and Carn a' Chlamhain on the west. Beyond Forest Lodge, the River Tilt narrows into a rocky gorge and there are some fine falls near where the Allt Fheannach rushes in from Beinn a' Ghlo. About 2 kilometres beyond this, a bulldozed track slants uphill to your left between Dun Mor and An Sligearnach. Your path keeps on up Tilt-side, crossing the Tarf at the Bedford Bridge below its rocky gorge, near the old ford at Poll Tarbh. Beyond, you climb gently up the slope on the west side of the ravine of the Allt Garbh Buidhe or rough yellow burn. Further up this burn, there comes a dramatic change from a steep, green, grassy glen to a wide moorland valley.

Out on the open moor the path avoids the wet peat by climbing a little to the west, towards, but not actually in sight of, the secluded Loch Tilt. It then reaches the highest point at just over 500m, and later becomes a bulldozed track down the wide glen to Bynack ('beinik). Standing at about 460m on a green knoll and surrounded by windblown conifers, Bynack Lodge is now a ruin, spoiled by selfish visitors who broke it up for firewood. You next cross Bynack Burn which trickles low in summer heat but sweeps dangerously in high water; in spate, you will find it safer to cross to the east side of the glen and stay on that side all the way down to the Linn of Dee, as the burns on that side are much smaller. North of Bynack Burn the track leads down a pleasant grassy flat to a wide rough ford over the water of Geldie to the partly ruined stables at Ruighe Ealasaid, at the beginning of the rough road down the Geldie to White Bridge over Dee. From Bynack on a wonderful view opens out up Glen Dee to the crags of The Devil's Point, to the even higher central Cairngorms, and through the Lairig Ghru to a remarkably distant-looking Creag an Leth-choin. The road below White Bridge continues past green flats with ruins of old farms and through pine woods to the locked gate at 373m at the beginning of the public road beside the Linn of Dee.

WALKING ROUTES IN THE KIRKMICHAEL AREA
A fine old cattle-droving route goes from Kirkmichael west up Glen Derby ('derrbee) to Loch Broom and Ballinluig. Distance: from Glen Derby to the public road at 000 525 at Tulliemet 12½ kilometres, 110m ascent. Another old route goes from Balch-rochan south of Kirkmichael up over Creag Gharbh to Lochan Oisinneach Beag and south via Riemore Lodge to Birkenburn and Dunkeld. A third runs north-east from Kirkmichael to Ashintully Castle, across Coire a' Bhaile, and down to Lair in Glen Shee.

Looking north from Ben Vuirich to Loch Loch and the distant Cairngorms

CLIMBING

Most high-level crags in the area are broken and lacking in defined lines. Strath Ardle, Glen Brerachan and the tract around Ben Vrackie and Loch Valigan contain many steep small crags which offer short routes. The area has plenty of easy winter climbing on mixed rock and snow, giving more sporting ways up to the summits.

Craig a Barns (337m), usually called kraigee'barns, is the finely wooded rocky hill 1½ kilometres north-west of Dunkeld. Its short but steep crags of Dalradian schist provide a great variety of excellent climbing which is described fully in a guide (Further Reading).

SKIING

The Beinn a' Ghlo hills give very good ski-mountaineering, and the generally easier slopes of the other high hills offer ideal conditions for Nordic ski touring. When snow cover is general, touring is also good on the lower hills and wide glens. Between Pitlochry and Strath Ardle the moors and rocky hills are interesting to explore on skis, but dense tree plantations in recent years have unfortunately blocked access to some former great sweeps of moor with distant spacious views.

Ski touring above Glen Tilt, looking towards Beinn Mheadhonach

FURTHER READING

W.M.Alexander and others *The Sgarsoch market.*   CCJ 8, 166, 215, 262.

H.T.Munro *Notes on Ben-y-Gloe.*   SMCJ 2, 239.

W.Douglas *Beinn a' Ghlo   (Guide Book article). SMCJ 8, 172.*

H.T.Munro *Beinn Dearg, Carn a' Chlamain, An Sgarsoch and Carn an Fhidleir   (Guide Book articles). SMCJ 8, 174.*

D.Cuthbertson *Creag Dubh and Craig-a-Barns.*   Climbers' Guide. SMC (1983). This guidebook is due to be published in a revised and enlarged version in 1994 under the name *Highland Outcrops.* Until then, K.Howett's *Rock Climbing in Scotland* (1990, Constable) is the best source of information for recent routes.

CHAPTER 8

The Braes o Mar

Morrone	859m	133 886
Creag Choinnich	538m	160 919
Carn na Drochaide	818m	127 938
Craig Leek	635m	185 931
Culardoch	900m	193 988
Carn Liath	862m	165 977
Sgor Mor	813m	007 914

These are all Corbetts except the two below 800m

ACCESS, PUBLIC TRANSPORT, ACCOMMODATION AND BOTHIES
See Chapter 2.

MAPS
Ordnance Survey 1:50,000 Sheets 36 and 43

Braemar (bri'mar), one of the highest and most attractive villages in the Highlands, nestles at about 340m among woods and lower hills, close to the high Cairngorms, Lochnagar and the Mounth. It makes the best centre for the Aberdeenshire Highlands and most of the Cairngorms massif. The name comes from Braigh Mharr or upland of Mar, Mar being an old district name, but the actual village consists of two parts with Auchendryne west of the Clunie Water and Castleton on the east bank.

The approach to Braemar from Ballater leads through some of the finest scenery in the Highlands. That part between Gairn and Invercauld, formerly called Strath Dee, is best. Here, big woods of native pine and birch run down to the banks of the Dee, and a multitude of complex small hills and side glens with fine burns leads up to the great bulk of Lochnagar. Shortly after passing over the new Invercauld Bridge which stands upstream from the more beautiful older bridge, you will see the corries of Beinn a' Bhuird coming into view beyond the tree-dotted parkland haughs of Invercauld, framed by steep wooded bluffs on either side. The reverse journey, with golden evening light on the dark green pines, on Lochnagar's plum-coloured west flanks and on the incredibly blue Dee, looks even better, a feast of colour.

The Braemar Highland Society runs the 'Gathering' - locally called the Games - every September, and publishes an annual, *The Book of the Braemar Gathering* which often contains articles and photographs on the whole Cairngorms region as well as the Braemar district.

The lower hills offer good walking routes with magnificent views of the Cairngorms, Lochnagar and part of the Mounth. The glens are the most varied in the region covered by this guide, and the old native forests outstanding for their beauty. The big burns coming down the glens add much to the unusual landscape of the area.

GEOLOGY, LANDFORMS AND WILDLIFE

The rock structure around Braemar is very complicated. Bands of limestone run along Morrone and north-east of Invercauld, but quartzite makes up most of Morrone. However the main rock of the Braemar district, especially around Inverey, Glen Quoich and Slugain, is Moine schist, with rich dark schist at Creag Clunie and Glen Feardar. These schist rocks account for the steep rocky bluffs near the main valley, which make the Braemar area unusual for the North-East.

The old pine woods, although in scattered smallish blocks, are the finest in Scotland for ancient, uncut and unburned forest, but red deer have for decades prevented young trees from growing. Lower Glen Lui and lower Glen Derry carry particularly impressive old trees. On the east side of lower Glen Lui towards Mar Lodge, you can see ancient gnarled pines with a girth surpassing anything in Scotland, and also some extremely old birches. On Morrone's north side, where there is a National Nature Reserve, fine old birch groves with juniper climb to 610m. The planted larches on Carn nan Sgliat, which you can see well from Braemar village, reach 640m. Some of the best larches and spruces in Scotland grow on either side of the Mar Brae, by the road down to the Victoria Bridge from the grand high waterfall at the bridge of Corriemulzie. Good spots for small flowering plants occur at lime-rich patches on the lower slopes of Morrone, Glen Lui and especially on the rocks of Creag an Dail Bheag to the west of Culardoch. The Braemar district is well-known to entomologists as a place for rare arctic-alpine insects; indeed, the subarctic mountain burnet moth occurs nowhere else in Britain. The surrounding district, along with Atholl and Balmoral, supports some of the largest herds of red deer in the Highlands.

ESTATES

Mar Lodge Estate has the land west of Carn na Drochaide and north of the Dee, and Mar Estate has ground south of the Dee, east of Connie, and west of Morrone. Invercauld (inver'kal) has the ground east of Carn na Drochaide and north of the Dee, and includes the Clunie and Callater drainages. Balmoral Estate has Ballochbuie Forest.

HISTORY

The history of the Braemar district is very rich, but here we have space for only the briefest sketch. Interested readers should refer to Simpson's *The Province of Mar* and Grant's *Legends of the Braes o' Mar*, noting that the later *The Braemar Highlands* by Elizabeth Taylor was largely a plagiarism of Grant.

The ancient castle of Kindrochit or bridge end, which gave Braemar its original name of Baile Chaisteil or Castleton, stood close to the bridge over the Clunie, but only its foundation now remains. Braemar was a Jacobite stronghold, and the Invercauld Arms Hotel now stands on the spot where the Earl of Mar started the 1715 rising; the Jacobite song beginning *'The standard on the Braes o' Mar'* commemorates it. After the '45, the new Braemar Castle was re-fortified and used as a base by English occupation troops who stayed here as late as 1831.

The farmers of Glen Lui were forcibly evicted in 1726, but people re-occupied the farms there later on, only to leave once again in a clearance to make way for deer. The farmers of Glen Ey and Glen Dee were cleared last century to make way for deer, and you can still see their many old stone ruins. However, clearances did not occur in most glens, which became empty later on due to folk moving out without being forced, a process that still continues. Just west of Corriemulzie stands the former farm of Braegarrie. Here was the scene of a lively poem in the now virtually extinct Braemar Gaelic, in praise of 'O mo chailin donn Braigh-Gharraidh' or 'O my brown haired lass of Braegarrie', recorded by F.C.Diack in his *Inscriptions of Pictland*.

THE HILLS

Morrone (859m)
The name comes from Gaelic, probably Mor-bheinn or big hill, now pronounced mo'rone. Morrone is the great sprawling mass, brown and heather-covered, which rises south-west of Braemar. You can motor up Chapel Brae to the car park beside the pond and then walk one kilometre up to Tomintoul, or better still reach there from the Princess Royal Park - locally called the Games Park - by paths which wind up through the birches. The prominent knoll at 472m above Tomintoul gives a fine view of the Cairngorms. Near here, a path starting at 144 904 goes for 2 kilometres to the summit of Morrone (490m ascent from car park). You can also ascend from Glen Clunie by a vehicle track going from the Coldrach opposite Auchallater all the way to the top. North of Morrone grow fine birch and juniper woods, offering interesting ways back off the hill by an upper and a lower track going along the level wide shelf back to Chapel Brae.

Creag Choinnich (538m)
This is pronounced kraig'koinich, and probably means crag with the moss. The summit stands one kilometre from Braemar (200m ascent). On the Aberdeen side of Creag Choinnich, the steep rocky bluff The Lion's Face rises boldly above the main road; it used to be named Creag a' Mhurtair or rock of the murderer. The fine path

of the Queen's Drive winds below it, after starting from the Glen Clunie road south of the youth hostel and passing below Creag Choinnich to the Aberdeen road.

To the south-east of Creag Choinnich, Carn nan Sgliat (locally karn'sklaitsh) or hill of slate continues as a long heathery ridge. Its north-east shoulder sticks out at Creag Clunie, a remarkably fine viewpoint with a dense growth of scrubby pines. About 2 kilometres to the south of Carn nan Sgliat rises Creag nan Leachda with lochans on its 784m summit - called Creag Leacach ('laikach) locally - and 3 kilometres further on the 849m Meall an t-Slugain or lump of the gullet. From Meall an t-Slugain you can return down Ballochbuie Forest or descend by the high, lonely Loch Phadruig ('farik) or Patrick's loch to Glen Callater.

One of the best walks near Braemar goes from Ballochbuie Forest up Glen Beg and through the gap of An Slugan to Loch Phadruig at 685m, and then over to Loch Callater Lodge (8 kilometres from Invercauld Bridge). You can also continue for 5 kilometres beyond Callater by an old drove path which runs up the Allt a' Bhealaich Bhuidhe, and next over the col between Carn Dubh and Creag nan Gabhar. You then

The Dee valley at Braemar, looking towards Morrone

drop down to Glen Clunie by the good path along the south side of the little steep glen of the Allt a' Mhaide (alt'veetsh) or burn of the stick.

Carn na Drochaide (818m)

Pronounced karn'drochitsh, the name means hill of the bridge. This top is another fine viewpoint, 4½ kilometres from Braemar. When the Dee runs low you can wade across; go half a kilometre out the Linn of Dee road to where the River Dee goes close to the road and then turn downstream a short distance to a ford over shingle. Beyond, an extensive marsh stretching almost to Mar Lodge forms an interesting habitat for birds and mammals; a path runs along it going up the bank of the Dee and then north along the edge of a birch wood to the foot of Carn na Drochaide. A good route back from the top (2½ kilometres) is to descend to 333m at Allanaquoich. From here a public road goes west to Mar Lodge. On the way you should first visit the Linn of Quoich where the water has a beautiful

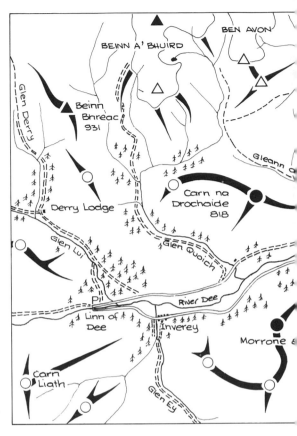

blue green colour, flowing over smooth slabs beside the Punch Bowl. Above the Linn looms the impressive wild face of Creag Bhalg ('valig), with its broken schist rocks thickly clad in larches.

Craig Leek (635m)

This is the best viewpoint near Braemar, rising behind Invercauld House. The name comes from Creag Lice or rock of slab, and indeed the hill throws out a bold bluff of smooth diorite on its east side above the boggy flats of Felagie and Aberarder. You reach it by going to the end of the public road at the Keiloch, and then climb north for 1½ kilometres through pines to the open ground on the top. The view of Ballochbuie, Lochnagar and Braemar is magnificent.

Culardoch (900m)

This windswept heathery dome (pronounced kil'ardich) lies to the north of Craig Leek. It rises to the summit at Cul Ardach Mor which means the big back high place, Cul Ardach Beag being the spur towards Loch Builg. A good cross-country walk is to go from the Keiloch up by Craggan Rour just north-west of Craig Leek, where a rough road leads north by the old right of way from Braemar to Tomintoul by the Bealach Dearg (byalach'jerreg) or red pass, over the west side of Culardoch. Beyond

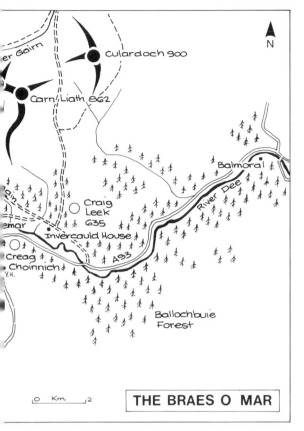

THE BRAES O MAR

the stable at the pass summit at 690m, which lies 7½ kilometres from the Keiloch, the old route drops into Glen Gairn and so 5½ kilometres to Loch Builg. One of the most interesting places in the district is the secluded Glen Fearder (Feith Ardair, 'fyarder) or glen of bog of high water, which runs south of Culardoch towards Dee at the Inver (8 kilometres from Culardoch via Auchtavan). Once populated by many farmers but now deserted, it has a sad haunting beauty, with old birches and lonely greens where stone walls show the sites of former farms.

Carn Liath (*grey hill*) (862m)
This hill is easily climbed in conjunction with the higher Culardoch (see above), by leaving the Bealach Dearg track near the stable at 650m and climbing due west for 1½ kilometres and 200m ascent. The main cairn at 860m stands nearly 400 metres south, near the north end of a prominent stone dyke.

Sgor Mor (*big rocky hill*) (813m)
This hill between Glen Dee and Glen Luibeg offers splendid views of the Cairngorms and southwards into Geldie and Atholl. It is easily reached from the Linn of Dee (see Chapter 2) and then the private road up Glen Dee to the White Bridge (Chapter 3, Glen Feshie). From there, a path leads past the Chest of Dee and up the east side of Dee. It is best to leave that path at 002 895 and then climb northwards to the summit (8 kilometres from Linn of Dee, 450m ascent). Sgor Mor has interesting granite tors and potholes at altitudes much lower than the better known ones on Ben Avon. The wind-scoured ridge, gravelly and with crisp heather, continues 3 kilometres east to Sgor Dubh. Local folk call the whole of this hill group Feith nan Sgor (fainna'skor) or bog-stream of the rocky hills.

Inverey (inver'ei) at 350m lies 8 kilometres west of Braemar. The last place in Aberdeenshire where Gaelic remained an everyday speech till about 1930, this pleasant string of houses has now been taken over largely by city dwellers with holiday houses. It is a good starting place for the Cairngorms. From Little Inverey, just west of the old Ey bridge, there opens out a particularly fine view of the Cairngorms rising beyond great pine woods. Ben Macdui and its pointed crag above

Carn Liath and Culardoch from Creag Choinnich

Lochan Uaine seem lower than the dramatic cone of the nearer Derry Cairngorm, while to the left you can see the top of Braeriach above the great cliff of Coire Bhrochain. West of Inverey is the Linn of Dee, a spectacular place where the river rushes through a one metre-wide channel cut in the schistose rocks, afterwards opening out into a series of deep circular pools.

Glen Lui and the Derry. To reach Derry Lodge, you cross the bridge at the Linn of Dee and go 700 metres east to the foot of Glen Lui, where a locked gate at 366m bars all but walkers and those with cycles or motor bicycles. Alternatively, after crossing the bridge you can go to the car park to the east and then use a footpath from there to join the Derry road a short distance up from the locked gate (see Chapter 2, Access). To the north and hidden from the road, Lui Water (laoigh or calf) rushes over a series of beautiful falls and pools where the water has a wonderful blue-green colour from the shelves of schist underneath. Lower Glen Lui is finely wooded with old pine and birch, but beyond the grand viewpoint at the Black Bridge, 2 kilometres up, you enter a more open glen with beautiful greens where folk farmed in the 1700s. On the green above the Black Bridge rise two beautifully symmetrical knolls named Da Shidhean or two fairy hillocks. About one kilometre beyond the Black Bridge, the road crosses the Allt Mhad-allaidh (vat'aalie, pronounced as in alley) or burn of the wolf. Immediately before you reach the road crossing, a path strikes uphill to the right. It leads to Glen Quoich by the rocky trench of Clais Fhearnaig (klash'yarnik), in whose floor lies an artificial loch for fishing, made by a dam at the Quoich end.

About 2 kilometres beyond the Allt Mhad-allaidh you come to Derry Lodge, after passing Bob Scott's Bothy shortly before on the left. Local people always talk of The Derry, like 'Dairy' pronounced quickly; it comes from An Doire, meaning the grove. Nearby to the west stands the cottage of Luibeg at about 420m. The 741m Sgor Dubh (skor'doo), or black rocky hill, rising immediately behind Luibeg, offers a good way back for 5 kilometres to the Linn of Dee and is a magnificent viewpoint for the Cairngorms.

CLIMBING

There are no big crags near Braemar. Various small cliffs of schist, diorite, quartzite and limestone occur, but the shortness of the crags has discouraged serious climbing. Try to avoid these small cliffs in Dee, Spey or Angus in any case, as they often harbour birds of prey which may have their breeding ruined by inadvertent disturbance from climbers. However, there are plenty of boulder problems and short routes on much smaller crags, varying from the boulder just west of the Invercauld Bridge, called the Muckle Steen o Clunie, to a few quarries and river gorges. Above Luibeg, Creag Bad an t-Seabhaig (kraik patin'jooik) or rock of the hawk's clump, rises out of the pines on the way to Carn Crom. It offers short climbs on dry rough granite, from Moderate to VS.

SKIING

As this area stands at a fairly high altitude in one of the snowiest parts of Scotland, conditions for ski touring are often good. In periods with general snow cover the whole area offers excellent potential through the forests, up the glens, and over the lower hills. The Sgor Mor - Sgor Dubh ridge is well worth going to in such conditions for its views of the snowy high Cairngorms. Culardoch often provides good snow, and ascents and descents are frequently easier in light snow cover if one uses a road or track where big stones or tall vegetation do not project through the snow.

FURTHER READING

H.Alexander *Hill excursions from Braemar*. Deeside Fld 2, 7.

A.E.M.Geddes *The climate of Braemar*. Deeside Fld 2, 14.

J. Dow *Some road reconnaissances from Braemar*. SMCJ 19,96.

A.Watson & E.Allan (1990) *Depopulation by clearances and non-enforced emigration in the north-east Highlands*. Northern Scotland 10, 31.

CHAPTER 9

Ben Avon and Beinn a' Bhuird

Ben Avon	1171m	132 018
Beinn a' Bhuird	1196m	092 006
Beinn a' Chaorainn	1082m	045 013
Beinn Bhreac	931m	059 971

ACCESS
The best access and finest approach to these hills is from Braemar in Deeside (see Chapter 2), but public roads to Delnabo near Tomintoul, to Cock Bridge in Strath Don, and over the hill from Crathie to Gairnshiel offer useful starting points for Ben Avon. Beinn a' Chaorainn and Beinn Bhreac rise above Glen Derry (for routes to Derry Lodge see Chapter 2).

PUBLIC TRANSPORT
See Chapter 2 for the Braemar area.

ACCOMMODATION, BOTHIES AND SHELTERS
For the Braemar area see Chapter 2. There are hotels and bed and breakfast places and a youth hostel at Tomintoul, and a hotel near Cock Bridge. Faindouran Lodge at 081 061 in Glen Avon is now a bothy. Loch Builg Lodge at 188 028 and Slugain Lodge at 120 952 are roofless ruins with meagre shelter. The Fords of Avon Refuge stands at 042 031 on the north side of Avon. There is a bivouac at 097 995 in a recess under one of the bigger boulders below Dividing Buttress on Beinn a' Bhuird; it holds 2-3 people. There is a bothy at Corndavon Lodge at 227 021

MAPS
Ordnance Survey 1:50,000 Sheets 36, 37 and 43

Ben Avon and Beinn a' Bhuird are among the less-visited of the higher hills in north-east Scotland. Both rise close to 1200m, and, being at the east end of the Cairngorms, both of them - and especially Ben Avon - give magnificent views to the north-east and east. You look out over the multitude of low hills and glens of upland Banffshire and Aberdeenshire, far away to Buchan and the North Sea. For the same reasons, Ben Avon appears one of the most prominent hills from the great sweeps of high farmland in Buchan. Both hills are enormously bulky, with great convex shoulders and slopes bulging steeply into wild unfrequented glens. Both excel in having the biggest stretches of ground over 1000m on any pair of hills in Britain. Here, on the great tracts of short grass, granite grit and mossy turf, is country where you can stroll easily for miles. But there also come many surprises, for these two hills are in places rent by corries among the wildest in the country. To the west, Beinn a' Chaorainn and Beinn Bhreac are at either end of a long plateau east of Glen Derry.

GEOLOGY, LANDFORMS AND WILDLIFE

Virtually all the rock is Cairngorms granite. The many tors of Ben Avon form one of the most interesting geomorphological features in the Highlands. You can see very fine examples of dry rocky gaps, which were cut in the distant past by glacial meltwater rivers, in Clais Poll Bhat south of Beinn Bhreac, at Clais Fhearnaig and in the beautiful little gorge at the head of Gleann an t-Slugain.

The slopes west of Bruach Mhor are a particularly good place to see stepped terracing of alternate vegetation and gravel, and Moine Bhealaidh is notable as an extensive high-altitude peat moss. Glen Quoich shows one of the five best stretches of ancient pine wood in Deeside and some fine old birch. As it lies far from houses and people searching for firewood, it has far more dead standing trees - an important part of a natural forest - than most Scottish pine woods. Ben Avon and Beinn a' Bhuird support more extensive tracts of windswept high gravelly barrens, studded with that common northern species the three-leaved rush, than any other two hills in Britain; Carn Eas and the North Top of Beinn a' Bhuird are good examples. In the hollows they also have unusually big expanses of continuous arctic-alpine grassland without bare gravel, as on Cnap a' Chleirich and Allt an Eas Bhig. Tiny lime-rich patches on the high crags of Beinn a' Bhuird and Ben Avon form the micro-habitats for two arctic plants, the rare brook saxifrage and tufted saxifrage. The limestone of Inchrory supports a fertile green vegetation rich in flowers, including some that grow commonly here at low altitude but elsewhere occur usually as uncommon mountain species, such as purple saxifrage. Ben Avon and Beinn a' Bhuird are home to great numbers of ptarmigan, and dotterel nest on both hills. Loch Builg is well-known for its arctic relict fish, the char.

ESTATES

The Banffshire part belongs to Inchrory. The Aberdeenshire part lies on Invercauld, except for the area west of a line from the North Top of Beinn a' Bhuird to Bruach Mhor to Carn na Drochaide, which is on Mar Lodge Estate. All this country is deer forest, with some grouse shooting.

HISTORY

In Blaeu's *Atlas* (1654), Robert Gordon of Straloch refers to the river Avin 'which Timothy Pont, who had surveyed all these parts, told me is the clearest and of the purest waters of all our Kingdom'. Men are said to have gone into the water thinking it was shallow, and been drowned, hence the old rhyme:

> The watter o Aan, it rins sae clear
> Twad beguile a man o a hundred year

Carn Eas and Creag an Dail Mhor from the south-west

The summit of Ben Avon

In *The Pennyless Pilgrimage* in 1618, John Taylor describes how he 'saw Mount Benawne, with a furr'd mist upon his snowie head instead of a night-cap: for you must understand that the oldest man alive never saw but the snow on the top of divers of these hills, both in summer as well as in winter'.

In the 18th and 19th centuries Ben Avon became well known as a place for digging out 'cairngorm' crystals, Allt an Eas Mhoir being a favourite spot, and in 1788 a Braemar woman found one of the largest recorded, on the top of Ben Avon. An old tale was that some of the crystal seekers died from drinking the gravelly water of the streams. You can still see the diggers' stone workings on the plateaux and by some of the streams on several of the hills of the Cairngorms. Another old legend spoke of gold lying below the waters of Lochan Oir (orr) or lochan of gold south of Loch Builg; it was said to be guarded by a water kelpie which has more than once driven off rash searchers for the treasure! On Ben Avon, an old legend which persisted very late was that Fingal's lady went to Clach Bhan to bathe in one of its rock pools. Pregnant women who were near confinement used to visit Clach Bhan and sit in one of its worn potholes, in the belief that this ensured an easy labour. In a *New History of Aberdeenshire*, Smith wrote that in August 1836 he saw the chairing of 12 women who had that morning come over 20 miles from Speyside to sit in the chair, and the custom lingered on as late as the 1860s.

There is less early history about Beinn a' Bhuird. Pennant, who visited Deeside in 1769, mentions the hill in his *Tour of Scotland* 'under Ben y Bourd is a small loch, which, I was told, had ice the latter end of July'. Later, about 1820, a herd of cattle which had been driven by bad weather from Glen Avon fell to their deaths over the cliffs above the loch.

THE HILLS

Ben Avon (1171m)

Locally called bain'aan, the name Ben Avon obviously comes from the river below it. Some Celtic scholars have thought the river to be Ath-fhinn, meaning bright or fair one, after an old legend that told how Fingal's wife fell on the slippery stones and drowned, whereupon he named the river Ath-fhinn in her memory.

Ben Avon is by far the most complex hill in the entire region described in this book. It is also the biggest, approaching a small hill range in size. From its lower slopes south of Linn of Avon in the north-east to its south-west corner above Glen Quoich it stretches 12 kilometres in a straight line, and 9 kilometres from north to south between Da Dhruim Lom and Creag an Dail. Ben Avon forms a vast sprawling mass, with bulging convex stony shoulders spreading out in various directions. It has more ground above 900m than any other hill in Scotland, and an extensive summit plateau which projects out in several huge curves and offshoots. The highest plateaux are gravelly, studded with wiry rushes, but lower down they lead to very gentle, stream-watered slopes with wide stretches of grass which make it one of the greenest of hills in the main Cairngorms massif. On the north side, big shoulders

project northwards, exposed,
scoured by great winds, showing
unusually large patches of bare granite grit, and with some fantastic
combs of rock. These ridges enclose
a few remote wild corries. Ben
Avon's chief characteristic, however, is the scores of extraordinary
granite tors of varied shape and size
which are scattered like plentiful
warts over its summit whalebacks
and flanks.

WALKING ASCENTS TO BEN AVON

From Invercauld. Distance: from
the Keiloch to Slugain Lodge 8km,
to the summit by the Sneck 16½
kilometres, total ascent 850m. The
public road ends at 330m at the Keiloch, near Invercauld Bridge east of
Braemar. A private road leads 3 kilometres from here to Allt Dourie
('dooree'). For another 3 kilometres
beyond, a rough road runs, at first
through pine woods and then ending about halfway up Gleann an
t-Slugain. Beyond the road end, the
path carries on up An Slugan or the gullet, a beautiful rocky ravine with sheltered
turfy meadows, a lovely winding burn and birches, to the ruined Slugain Lodge at
about 570m. Above here you come to an open moor that slopes west down to Quoich
Water and gives grand views of Beinn a' Bhuird.

You now climb very gradually on the path for 5 kilometres north up the glen to
760m at Clach a' Chleirich (klach'chleerich) or stone of the clergyman, a big boulder
on the hillside. Go 1½ kilometres north-north-east of here up the grassy glen leading
to the saddle at about 970m between Cnap a' Chleirich and Ben Avon. This saddle
is the Sneck (Scots for notch). Here you suddenly look north down one of the wildest
corries in the Cairngorms into An Slochd Mor or the great pit. A rugged glen coming
up from Glen Avon, the Slochd Mor falls deeply, hemmed in by the craggy and
gravelly slopes of Ben Avon on the east side and Stob an t-Sluichd or point of the
Slochd on the north-west side. At its head Slochd Mor widens into an upper recess
called the Garbh Choire or rough corrie, where splendid rock buttresses soar to the
green plateau of Cnap a' Chleirich. From the Sneck you can easily walk down scree
slopes into the Slochd Mor and so to the River Avon, along an old right of way
between Inverey and Tomintoul by Inchrory.

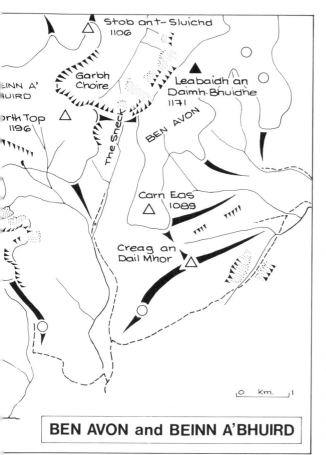

BEN AVON and BEINN A'BHUIRD

If going to Ben Avon, however, you walk half a kilometre east from the Sneck up a slope of loose gravel, turf and stones to the plateau at 1070m, and then for 1½ kilometres along the plateau north-east to the highest point of Ben Avon at 1171m. The actual summit is a huge black tor whose name appears on the map as Leabaidh an Daimh Bhuidhe, meaning couch of the yellow stag. The old local name was Stob Dubh Easaidh Mor or black point of the Muckle Essie burn. You can easily scramble from the neck at the north-west side up the rough granite to the cairn, which overlooks a 15 to 20m drop on the south side.

To vary the return by the Slugain to Braemar, a good way in summer and autumn is to head south-south-west over the green rolling plateau past the 1063m black tor of Stob Dubh an Eas Bhig (a map error for Stob Dubh Easaidh Beag), so conspicuous from Braemar, to the gravelly flat plateau top (1089m) north-west of the steep slope at Carn Eas (karn'yes) and so to the Slugain. Avoid this steep slope in winter and spring as the steep south face at the plateau rim often carries a giant cornice which occasionally slides down in avalanches. A safer way at that season is to walk south-east into the beautiful green bowl of the upper Allt an Eas Mhoir, which is a map error for Easaidh Mor or big cascading one, now often called the Muckle Essie. Take care in mist here, as the hillside immediately to the west of the burn at about 900-950m altitude often carries a vertical snow wall. Lower down you enter a delightful secluded little glen with steep hillsides rising from the cascades of the burn, and then come on an old stalkers' path leading to the River Gairn.

This upper part of Glen Gairn, lonely, treeless and remote, is one of the wildest glens in the Cairngorms. Up the long glen goes a track from the ruined Lochbuilg Lodge to join the path 1½ kilometres north of Slugain Lodge on the way to the Sneck. In its upper part, Glen Gairn passes through a huge U-shaped gap between steep slopes of broken rock and scree, with Creag an Dail Mhor or big rock of the haugh on the north-west and Creag an Dail Bheag on the south-east. Just below where Allt Bad a' Mhonaidh (a map error for the local name of Allt Bad Tomaigh) enters the

River Gairn, a small footbridge crosses to a vehicle track that leads south to the Bealach Dearg pass at the stable below Culardoch (for the rest of the way to Braemar see Chapter 8).

From Loch Builg. If you wish to visit most of the many tors and tops of Ben Avon, this forms the best route from Deeside. Distance: from public road north of Crathie to Corndavon Lodge 6 kilometres, to Lochbuilg Lodge 11 kilometres, to summit 17 kilometres. From Lochbuilg Lodge, total ascent 670m. At the public road north of Crathie, at 260 981, a private rough road leads to the largely ruined Corndavon Lodge. Beyond, the road goes to the ruined Lochbuilg Lodge. An alternative way to Lochbuilg Lodge starts from the Inver, climbing up the east side of Glen Fearder by an old drove road which goes over Carn Moine an Tighearn, east of Culardoch and down Tom a' Chuir. Lying at about 485m, with a fine beach at its south end, Loch Builg ('boolig) or loch of bag (shape) gives a feeling of great remoteness and open space. Beyond the loch, the water runs north into Glen Builg, where brilliant green hills contrast with the generally brown, heather-covered landscape around the loch. The path along the loch's east side continues to Inchrory as a bulldozed track, part of the old right of way from Braemar over Bealach Dearg to Tomintoul.

From Lochbuilg Lodge at 488m, you head uphill to Ben Avon by an old path which ends on the flat moor south-west of Carn Dearg. However, just beyond there you can connect with another path (an alternative way from Lochbuilg Lodge), which comes round Carn Drochaide after starting from higher up Glen Gairn. It ends at 890m beside Allt Phouple. Above, you climb easily past some small tors till you reach the pair of large tors on the south-east end of the great high crescent enclosing Allt an Eas Mhoir. This pair, so prominent from Braemar, lies at 1120m on the stony dome of Stuc Gharbh Mhor or big rough point. About 350m in distance to the north rises the enormous black wart of Clach a' Chutsaich or Coutts's stone, also at 1120m. A stroll follows around the high crescent to the summit of Ben Avon at Leabaidh an Daimh Bhuidhe.

A good way back is to descend the eastern tops by the Tomintoul route towards Inchrory and then come back southwards up Loch Builg side. Avoid the descent of the north branch of Feith Laoigh to the south of the Big Brae, a place of broken crags and very steep vegetation, often snow-corniced in winter and spring.

From Tomintoul. Distance: from Delnabo to Inchrory 10 kilometres. From Inchrory to summit 9 kilometres, total ascent 760m. The public road ends at Delnabo, just south-west of Tomintoul. A private road beyond a locked gate runs up to Inchrory Lodge going up the side of the River Avon, a beautiful narrow valley with old birch woods, steep green sides, screes and deserted farms. You can also reach Inchrory from Cock Bridge in Strath Don, 9 kilometres to the east where the public road ends at 255 089 on the valley below Corgarff Castle. From there a private road runs for 3 kilometres to Delnadamph Lodge, from which a vehicle track leads up the fertile green bowl of Feith Bhait (fay'vatsh) to Inchrory at about 405m.

The summit plateau of Ben Avon

Glen Avon below Inchrory Lodge

The best way from Inchrory to Ben Avon climbs over the 914m Meall Gaineimh. Take the rough road leading to Glen Builg and cross by the footbridge over the Builg Burn, west of which you should diverge to see the fine rocky Linn of Avon. Before you reach the Linn, a path leads south to a little grassy col at 845m, just west of the top of Meall Gaineimh or sandy lump, a good name for this rounded hill with its extensive patches of bare granite grit. Only 250m in distance north-west of this col stands the fantastic Clach Bhan (van) or stone of women, which really forms a complex long outcrop of rock. The most extensive of all Ben Avon's tors, though not the highest, it has 'by far the most extraordinary variety of channels, passages, recesses, potholes, and other forms of rock weathering to be seen in the Cairngorms' (Alexander, first edition). Many of the potholes contain water, others that lay near the edge of the rock have been eroded by drain holes and are now dry, and in others a whole side has worn away to form a large chair. These cavities are symmetrical, either oval or circular, some being deep enough to hold a man standing up to his waist.

The way now lies up the easy broad gravelly whaleback south of Clach Bhan, but you can get some interesting scrambling on its side along the 935m East Meur Gorm Craig (meur gorm or blue finger). This cock's comb of rock runs along the ridge, throwing broken buttresses to the west. After crossing the flat plateau of Big Brae at 937m, you climb easily to the dome south of West Meur Gorm Craig at 1021m. It is worth diverging to the west here to look into the beautiful corrie of steep green grass, red gravel and broken slabby black rocks, down to Lochan nan Gabhar (gower) or lochan of the goats at about 770m. A gentle rise now follows to 1122m at the group of tors south-west of Mullach Lochan nan Gabhar (mullach means summit), and from there along the high crescent running round to the top of Ben Avon.

Across a green hollow north-west of Mullach Lochan nan Gabhar stands the fine 1076m spur of Stob Bac an Fhuarain or point of the bank of the spring. Tucked high up on its west side lies the remote Slochd Beag or little pit, a colourful place where Allt an t-Sluichd Bhig cascades over broken rocks among pink gravel and patches of bright green vegetation. To the north of the Stob, you will see the conspicuous Clach Bun Rudhtair, a group of rocks standing up like gigantic rhinoceros horns to 914m. These and Sabhalan Beithneag on Bynack More are the highest and most impressive tors in the Cairngorms. Of the three masses at Clach Bun Rudhtair, the middle one sticks up highest, reaching 25m, and has a window right through it. North of Clach Bun Rudhtair, a long spur with great patches of bare pink granite grit thrusts out to Da Dhruim Lom ('dagrum'lom) or two bare ridges, above Glen Avon.

The walk from Inchrory to Loch Avon. Distance: from Inchrory to Faindouran Lodge 11½ kilometres, to Ath nam Fiann 17 kilometres, to Loch Avon 19 kilometres, ascent 320m. This makes a fine walk through some of the least-visited country in the Cairngorms. Glen Avon is a narrow glen, steep-sided and with broken rocks in places. From 600 to 700m altitude on the north side a huge undulating plateau stretches north over the wild expanse of the Caiplich, whereas on the south side you look up to the lonely corries and ridges sweeping up to the high Cairngorms. At the Linn of Avon beside Inchrory the river comes over a series of falls with deep translucent pools of great purity and beauty. A bulldozed track runs up the south side to just west of where Glen Loin breaks off to the north (footbridge over the Avon here), and another rough road from Inchrory comes up the north side to about 2 kilometres south-west of Faindouran Lodge. A bulldozed spur of this northern road goes up the east side of Glen Loin to the col south of The Castle rock on the Water of Ailnack, and a second bulldozed spur climbs Druim Loin and runs along the top of the rocky escarpment of Creag a' Chadha Dhuibh high above Glen Loin. Glen Loin is a remarkable curving glen, steep and craggy and so impressive that from the plateau of Ben Avon you might easily mistake it for Glen Avon itself.

Between the Linn and the opening of Slochd Mor, the clear water of Avon hurries on over shingle beds among grassy haughs. You will enjoy the fine view up Caol Ghleann or Sma (Scots small) Glen to the wind-scoured gravelly ridges and corries of Ben Avon and the fantastic horns of Clach Bun Rudhtair. Even more impressive is the outlook up wild Slochd Mor and its many rock faces. Stob an t-Sluichd and Stob Bac an Fhuarain, which run as level spurs from the higher hills behind, from below look impressive sharp peaks shielding the entrance to the huge Slochd Mor. Further on up the glen you can look back to Clach Bun Rudhtair and see light through its window.

Beyond Allt an t-Sluichd the road continues about 2 kilometres past Faindouran Lodge (Feith an Dobhrain (fain'doorin) or bog stream of the otter), where the cottage and stable at about 590m have been renovated by the Mountain Bothies Association. In this upper part of Glen Avon you look south past the curious little Spion Rocks into the enormous open corries on the north sides of Beinn a' Bhuird and Beinn a' Chaorainn. Eventually, 2 kilometres east of Loch Avon, the path from the end of the Faindouran vehicle track takes you to Ath nam Fiann, where the Lairig an Laoigh route crosses the River Avon beside the Fords of Avon Refuge hut.

Beinn a' Bhuird (1196m)

Although spelled Beinn a' Bhuird on maps, probably it should be Beinn Bord or table hill; Gaelic speakers on Mar used to call it ping'bord, and older local folk still say bainna'bord. Whether you look from Dulnain Bridge, Invercauld or the central Cairngorms, it makes a good name for this great top with its huge flat summit plateau. Beinn a' Bhuird is a hill of contrasts. On its west and north sides, vast heathy slopes fall gently to the peaty plateau of Moine Bhealaidh above Glen Derry and to lonely Glen Avon. On the south it rises commandingly in great steep bulging flanks high above the magnificent old pine forest of Quoich. All along the east side runs a series of wild craggy and snowy corries which you see well from Invercauld. In the north-east, the huge plateau rolls on over the green Cnap a' Chleirich and then ends abruptly at the great wall of cliffs above Slochd Mor. The grand high-level walk from the South Top to the North Top gives some of the finest views in North-east Scotland. Although the central Cairngorms bar you from seeing the peaks on the Atlantic

The South Top of Beinn a' Bhuird from Glen Quoich

seaboard, the rest of the view, of innumerable wild hills beyond a vast tract of lonely glens and rolling lower foothills, is unusually impressive.

WALKING ASCENTS TO BEINN A' BHUIRD

From Invercauld.   Distance: from Keiloch to Slugain Lodge 8 kilometres, to the South Top 13 kilometres, to the North Top 16 kilometres, total ascent 940m. The first part of this route, up to Slugain Lodge, is the same as to Ben Avon (see above). Beyond the col above the ruined lodge, a path breaks off to the left to Quoich Water and then climbs around Carn Fiaclach ('feeaklach) or toothed hill to end at 800m. From there you climb easily on short vegetation and stones straight uphill. Nearby, the shallow hollow at the top of the stream to the west is Ear-choire an t-Sneachda ('err choran 'drechk) or east corrie of the snow, where snow lies late into the summer. You will find it worth going to the edge of the cliffs to the east, so as to look into Coire na Ciche and see the huge slabby rock of A' Chioch or the pap, which sticks high up from a tail spur of the plateau and looks so prominent from Invercauld.

From A' Chioch a stroll along the plateau takes you to the cairn on the South Top at 1177m, and then along the 3 kilometres of plateau north to the North Top at 1196m. If you go along the cliff edge, grand views open out into the two huge eastern corries, Coire an Dubh Lochain and Coire nan Clach. You can walk east along the cliff edge

Coire an Dubh Lochain, Beinn a' Bhuird

from the North Top, but a better way leads further north across the beautiful spacious green hollow at the head of Feith Ghiubhasachain or stream of the little fir wood. From there you stroll easily over the delightful flattish plateau to the highest 1172m point of Cnap a' Chleirich (knap'chleerich) or knoll of the clergyman. You should diverge north of here, passing on the way a very high small lochan, to look into Garbh Choire. Alternatives are then to descend to the Sneck and continue to Ben Avon (see above), or go south to Clach a' Chleirich and Slugain. If you go south, the Allt Dearg south-west of Cnap a' Chleirich makes a good route, but watch out for a deep sandy pocket in the stream bed at about 104 003, which often contains a vertical snow bank right through the summer, and remember that the slope to the east of this burn carries steep broken crags. Distance: from North Top to Cnap a' Chleirich 1½ kilometres, to the Sneck 2½ kilometres if you avoid detours.

From Cnap a' Chleirich, the walker with plenty of time should not miss the 2 kilometres long spur north-east out to Stob an t-Sluichd where a comb of broken rocks and small tors of rough granite leads out along the spur to this fine point overlooking Glen Avon. You can also reach it from Glen Avon by going up the road to Allt an t-Sluichd and then taking a path up Cul na Bruaich to a point west-south-west of Stob an t-Sluichd.

From the Dubh Ghleann. This is the finest approach to Beinn a' Bhuird. Distance: from Quoich road bridge (333m) at Allanaquoich to Allt an Dubh Ghlinne 6 kilometres, to North Top via An Diollaid 13 kilometres, total ascent 800m. The public road from Mar Lodge and Linn of Dee ends at Allanaquoich, where a footpath runs above the rocky Linn of Quoich to a footbridge beside the now broken pothole of the Punch Bowl. To the west of here on the flat above the river you come on a private vehicle track. This leads to a bulldozed track up the west side of Glen Quoich through a beautiful natural forest of mixed old pine and birch, to cross Allt an Dubh Ghlinne at a ford at about 450m. Here Glen Quoich divides. The Dubh Ghleann ('dooglin) or dark glen is the west branch, and Am Beitheachan (m'bay-achan) or the little birch place is the glen to the east. Although local people always call this east part the Beitheachan and not the Quoich, all the maps have omitted it. You can also reach this glen junction by going from the Derry gate at the foot of Glen Lui and taking the path through the rocky Clais Fhearnaig (Chapter 8), a way that is half a kilometre further than the route from Allanaquoich.

Beyond the junction of the streams, the bulldozed track also divides. The east branch runs up the Beitheachan to a ford at about 093 952, where it loops round and eventually back to Allanaquoich down the east side of Glen Quoich. The west branch goes straight ahead into the pine wood clothing the rounded hill of Carn Alltan na Beinne, and then winds round and climbs this hill by a series of spectacular zigzags before dropping slightly down to An Diollaid at 074 967. You will come on an alternative and better walking route if you trace the old stalkers' path which slants uphill below most of the zigzags. On the opposite steep hillside of Bruach Mhor, the first burn of Alltan Tarsuinn or cross streamlet rushes down a steep green stripe, while the next one up falls from the wide green upper corrie of Coire Gorm (kor'gorom). The main burn is Alltan na Beinne (altana'peeng) or streamlet of the hill. Cornices often ring the steep lower slopes west of Alltan na Beinne and Allt a' Choire Ghuirm, and an avalanche at Alltan Tarsuinn killed two men in 1964. An Diollaid or the saddle is an impressive and unusual narrow neck at 744m where you look down steeply into the wild depths of the Dubh Ghleann. Ahead, the bulldozed track climbs to 1080m, just west of the head springs of Alltan na Beinne. Snow lies late along the shallow upper part of this burn and often builds up into a high vertical wall on its west side. From the track end you can stroll easily to either top of Beinn a' Bhuird.

A finer route is to walk up the deep and narrow Dubh Ghleann to its head, where streams fall tumbling down among steep grass, broken rocks and screes. The eastern burn, Allt Coire Ruairidh, comes down the shallow green Coire Ruairidh (kor'ooarie) or Rory's corrie, from near the North Top.

Beinn a' Chaorainn *(hill of the rowan)* (1082m)
Beinn Bhreac *(speckled hill)* (931m)
Connecting these two hills to one another and to Beinn a' Bhuird stretches a vast medium-level plateau, one of the fine wild places of the Cairngorms. Its old name was Moine Bhealaidh (mon'vyal) or peat moss of the broom, but local people now

call it the Yalla Moss. Here, several hills rise in the distance far beyond the great flattish expanses of bog, peat hags and stretches of crisp turf. Looking from Beinn a' Bhuird in the evening you will see its innumerable pools glint like silver, and from the moss itself the views into Coire Etchachan are magnificent.

The quickest way to the shapely cone of Beinn a' Chaorainn (bain 'hoorin) starts from Derry Lodge by the Lairig an Laoigh path for 7½ kilometres to the top of the path (Chapter 3). Distance: from top of path at 034 004 to summit 1½ kilometres, ascent 330m. To the east of the summit, 1½ kilometres away, the lower rounded top of Beinn a' Chaorainn Bheag stands beyond a set of tiny lochans along the Avon watershed.

Beinn Bhreac (bain'vraichk) is a dry spur rising at the south end of Moine Bhealaidh into two tops, the eastern being higher, 5 kilometres from Beinn a' Chaorainn. From here you can stroll north-west to Craig Derry at 040 980, the spur that drops sharply down screes to Glen Derry. It is then an easy walk south to the Derry down the shallow Coire an Fhir Bhogha, which the map makers mistook for Coire Cadha an Fhir Bhogha or corrie of pass of the archer. Another route off Beinn Bhreac goes south-south-west by the little rocky gully of Clais Poll Bhat (locally called klash pole 'va) and the curious hanging tarn of Poll Bhat to Glen Quoich. On the way down in spring, avoid the sudden drop of Coire Gorm to the south-south-east of the summit, as its steep upper green bank is often heavily snow-corniced. From the Clais, you can also descend easily over the rounded 777m Meall an Lundain (myal'lowntin) or lump at marshy place, to the pines of the Derry (5 kilometres from Beinn Bhreac to Derry Lodge).

WALKING IN THE CORRIES

Ben Avon shares the magnificent Slochd Mor with Beinn a' Bhuird, and its other corries have already been mentioned. Beinn a' Bhuird carries some grand wild corries with superb cornices and other snow scenery. In the south-east the shallow Coire Buidhe (kor'booee) north of Carn Fiaclach leads higher up into the much bigger Coire na Ciche. Coire na Ciche (korna'keech) or corrie of the pap, is a sheltered sunny corrie with fine buttresses of rough granite on the west side and the great tor of A' Chioch or the pap rising high above its eastern damp slabby rocks. Round the corner to the north spreads the huge Coire an Dubh Lochain - locally called Coire an Loch (korin'loch) - a wide corrie with many rocks and screes, and grassy shelves that lead easily but steeply to the plateau above. For its great variety of scenery and its air of remoteness, this corrie is one of the finest in the region described in this book. One of the highest lochs in the Cairngorms, the lovely Dubh Lochan or black lochan lies at about 935m among the corrie's great screes. To the north, the bold slabby Dividing Buttress separates the corrie from the even larger Coire nan Clach (korna'glach) or corrie of the stones, where cornices usually last into July.

The Mitre Ridge, Beinn a' Bhuird

Squareface, Beinn a' Bhuird

CLIMBING

The big high corries of Beinn a' Bhuird have some superb rock walls and steep snow, and offer many fine routes on good rock, snow and ice. The remote, north-facing Garbh Choire is especially impressive, and climbing there on short winter days is a particularly serious challenge. On Ben Avon the crags consist mostly of broken and short rocks. However, the tors give sporting scrambling on dry rough granite, especially at Clach Bun Rudhtair. All the climbs describd below are on Beinn a' Bhuird.

Coire na Ciche. This corrie has two parts which almost form a right angle with the wide South Gully in the corner. To the east of the corner a smooth sheet of slab called Slab Buttress stretches across under the great wart of A' Chioch. A' Chioch itself gives interesting climbing on good dark rock but lacking any obvious defined lines. The Slab Buttress below is partly vegetated, often wet, and prone to avalanches in spring, but in summer gives the good 200m climb of *Quartzvein Route* (Very Difficult) up a central dyke containing a vein of quartz. To the left of South Gully soars a 110m high crag, so tucked in on the west side of the corrie that much of it is hidden out of sight from the glen below or from Invercauld; indeed, only when you come right into Coire na Ciche do you fully realise its width. Good routes (both VS) are *Hourglass Buttress* and *The Carpet*. Hourglass rises just left of South Gully, easily recognised from its hourglass or 'egg-timer' appearance. The Carpet lies towards the left end of the crags, up an obvious big slab to the right of a huge alcove in the rock. *Three Step* (E1) goes up the gigantic steps below and to the right of The Carpet, and *Slugain Buttress* to its right is a popular winter climb.

Coire an Dubh Lochain. The main features here are the steep bulging wall of Bloodhound Buttress that culminates in a few prominent pinnacles near the plateau edge, the wide easy gully of The Main Rake further north, and north again the slabby Glaucous Buttress. *The Scent* (HVS), one of the best climbs in the corrie, goes up by a big hanging slab under the nose of Bloodhound Buttress. A popular climb is *Polypody Groove* (Very Difficult) on Glaucous Buttress, up an obvious, dark, left-slanting line between the smooth slabs on the right side of the buttress and the steeper granite pillars on the left side. The VS *Tearaway* goes up the slabs to the right, as do other good lines up part of the slabs. At the north end of the corrie, the great bulge of Dividing Buttress projects outward, hiding the remote Coire nan Clach further north. Dividing Buttress looks a grand sight but offers mostly indefinite though sporting climbing to the plateau; a more defined way is by the 140m *Slab and Arete* (Moderate) up the ridge on the dividing line between the two corries. The 110m *Streaker's Root* (HVS) is a fine climb on excellent granite up grooves to the right of a big corner in a stretch of slabs to the right of Slab and Arete. The gullies further north in Coire nan Clach offer Grade I snow climbs ending in big cornices.

Garbh Choire. Big continuous crags rise on the south or Cnap a' Chleirich side, with ribs and broken smaller buttresses on the Stob an t-Sluichd side. The finest feature is the Mitre Ridge, a wide, 200m high black wall projecting as a wedge into an outer ridge, and culminating in a series of fine towers. The Mitre Ridge was the scene of one of the main early breakthroughs in Cairngorms climbing in July 1933, when two parties climbed two separate routes up the wall; both were exposed face routes that are still among the finest climbs in the Cairngorms. The *Direct Route* (Hard Severe) starts between the lowest rocks and the outer corner of the Mitre wall, and goes up a great slab. The rest of this grand route goes near or on the edge of the ridge, first by chimneys, then up or around two fine towers, and finally over the knife-edged arete and pinnacles of the summit crest. The Mitre Ridge, which faces north at a high altitude, looks a magnificent sight in winter, when the Direct Route becomes a Grade V winter ascent that is one of the finest in the massif. Round the corner to the west and past the outermost wedge of the Mitre Ridge, the *Cumming-Crofton Route* (Severe) was also first climbed on that same great day in 1933. It takes a dark line running right up the steep face just west of the corner. On the remote, steep and spectacular west face of the Mitre Ridge, the superb *Slochd Wall* (HVS) starts at the foot of North-West Gully, the gully which bounds the west side of the ridge.

The other outstanding feature of the Garbh Choire is *Squareface,* which projects outwards about halfway between the Sneck and the Mitre Ridge. This high-lying black buttress has a largely hidden west face of dry, rough, clean rock that offers one of the best climbs in the massif. The 100m route goes up on or near the arete where the north and west faces of this buttress meet in a prominent edge. The original route (Very Difficult) slants off the arete to the right, on to the west face, for the final pitch. *Angel's Edgeway,* a later VS variation to the second pitch, goes right up the steep top part of the arete by a delicate and spectacular finish on superb rock.

SKIING

The entire area is excellent for cross-country skiing up the glens on the long approaches to the hills, across the wide moors, and on to the high plateaux and corries. Some high slopes are steep and others corniced, so ski-mountaineering techniques may be needed. Superb descents are down Coire Ruairidh west of the North Top of Beinn a' Bhuird and down Feith Ghiubhasachain north of it, off Beinn a' Bhuird into Glen Quoich by Coire Gorm, Alltan na Beinne and Ear-choire an t-Sneachda, off Cnap a' Chleirich (sometimes corniced) to Clach a' Chleirich, and down the slopes of Ben Avon to Allt Phouple and Feith Laoigh.

FURTHER READING

A.I.McConnochie *The eastern Cairngorms*. CCJ 1, 236.

Prof Heddle *Ben Avon*. SMCJ 2,225.

L.W.Hinxman *In ptarmigan land*. SMCJ 4, 214.

The eastern Cairngorms (Guide Book article). SMCJ 8, 41.

CHAPTER 10

The Mounth from Callater to Glen Ey

Carn an Tuirc	1019m	174 805
Cairn of Claise	1064m	185 789
Tolmount	958m	210 800
Tom Buidhe	957m	214 788
Glas Maol	1068m	167 766
Creag Leacach	987m	155 745
The Cairnwell	933m	135 774
Carn Aosda	917m	134 792
Carn a' Gheoidh	975m	107 767
An Socach	944m	080 800
Beinn Iutharn Mhor	1045m	046 973
Beinn Iutharn Bheag	953m	065 791
Mam nan Carn	986m	050 781
Carn Bhac	946m	051 833
Glas Tulaichean	1051m	051 760
Carn an Righ	1029m	028 773
Ben Gulabin	806m	101 722
Mount Blair	744m	167 629
Monamenach	807m	176 707
Creag nan Gabhar	834m	154 841

This chapter describes that grand part of the Mounth from Glen Callater and Glen Isla west to the Glen Ey hills, Fealar Lodge and Glen Shee. Here the Mounth separates upper Deeside from the low ground of Perthshire and west Angus. This makes very good walking country on smooth green hills with vast rolling plateaux and broad ridges; even at 1000 to 1050m you tread on a springy continuous turf of sedge and moss almost like a lawn. The glens have a wild open beauty, each with a distinctive character all its own. In the centre of the district the signs of roads, tracks and other works of man are so few, the wildlife so rich, and the feeling of space so strong, that the highest hills are almost as good as the Cairngorms massif as a wilderness area.

ACCESS
Braemar is the best centre for the north side of this part of the Mounth, and Spittal of Glenshee for the south side. The public road from Braemar to Perth brings many hills closer. Useful public roads go from Braemar to Inverey, from Pitlochry to Kirkmichael, and up Glen Isla to Auchavan. There is a chairlift on The Cairnwell.

PUBLIC TRANSPORT
See Chapters 2 and 7. A bus runs between Braemar and Glen Shee on some days in summer (check details locally).

ACCOMMODATION
See Chapter 2. There are also hotels at Kirkton of Glen Isla, Spittal of Glen Shee and the nearby Dalmunzie, and at Kirkmichael, and a cafe at Glenshee Ski Centre near the top of the Cairnwell Pass.

MAPS
Ordnance Survey 1:50,000 Sheets 43 and 44

These hills offer an infinitely varied set of cross-country walks over the tops, starting in one glen and finishing in another. Although usually easy for hillwalking in snow or for ski touring, they can be inaccessible and very snowy hills in some winters. In hard winters with south-east winds, as in 1947, 1963 and 1972, they become far more deeply covered than the higher Cairngorms massif to the north. Huge cornices and great convex bulges of snow often build up on otherwise easy slopes, and avalanches are common. Avalanches have occurred even on gentle slopes, like the one east of Sron na Gaoithe on the route of the Monega path over Glas Maol.

GEOLOGY, LANDFORMS AND WILDLIFE

The rock consists mostly of schist with some quartzite and big patches of limestone and epidiorite, and with granite on Creag Caorach and Creag an Fhir-shaighde. Glen Callater and Caenlochan are fine examples of glacial trenches with precipitous corries at the top, the glens of Ey, Clunie, Taitneach and Shee being more typical U-shaped valleys with steep sides. Many of the high corries have beautiful cups or basins with steep slopes but little or no rock. Just north of Blairgowrie, the River Ericht runs through a remarkable beautifully wooded canyon with cliffs of conglomerate and sandstone.

Because of its lime-rich rocks, the district is far more fertile than the Cairngorms massif, with a deeper richer soil, a more fertile and varied vegetation with more grass and blaeberry and less heather, and a more abundant and varied animal life. The lime-rich rocks of Caenlochan rank with Ben Lawers as one of the two best places in Britain for uncommon arctic-alpine plants. Here you may see snow gentian, blue sow thistle, woolly willow, boreal fleabane and other rarities. Loch Kander is another very good spot for rare arctic-alpines, although less varied than Caenlochan. Over the limestone there are also a few rich places on open ground where mountain avens, alpine cinquefoil and purple saxifrage grow on the open hillside away from cliffs.

The Glas Maol summit plateau has an interesting arctic-alpine grassland that is typical of dry climates, being dominated by stiff sedge with some viviparous fescue, a little woolly hair moss and much lichen. The Glen Ey hills further west, as on Carn an Righ and Carn Bhac, support a more western type of vegetation like that on the Drumochter hills, with more moss and less lichen. A feature of all these fertile hills is that vegetation covers far more of the ground than at the same altitude in the Cairngorms, with very little bare gravel or screes. Ptarmigan, red grouse, skylarks and mountain hares reach a greater average abundance on some of these hills than anywhere else in the arctic-alpine zone in Scotland, and ptarmigan and red grouse tend to rear bigger broods here than elsewhere, which again indicates the underlying fertility. On some of these hills, several species of animals live at much higher altitudes than usual, for instance moles and breeding frogs. This part of the Mounth is therefore unique in Scotland for its wildlife interest, both plant and animal.

ESTATES
Invercauld has Callater, Clunie and most of the Glen Shee and Glen Taitneach hills. Fealar is a separate deer forest running up to Carn Bhac and Beinn Iutharn. Glen Ey and Glen Connie lie on Mar Estate, Glen Lochsie on Dalmunzie, and Caenlochan on Tulchan Estate. All the ground is deer forest, with hill sheep in summer and grouse shooting on the lower ground.

HISTORY
Glen Shee shares with Kinveachy near Aviemore and several other places in Scotland and Ireland an old Celtic legend of Fionn or Fingal who took vengeance on Diarmaid for stealing the love of Grainne, Fingal's queen. After Diarmaid slew the great boar of Beinn Gulbain (in this case Ben Gulabin near the Spittal), Fingal bade him measure the monster from tail to snout with his bare foot, whereupon the poisoned bristles pierced his foot and he died in agony. Grainne in despair flung herself on an arrow, and she and Diarmaid and his white hounds were said to be buried on Tom Diarmaid or Diarmaid's hillock, beside the farm of Tomb (i.e. Tom) across the river from the Spittal (T.D.Miller, *Tales of a Highland Parish, Glen Shee*). Later on, during the period of recorded history, many feuds and minor battles occurred in the Cairnwell district on both sides of the pass, possibly because it was in a boundary area lying between different communities. Grant's *Legends of the Braes o' Mar* is a good source for this history. At Loch Callater, beside the Tolmount path just east of the Lodge, you will see the Priest's Well or Fuaran an t-Sagairt; legend has it that water flowed freely after a priest prayed here during a spell of severe frost when all wells in the district were frozen over.

In old times people travelling from Tomintoul to Pitlochry walked by the Bealach Dearg and the Cairnwell. Before Gaelic died out here, F.C.Diack noted an ancient verse among Gaelic speakers at Tomintoul, Deeside, and in Strath Ardle. It runs:

> Cuir is cathadh am Bealach Dearg,
> Sneachd is reoth air Charna Bhalg,
> Cul ri gaoth air Lairig bhealaich,
> Grian gheal am Maoilinn

which means, 'snowing and drifting in Bealach Dearg, snow and frost on the Cairnwell, back to the wind on the Lairig pass, bright sun in Moulin'. The Lairig of the verse is An Lairig, which travellers on foot used from Glen Shee to Pitlochry.

THE HILLS

Carn an Tuirc *(hill of the boar)* (1019m)
Cairn of Claise (1064m)
Tolmount (958m)
Tom Buidhe *(yellow knoll)* (957m)
These are the big tops on the west of Glen Callater, forming a vast grassy tableland that is peaty and damp in the hollows but well drained and springy on the ridges. From Glen Callater a bulldozed track climbs on to them up to an altitude of 940m on Carn Tuirc Beag, which projects out as a spur of dry tundra north-west of Loch Kander.

For Carn an Tuirc (kairn'turk), one of the best routes up (3 kilometres, 520m ascent) starts from the corner of the Cairnwell road at 147 799. Immediately down-hill stands the old bridge at the site of An Seann-spideal or the old spital, that carried the first military road. Here you stand in a great amphitheatre which runs from Carn an Tuirc round to the Cairnwell and divides into separate glens or corries further up; it is called Coire Bhuth (voo) and has long been regarded as an excellent grazing. Across the old bridge a path winds up the stream along the fine rocky gorge and pools of the Linn of Allt a' Gharbh Choire, and then past some old shielings to the foot of Carn an Tuirc. Here the burns divide, and you take the north-east burn up the hollow of Coire na Coinnich or corrie of the moss, to the summit plateau.

South of Carn an Tuirc, you pass the top of Coire Loch Kander beside an old stone wall and then climb up a gradual green damp slope to Cairn of Claise (2 kilometres from Carn an Tuirc, 110m ascent). This name comes from Carn na Glaiseath (kairna'glasha), meaning hill of the green place or of the stream place. A broken wire fence with wooden posts runs for miles along the county boundary here, stretching from Creag Leacach of Glen Shee to Cairn of Claise where a big stone dyke replaces it at an unusually high altitude. Cairn of Claise has a southerly top called Druim Mor (961m) at the end of a long flat grassy spur extending near the Caenlochan cliffs. Below it the cliffs fall abruptly in the prominent triangular face of Creag Caorach (locally called kraig'herrich). At its lowest point at about 950m the main ridge that goes 3½ kilometres round to Glas Maol passes near the edge of a great steep basin falling to the north, which is the Garbh-choire ('gar chorrie) or rough corrie.

Tolmount, a conical top 3 kilometres to the east of Cairn of Claise (60m ascent), sweeps up from an expanse of high tableland that runs out to the hills west of Glen Clova and round to Lochnagar. The name, which is the same as that of the nearby Mounth road, comes from An Tul-monadh, probably meaning the brow mounth or hill ('tole-munth). The lowest point on the watershed lies at the col east of the top, at 874m. One of the best routes is to climb all three hills from Loch Callater via Loch

Creag Leacach from the north-east

Kander and then go down Jock's Road (see Chapter 13, The Tolmount). Two other fine alternatives are to walk from the Seann-spideal up Carn an Tuirc to Tolmount, Cairn of Claise and round the head of Garbh-choire to Glas Maol (8½ kilometres) and back 5 kilometres by Sron na Gaoithe, or else to go from Caenlochan up Glen Canness and then to Tolmount, Cairn of Claise, Glas Maol and Monega Hill.

On the rounded hill of Tom Buidhe you stand in the centre of a great tableland, and can appreciate the comment of Sir Hugh T. Munro – the originator of our 'Munros' of today – 'So elevated and flat is the range that a straight line of 10 miles could be drawn from Creag Leacach to the Meikle Pap of Lochnagar, and, except for about half a mile on each side of the Tolmount, the elevation is everywhere about 3000ft, while even at these points it only falls to 2863ft and a dogcart could be driven the whole way.' Some find these uplands dull and featureless, but although at first sight they do seem uniform, if you pay closer attention and come on return visits you will find them all very different, with many varying kinds of terrain and vegetation. Getting to know the individual complexity and the sheer extent, spaciousness and peace of this wilderness is to realise its special character and charm.

To reach Tom Buidhe is an easy walk of 1.3 kilometres from Tolmount, 3 kilometres from Cairn of Claise, 5½ kilometres from Glas Maol, 4½ kilometres from Broad Cairn, and 9½ kilometres from Lochnagar; the choice in all directions from this central point on the tableland is varied. If you are returning to Glen Clova (Chapter 13) from Tom Buidhe, a good way goes east by remote Loch Esk, down to the ruined lodge of Bachnagairn and its old larches beside green meadows, and so to Braedownie (10 kilometres). Glen Canness also makes a fine approach to Tom Buidhe (see Caenlochan below).

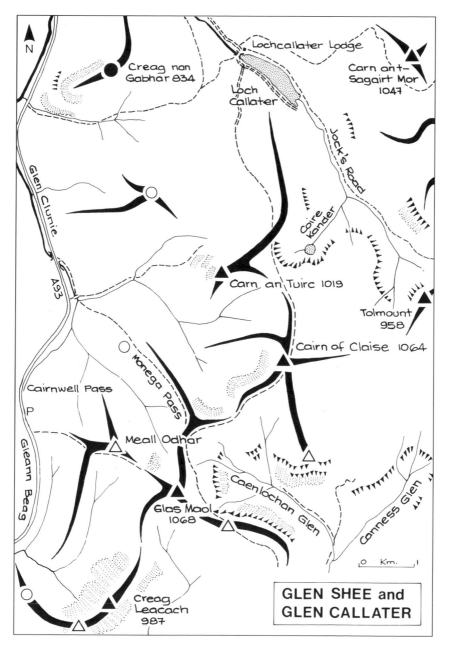

Glas Maol (1068m)
Creag Leacach *(slabby rocky hill)* (987m)
From the road over the Cairnwell, you can see these hills very well from the south end of the highest car park at about 670m. Creag Leacach looks a fine peak, soaring high out of Gleann Beag with steep slopes of contrasting blue-grey scree, black expanses of peat at an unusually high angle, and bright green grass. However, the best view of Glas Maol from the Cairnwell road is at the head of Glen Clunie near the Seann-spideal Bridge. On this side, Glas Maol presents its northern corrie of Fionn-choire (not Coire Fionn as on the map) as a beautifully symmetrical bowl, flanked by the steep Sron na Gaoithe on the left and Meall Odhar on the right. The name Glas Maol ('glas meel') suggests green bald top, but in local Gaelic speech the old words were A' Ghlas-mheall ('hlas vyal) or the green lump.

The easiest way to climb Glas Maol is to start from the top car park on the Cairnwell Pass (3 kilometres, 400m ascent). The route leads by a vehicle track over the heathery hill of Meall Odhar Beag (about 770m) or by paths up its south side, to the ski grounds in the basin of Coire Odhar beyond. There, a tow pulls skiers to the 922m top of Meall Odhar, whose local name is Meall Odhar Mor (mil ower 'more) or big dun lump. From here the horseshoe of Fionn-choire ('fyan chorrie) or cold corrie falls to the east (the 1:25,000 map erroneously locates it on Sron na Gaoithe). A curved horseshoe-shaped snow drift lies far into the summer here, and avalanches often occur in winter. A steepish climb straight ahead leads to the plateau, and along the broken remains of a fence you stroll across soft turf to the summit cairn of Glas Maol (no fence on the last part). Other broken fences which branch off this fence at two different points run out to Cairn of Claise and to Creag Leacach. Aberdeen, Angus and Perth counties meet on the top, where a very fine view opens out, especially towards the south and south-west. There is a pleasant 2½ kilometres walk from the cairn down to the stony ridge leading south to Creag Leacach, a fine sharp peak with scree slopes that fall steeply to the west into Coire Bhathaich or corrie of the shelter. The easiest way (3 kilometres) from there to Glen Shee goes down the subsidiary bulge to the south-west and then down Meall Gorm to the road above the house of Rhidorroch (Ruighe Dorch or dark shieling).

The Cairnwell (933m)
Carn Aosda (917m)
Carn a' Gheoidh *(hill of the goose)* (975m)
These hills stand west of the Cairnwell road summit and can be easily climbed as they form a series of hill tops. The Cairnwell is pronounced the 'kairnwall, and comes from An Carn Bhalg or the hill of bags (i.e. round-shaped hill). It gives a fine view down Glen Shee to lowland Scotland. To the west the huge basin of Coire Direach (kor'yeerich) or straight corrie slopes steeply, with the broken rocks of Creag a' Choire Dhirich on the far side. From the Cairnwell a broad ridge runs round for 2 kilometres north to the two stony summits of Carn Aosda, an erroneous map name which should be Carn Aoise (karn'oosh) or hill of age. A fine-looking hill from upper Glen Clunie, Carn Aosda sends out a long ridge down the east side of the Baddoch Burn.

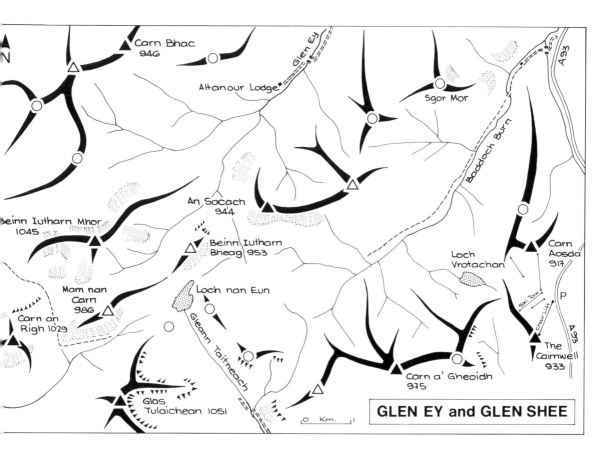

GLEN EY and GLEN SHEE

Between Carn Aosda and the ridge to the Cairnwell, Loch Vrotachan lies at about 750m in a fertile basin draining towards the Baddoch Burn, a fine loch for trout. You stroll easily along the broad ridge above Loch Vrotachan past the beautiful tarn of Loch a' Choire Dhirich among its rocky hillocks, and on to the tablelands beyond. Further on rises Carn a' Gheoidh ('yoe-ee) or hill of the goose, 3½ kilometres from the top of the chairlift. Beyond again for 2 kilometres is the 917m peaked Carn Bhinnein ('veenin) or hill of the pinnacle, on whose craggy front of Creag Dallaig (724m) a small rocky point sticks out, which you can climb easily from the neck behind it. Two good routes off these hills are to drop down to the Spittal of Glen Shee by Gleann Taitneach, or down to Braemar by Glen Baddoch (from Badach or clumps). Carn Bhinnein stands 5 kilometres from Dalmunzie Hotel, and Carn a' Gheoidh 8 kilometres from the A93 at the foot of the Baddoch Burn.

A number of high tops, described below, ring the head of Glen Ey. It makes a pleasant trip to climb all of them together, as they are connected by high cols where you lose little height; moreover a round trip like this gives you new scenery throughout the day.

An Socach *(the snouted one)* (944m)

An Socach ('sochkach) is a long stony whaleback with two tops, the east one rising to 938m and the slightly higher west top overlooking Loch nan Eun. A good walk starts on Morrone above Braemar and goes 10 kilometres to An Socach along the series of hills between Glen Ey and Glen Clunie, a route that nowhere drops below 700m. An Socach lies only 4½ kilometres from the top of the Cairnwell chairlift, and is easily climbed from there past Loch Vrotachan. A third approach begins from a bulldozed track going up the north side of the Baddoch Burn to 103 788. An Socach looks its best from Glen Ey where it throws out a bold northern spur at Creag an Fhuathais (kraig'nooish); this towers strikingly above the Ey bridge 3½ kilometres below Altanour.

The northern spur of An Socach above Glen Ey

Glas Tulaichean from Creag Bhreac

Beinn Iutharn Mhor (1045m)

The name should be Beinn Fhiubharainn Mhor or big hill of the edge-point (ping yoo-iring 'vore to folk with most Gaelic, now mostly bain yoorn 'more). Below Altanour in Glen Ey, the wide grassy flats give one of the best views in the district. Beinn Iutharn Mhor with its great bulging shoulders dominates the top of the glen. The 953m rocky rounded Beinn Iutharn Bheag lies across a corrie to the east, whereas the green 986m Mam nan Carn (mam na'garn) or round hill of the cairns (i.e. screes), standing between the other two, blocks the head of that corrie. A good way to all three tops starts from Gleann Taitneach. A bulldozed track runs up to the top of the glen below Creag Dallaig, from which you climb up to Loch nan Eun (loch nan'yain) or loch of the birds, where common gulls nest. Another walk goes from Glen Ey by a route that can also be varied to include An Socach, Beinn Iutharn and Carn Bhac. Apart from some peat hags on the cols, the walking is good on crisp heather and alpine mossy grassland with occasional sharp quartzite stones. Distance: from Dalmunzie Hotel to Beinn Iutharn Bheag 8½ kilometres, back to Loch nan Eun via Beinn Iutharn Mhor and Mam nan Carn 13½ kilometres, back to hotel 21 kilometres, total ascent 880m. Cars should be parked at 105 702 nearer to the Spittal of Glenshee unless you have permission from the hotel to drive further up. From Altanour to Beinn Iutharn Mhor 5 kilometres, via Mam nan Carn to Beinn Iutharn Bheag 8½ kilometres, back to Altanour 12½ kilometres, total ascent 720m.

Carn Bhac *(karn'vachk, hill of peat banks)* (946m)
Carn Bhac is an unfrequented ridge which sends streams into Ey, Connie, Tilt and Bynack. It has three tops in a long line, Carn a' Bhutha at 907m, which was previously considered a 'top' over 3000ft but has now been relegated below that height, then Carn Bhac at 920m, and to the east the highest top, which is unnamed on the map. From the ruined farm that appears erroneously as Auchelie on the map but which local people always call ach'eeree, a vehicle track leads from the Glen Ey road up to 680m on the spur north of Carn Creagach. You will find it an easy walk from the track end across to Carn Bhac, 5 kilometres from Auchelie. Another bulldozed track runs up Glen Connie, and beyond climbs up the Allt Cristie Beag (criosda, 'creeos-tyee or swift) to 740m, south of Carn Liath. Two of the many other ways of exploring these hills begin at Bynack Lodge and at Fealar Lodge.

Glas Tulaichean (1051m)
Glas Tulaichean (glas'tulchan) or green hill, is a beautiful shapely top with two fine corries of steep grass and a little broken rock, and many long ridges which give grand walking on springy turf. A good route comes from Dalmunzie Hotel at 370m in lower Glen Lochsie, then up Allt Ghlinn Thaitneich to Glas Tulaichean (9 kilometres, 690m ascent), and back 7 kilometres by a vehicle track from the summit along the ridge of Breac-reidh to Glenlochsie Lodge, and so down Glen Lochsie to the hotel (cars should be parked at 105 702 unless permission has been received from the hotel to drive further). You can also easily combine the ascents of Beinn Iutharn and Mam nan Carn with Glas Tulaichean. In Victorian times when deer stalking was in its heyday, a railway was built to take the shooters up to the now ruined lodge in Glen Lochsie. The railway operated until 1977, and many of the old rails still exist.

Carn an Righ (1029m)
It is locally called karn'ree, meaning hill of the king or possibly Ruighe meaning a shiel. A great round stony mass, it lies off the main chain of hills, so walkers seldom visit it. From Glen Ey you can reach it from Mam nan Carn (2½ kilometres), but have to drop and regain 250m of altitude on the way. A good way is to climb it along with Beinn Iutharn Mhor and Carn Bhac from the Glen Tilt path via Fealar Lodge. At the bridge over Allt a' Ghlinne Mhoir on the road to Enochdhu, 3½ kilometres south of Fealar, you are standing at about 600m altitude with Carn an Righ rising above (2 kilometres). A more gradual route takes the path running up the Allt a' Ghlinne Bhig to 780m, between Mam nan Carn and Carn an Righ. At 550m, Fealar Lodge is the highest occupied shooting lodge in the Highlands and one of the most remote. Fealar (Feith Laire, fi'lar) or mare's bog-stream, lies in a beautiful, sheltered, fertile green basin surrounded by lonely open hills. As well as coming in to Fealar by the long road over the hill from Enochdhu, you can also reach it by a 3 kilometres path from Glen Tilt which starts north-east of the bridge over Tarf Water, or else from Bynack by an old short-cut north-west of Fealar Lodge by the Allt Garbh Buidhe.

Ben Gulabin (806m)
Ben Gulabin ('goolabin) is the classic Fingalian name Beinn Gulbain from the legend of the death of Diarmaid, and appears in several place names in Ireland and

Scotland. The hill dominates Spittal of Glenshee on the north side. On the public road north of the Spittal at 114 714 on the A93, a track goes northwards to the col between Ben Gulabin and Creagan Bheithe. It is easiest to leave this track before the col, at the forkings of the burn, and head south-west to the top (3 kilometres from good car parking near the Spittal, 450m ascent). The hill gives very fine views up Gleann Taitneach to Glas Tulaichean.

Mount Blair (744m)
Mount is from Monadh meaning hill, and Blair possibly from Blar meaning white-faced. About 8 kilometres below Spittal of Glenshee, Mount Blair stands between Glen Shee and Glen Isla and can easily be climbed from 160 646 at about 360m on the B951 road between them (1½ kilometres, 380m ascent). An isolated hill, it gives outstanding views of the lowlands to the south and east.

Monamenach (807m)
This hill stands between upper Glen Isla and Glen Shee, as its name (from Monadh Meadhonach or middle hill) shows. It is a heathery hill in grouse-moor country. The easiest approach is from the end of the public road at Auchavan (park cars to the east). A track leads north-west from Auchavan to Glack Burn. Where the track turns leftwards at 610m altitude below a bend in a nearby fence, you leave the track and follow the fence steeply north-west to the top (2½ kilometres, 450m ascent). There are fine views west down Gleann Carnach into Glen Shee, north down Glen Brighty into Glen Isla, and beyond to Glas Maol and Caenlochan Glen.

Creag nan Gabhar (*kraig nan'gower, rocky hill of the goats*) (834m)
Creag nan Gabhar is the largest hill on the east side of Glen Clunie, and presents a steep face of broken rock above the public road up the glen. An easy and attractive way up is from the A93 road at 140 834, by a footpath going east up the south side of Allt a' Mhaide in a narrow glen. The path reaches a fine viewpoint at 680m before dropping into Glen Callater. From here it is easy walking, mostly on short wind-swept vegetation, to the top (3½ kilometres, 420m ascent).

WALKING IN THE GLENS

Glen Callater. The name comes from Caladair, meaning hard water. Approximately 3½ kilometres south of Braemar at Auchallater, at about 370m altitude, a private road goes up Glen Callater. At first it runs alongside a fine little rocky gorge and then for 5 kilometres up the treeless glen, twisting around bare stony hills to the locked lodge beside Loch Callater, where a bridge crosses the river and a bulldozed track runs along the south side of the loch. Lying just below 500m and dammed up by glacial deposits, Loch Callater stretches for 1.3 kilometres long and covers 30 hectares in area; nearly half of it is less than 3m deep but the water reaches 9m in depth near the south-west shore. The loch supports many pike which live unusually high up here. Feral goats lived on some of the nearby crags earlier this century but have not been seen in recent decades.

Loch Callater, looking towards Tolmount   ·

At the lodge the path to Lochnagar slants up to the left. The Tolmount path goes 1½ kilometres along the east side of the loch, then up the grassy flats beyond, and finally climbs over fairly steep grass and boulders out to the plateau at a dip (883m) on the east side of the hill of Tolmount (for the continuation to Glen Clova, see Chapter 13). This upper part of the glen beyond the loch becomes gradually hemmed in by crags, steep slopes and corries. It is a wild impressive place, unusual in the Braemar district for being so bright green in summer. About 2 kilometres up from Loch Callater, the burn from Loch Kander comes in on the west side. The main glen continues for another 1½ kilometres until it stops under the steep broken rocks of Tolmount, in the vast green basin of Coire Breac or speckled corrie.

The hills on the east side of Glen Callater carry a long face of steep slopes and rocks locally called the Devil's Kitchen. Forming part of this face, imposing cliffs rise at Creag Leachdach or locally Creag Leacach ('laikach), and particularly on the 100m granite crags of Creag an Fhir-shaighde. The maps err here also, as the local name for Creag an Fhir-shaighde is Creag an Fhleisdeir (kraigin'leeshter) or rock of the arrowmaker. On the west side an almost continuous escarpment of cliffs stretches from Tolmount to north of Loch Kander. Just east of Loch Kander on the corner plunges an impressive high waterfall, Eas Allt Briste-amhaich or waterfall of burn of broken neck, now often called breakneck falls.

An easy climb of 120m takes you up beautiful green grass and blaeberry from Glen Callater to Loch Kander (Ceanndair, 'kyander or head water) at about 670m. This dark little loch lies in the striking green Coire Loch Kander with its fine broken cliffs of schist, including one steep buttress that soars from just above the water line. You can easily climb out of the corrie at its head by a wide gully which leads to the lowest rim on the plateau between Carn an Tuirc and Cairn of Claise.

The Monega Road. Crossing from Glen Clunie to Glen Isla, this is the highest of the old rights of way across the Mounth. Distance: from the start at the Cairnwell public road to the county boundary 4 kilometres, to the summit of the track 5 kilometres, to Tulchan 10 kilometres, total ascent 520m. The Monega (mon'aigi) leaves the Cairnwell road at 145 805 on the east side of the bridge over the Uisge Bhruidh. The path is indistinct up the north side of the conical 814m spur of Sron na Gaoithe (stronna'gooee) or nose of the wind, from which you have a fine view of the big horseshoe-shaped Fionn-choire of Glas Maol. After reaching the county boundary, the indistinct path suddenly becomes a clear vehicle track which runs from Monega Hill to beyond Cairn of Claise. Just before you reach the highest point at almost 1020m, half a kilometre east of the Glas Maol summit cairn, the track passes through a stretch of subarctic-like hummocks 15 to 25cm high, caused by alternating frost and thaw. It then skirts the west edge of the corrie of Caenlochan to 960m on Little Glas Maol, and drops down a long dry ridge to Monega Hill and finally to the stalker's house of Tulchan at 426m in the head of Glen Isla. Further west, another track climbs from Tulchan up to Little Glas Maol by Glen Brighty and the broad ridge west of Sron Saobhaidhe.

Caenlochan Glen. About 2 kilometres above Tulchan, Glen Isla becomes a green basin hemmed in by crags, a place well worth exploring for its wild scenery. Further up this basin, the valley divides at about 460m. The smaller east branch is Glen Canness (Cadha an Eas, ka'ness) or pass of the waterfall, the west branch being Caenlochan (Cadha an Lochain, kan'lochan) or pass of the lochan. A few straggling larches still remain from the big wood that was once planted and later felled on the lower slopes. A bulldozed track now runs well up Caenlochan. On every side, except the way in from the south, you are hemmed in by steep walls of broken rock and scree, which look especially impressive on Monega Hill to the south-west and on Creag Caorach to the north. One of the easiest ways to climb out passes near the lochan at the north-west corner where a grassy scoop with a zigzag path leads up to the col between Glas Maol and Cairn of Claise. Another goes by a good path that zigzags steeply right up to the plateau beside Caderg (Cadha Dearg, ka'derg) or red pass, which forms the projecting spur between Creag Caorach and Glen Canness. A third way by a steep gully of scree, leads out to Little Glas Maol.

Glen Shee. The longest of the southern glens of Angus or Perth, Glen Shee via Glen Clunie formed the chief route in the old days for travellers walking over the Mounth from upper Deeside to the south. Many used it, and like the Cairn o' Mount it was notable in having a hospice at either side of the high crossing: the Spittal of Glenshee and the Seann-spideal in Glen Clunie. The road across the Cairnwell is the highest public road in Scotland at about 670m. For most of its way it follows the line taken by the old military road which was built from Blairgowrie to Grantown in 1750-54. Many people call this a Wade road, but General Wade left Scotland before the 1745 rising. The famous Devil's Elbow, a double bend on the Glen Shee side, has now been bypassed by a wide straight road built in 1972 and 1973.

At the Spittal of Glenshee the old road goes over a fine stone bridge. The glen divides here, with the steep face of Ben Gulabin at the division. The east branch, Gleann Beag or little glen, leads towards Glen Clunie, becoming hemmed in by Creag Leacach, Glas Maol and the hill of the Cairnwell which from here looks a fine peak. The west branch, upper Glen Shee, itself divides 2 kilometres up beside the Dalmunzie Hotel. Its east sub-branch is green Gleann Taitneach (glin'tatnach) or delightful glen, and its west one Glen Lochsie (lochsaidh or black river goddess). Gleann Taitneach runs, steep-sided and craggy, for 8 kilometres up to Loch nan Eun, beyond which a pass at about 790m leads into upper Glen Ey. In Glen Shee and all its side glens, the green hills, the rocky bluffs of varying colour from pink to black, the many fine big burns and the fertile grassy river flats give the scenery a distinctive character and charm. The Forestry Commission have planted up many of the rolling moorland and smooth low heathery hills between Glen Shee and Glen Isla, and eastwards to Glen Prosen. Glen Shee you will find much more rocky, like the nearby hill country of Strath Ardle. There are no high hills in this countryside, but a great variety of interesting moorland and low hills, many of which carry small crags.

Glen Clunie. The fertile green ridge of Strone Baddoch (sron or nose) separates the Baddoch Burn from the stream of Uisge Bhruidh that runs beside the road down from the Cairnwell. Below here, Glen Clunie (Gleann Cluainidh or glen at a plain) opens out into a wide green valley, with heathery slopes on both sides running steeply up to high ridges over 750m; it has something of the same open character as the Pass of Drumochter. Only one farm survives from what was once a fairly big farming community in the 19th century, and no one now lives in the glen above Auchallater. Well down the glen, the beautifully made Fraser's Brig carries the old military road which winds pleasantly down the west side of Clunie Water from there to Braemar.

Glen Ey. Glen Ey (glin'ei) drains a large tract of rolling hills stretching from near the head of Glen Baddoch to the Dee west of Braemar. A good cross-country walk goes from the Cairnwell cafe for 8 kilometres over to Loch nan Eun at about 785m, and then 5 kilometres down to Altanour in Glen Ey. At Altanour (Alltan Odhar, altan'ower or dun streamlet), an isolated plantation of larch and spruce conceals a ruined shooting lodge at about 500m. A track runs down Glen Ey from here, passing the weird upright rock of A' Chailleach or the old woman. Further on, the Ey Burn winds sinuously in beautiful dark pools through a grassy flat, and in the lower glen below Auchelie hurries faster through a fine long gorge fringed with trees. There a path leads off the track downhill to the Colonel's Bed, a recess by the Ey Burn where John Farquharson of Inverey or the 'Black Colonel', who was a famous figure in the legends of old Deeside, lay hidden after the Battle of Killiecrankie. Much of the old track has been obliterated by a massive wide bulldozed road, which drops down through scattered birches to where the Allt Connie meets the Ey Burn, just below the fine Falls of Connie. The road from Inverey up Glen Ey has a locked gate just south of the Knock house at 088 888, 8 kilometres below Altanour Lodge.

An Lairig. This fine old route goes by a path up Coire Lairige south-west of the Spittal of Glenshee to a col at 648m, and then as a vehicle track gradually down the glen of Allt Doire nan Eun (dernan'ain as in the name Dirnanean at the foot of the glen), to Enochdhu (10 kilometres, 320m ascent).

CLIMBING

Although plenty of rocks give interesting scrambling and even - at the head of Glen Callater and Caenlochan - some sporting climbs, the routes are mostly rather contrived as you can usually escape along grassy or heathery ground or broken rocks nearby. This is true even above Loch Kander at the biggest cliff in the area (200m); the best buttress there carries many grassy ledges which make climbing indefinite. In winter, however, many corries give plenty of easy but sporting Grade I snow climbs, such as the gullies at Loch Kander. A few other climbs have been done on winter ice on other crags, and some short routes on rock in the north corrie of Glas Tulaichean.

SKIING

The large development of the Glenshee Ski Centre reflects the relative dependability of snow in these hills. There is excellent ski touring over the higher hills and corries, and often down in the glens. The area lends itself to long ski tours starting in one glen and finishing in another, or going along all the tops on one side of a glen, such as from Morrone to An Socach on the west side of Glen Clunie. Particularly good descents with generally wide snow cover are the burn off Carn an Tuirc towards the Cairnwell road, the burns in Glas Choire and Fionn-choire on Glas Maol, off Carn a' Gheoidh into Glen Baddoch, and off Glas Tulaichean towards Glen Lochsie. There are marked ski trails along forest roads at Glen Isla.

FURTHER READING

H.T.Munro *The Cairnwell and Glas Thulachan groups* (Guide Book articles) SMCJ 8, 167.

CHAPTER 11

Ballater and Creag an Dubh Loch

Craigendarroch	402m	365 965
Morven	871m	377 040
The Coyles of Muick	601m	329 910
Broad Cairn	998m	240 815
Cairn Bannoch	1012m	223 825
Brown Cow Hill	829m	221 044

ACCESS
Ballater is the best centre for Creag an Dubh Loch and Lochnagar, and for exploring upper Deeside except the highest parts in the Braemar area. The town stands at 200m altitude near where the two major glens of Glen Muick and Glen Gairn open into the wider strath of Dee. A public road from Ballater goes up the east side of Muick to a car park just short of the Spittal of Glenmuick, and another public road runs halfway up the glen on the west side. A public road runs up Glen Gairn and divides at Gairnshiel, with the left loop heading round to Crathie and the right one going over to Corgarff on Don.

PUBLIC TRANSPORT
Bus: Aberdeen to Braemar via Ballater and Crathie.

ACCOMMODATION AND BOTHIES
Ballater has a wide variety of hotels, boarding houses and other accommodation, as well as cafes. A small boulder bivouac lies in the screes below Central Slabs at Creag an Dubh Loch. Open bothy at Glas-allt-Shiel 276 824 behind main building on east side. Locked hut at Allt-na-giubhsaich 299 858, enquiries to University of Aberdeen's Department of Physical Education, Butchart Recreation Centre, Old Aberdeen.

MAPS
Ordnance Survey 1:50,000 Sheets 37 and 44

The lower hills and big glens in the area are heavily wooded, with a fine variety of river and loch scenery. Here you will find a complex fascinating piece of country where a multitude of low hills and glens generally bars widespread views to the higher Cairngorms and allows only occasional tantalising glimpses of small parts of them. However, the view of Lochnagar is superb and largely uninterrupted, as it rises high above a wide skirt of lower ground on the Balmoral and Abergeldie moors. The head of the glen up from Loch Muick is one of the wilder places in the Highlands, with the massive dark cliff of Creag an Dubh Loch rising far above, one of the most impressive rock walls in Britain. The great moors of the upper Gairn are unusual for their scale and sense of vast space, leading up to Brown Cow Hill and Ben Avon.

GEOLOGY, LANDFORMS AND WILDLIFE

Much of the district lies over hard pink granite, for instance on Craigendarroch, the Pass of Ballater, Creag Ghiubhais, Geallaig, and Culblean with its disused granite quarries. A wide strip of fertile epidiorite runs through Glen Muick and Morven, patches of limestone occur in Glen Gairn, and the green knobbly Coyle at Glen Muick looks unusual due to its magnesium-rich serpentine. Craigendarroch and Creag Ghiubhais are two great lumps of ice-smoothed granite and another good place to see ice-smoothed rock is Cnoc Dubh north of Cambus o' May. Channels that were cut by big rivers roaring off melting glaciers are especially deep at the Burn o' Vat and the Slacks of Glencarvie. The best example of a big glacial mound is at Tom Mor on the flats below Creag Ghiubhais.

The moors support more flowering herbs than in most parts of the region. You see relatively few red deer except on the Glen Muick drainage and Corndavon, and the farmers cannot maintain high sheep stocks on even the lower moors because of the hard winters. The result is that pine, birch and juniper regenerate very well, the most spectacular examples being the dense birch scrub at Muir of Dinnet, and the pines coming in above Coilacriech (keila'chreech) where you will also see one of the highest timber lines in Scotland. A rich variety of pine grows at Coilacriech and Creag Ghiubhais, and of birch in Glen Gairn, Glen Muick and Dinnet. The biggest alder wood in Deeside stands east of Ballater on the north bank of the Dee, and the biggest aspen wood in north-east Scotland at Crathie. Parts of the basin around Morven Lodge are unique in Scotland for their extensive dense scrub of moorland juniper. The very fine oak woods of Ballater and Dinnet contain a varied ground flora and hold interesting summer birds such as the wood warbler. In summer the wild lupins tinge the shingles of Dee a lovely soft blue colour. Down at Dinnet the two fertile, very shallow lochs (greatest depths 3m at Davan and 4m at Kinord) support many waterfowl and a few uncommon insects, and nearby there are interesting marshes for birds beside Ordie and in the varied country of little hills around Braeroddach Loch. The varied and fertile moors of Glen Gairn and Morven are home to great numbers of moorland wading birds, red grouse and mountain hares.

ESTATES

Invercauld has Gairnshiel, Corndavon, Geallaig and Glen Gairn. Dinnet Estate has Culblean, Morven Lodge and Muir of Dinnet. The Deskry side of Morven belongs to Tillypronie, and the east side of Muick to Glen Muick Estate. All these are grouse moors with hill sheep. The Forestry Commission owns Glen Carvie. The Dubh Loch area and Creag an Dubh Loch form part of the White Mounth deer forest run by Balmoral Estate. Deer shooting also takes place on Corndavon and Glen Muick.

HISTORY

Loch Kinord is famous for its prehistoric crannog or artificial island, built for defence; it forms the smaller of the two islands in the north part of the loch. Michie, in his two books *Deeside Tales* and *Loch Kinnord,* and in his more detailed *Records of Invercauld* gave much information on the history of the district. The ring of low hills around Braeroddach carries many ancient cairns, whose history he also described in the book *Loch Kinnord.* The old site of Ballater lay near the east end of the Pass, the new village being a planned one which started only at the end of the 1700s on what was then a moor. Byron, who spent his boyhood in Aberdeen, lived in summer at Ballaterach (bal'aitrich), the farm on the south Deeside road opposite Cambus o' May (kamasa'mei).

THE HILLS

Craigendarroch *(rocky hill of the oak wood)* (402m)
The name comes from Creag an Daraich (kraigin'darich). Ballater's special hill, Craigendarroch is one of the priceless places of Deeside. Although a small hill with only 200m of an ascent, it towers steeply above the north side of the town, whose upper houses and school nestle among the fine woods at the foot. Craigendarroch protrudes as an isolated round mass of granite, with small crags and screes above Ballater and with ice-smoothed bedrock on its summit. The biggest oak wood in Deeside covers the lower one-third of the hill on its Ballater side, above which many self-sown birches and pines grow right to the top.

From Ballater's Square you go 400 metres along the Braemar road and turn right at Craigendarroch Road to the foot of the hill among some grand old oaks. A path zigzags up the hill, with a trend to the left. It continues leftwards, goes right around the hill above the Pass of Ballater and comes back to your starting point by the path that slants up to your right. Roughly at the furthest north-east and south-west points of this circular path, two other paths branch off uphill and meet at the summit. A good way goes up the left track, then right round the north side to the north-east end, up to the top, and down by the south-west end (3 kilometres). The variety of woodland and other scenery is extraordinary and the views very fine. On the north side of the road through the Pass of Ballater rise some steep crags of reddish granite among scattered pine trees, the grand rocks of Creag an t-Seabhaig (kraikin'jooik) or precipice of the hawk (see Climbing). Craig Coillich (from Creag Cailliche, kraig'keilich or witch's rocky hill), rises steeply above Ballater's Dee bridge. A good path goes up through a plantation to the 397m top. Craig Coillich gives a better view of the Cairngorms than does Craigendarroch.

Morven *(big hill)* (871m)
The Gaelic name was Mor-bheinn ('more-vin, often locally 'murr-vin). From lower Deeside, Morven's massive rounded bulk seems far bigger than the Cairngorms, and it towers above the Howe o Cromar to the east. It is the 'Morven of snow' mentioned

by Byron. Unlike the heathery hills around, Morven looks much greener and more grassy, as it lies on the long strip of fertile epidiorite rock which runs from Portsoy on the Moray Firth through Glen Muick into Perthshire.

The direct way from Ballater to this Corbett starts up the Tullich Burn. At the east end of the Pass of Ballater at 376 972 the right of way slants north-east through a plantation up the side of Creagan Riach; beyond there the route goes through natural pines by the Tullich Burn and heads past the ruined farm of Easter Morven to the top of Morven (7½ kilometres, 670m ascent). For a second route with the same distance and height, you can visit the old churchyard of Tullich with its sculptured stones and then take the track east of Crannach Hill. A third way from beside Ballater starts by the path which climbs from Abergairn near the Bridge of Gairn to the ridge of Craig of Prony. Round the west end of Peter's Hill it continues as a vehicle track coming from the west end of the rocks in the Pass of Ballater, and goes on over Tom Garchory to the east-west track running south of Morven.

On the Cromar side, the top of Morven stands only 6 kilometres and 500m in ascent from the highest point (370m) on the public road from Logie Coldstone ('kole-stin) to Boltenstone ('bowtinsteen or 'bowteez), near some artificial lochs. This public road, locally called the Birk Hill Road, takes a low line over the hills, cutting over to the east of the old drove road of Bad Chrasgaigh ('chraskie) which crosses the west side of Craig Glas over to Deskry Water at Badnagoach.

The shortest route to Morven starts at 411 043 on a public road in Cromar. From the deserted farm of Balhennie a path goes south-west up to 520m by the Coinlach Burn. From there the summit stands 2 kilometres to the north-west (4 kilometres, 650m ascent).

From the top of Morven you can descend easily westwards into the beautiful lonely green basin around Morven Lodge, and then down Glen Morven to the public road (7 kilometres) at Lary in Glen Gairn. Another interesting way down passes over Culblean to the extraordinary rocky gorge of Allt na Dabhaich, translated as the Burn o' Vat (7 kilometres from Morven to the public road). This takes you down to the Muir (locally meer) of Dinnet with its fine birch scrub and its pair of lovely lochs. Perhaps the best way back is to walk westwards along the watershed to the big jubilee cairn on Mona Gowan and beyond over Scraulac to the 551m top of the public road over the Glas-choille (9 kilometres). From this watershed, at first you look down north-east into Deskry and over the fertile green grazing of the Bunzeach ('boony-ach), now partly afforested, towards Strath Don. Further on this route takes you past the unusual rocky gap at the Slacks of Glencarvie. According to Grant's *Legends of the Braes o' Mar*, the old name was Sloc Cailliche after the supernatural old woman Cailleach Bheathrach, who bit out the Sloc with her teeth while trying to cut a way through for the water on the Don side to flow south into Dee! About one kilometre west of the Slacks, beyond Mona Gowan, you look south down Glen Fenzie (Fion-naidh, 'fingee or white one) to the birches of Gairnside. Glen Fenzie was an old short-cut for drovers going from Corgarff via Lary to Ballater.

The Coyles of Muick (601m)

The OS map errs here, as local people use the 'Coyles (pronounced keils) of Muick' to refer to the whole range of hills so obvious from Ballater, and not just the highest one as on the OS map. The highest is simply The Coyle (601m), a curious peak with knobbly bosses of serpentine and a dark green vegetation. The middle hill in the view from Ballater forms the steep dome of Craig of Loinmuie (lin'mooee), the third one being Meall Dubh. A good way to The Coyle starts from upper Glen Muick, where you can easily climb for 2½ kilometres up from the road at 328 891. It makes a fine walk to go the 4 kilometres along the whole hill range, finishing on Creag Phiobaidh at the east entrance to Glen Girnock. Alternative ways up are by the vehicle track passing just west of Loch Ullachie ('yoolachee) to the top of the ridge, or by the forest track going from the road bridge at 346 936 near Birkhall (locally birk'ha) straight up the burnside to the top of the wood near Meall Dubh.

Cairn Leuchan

The old Mounth Road called the Mounth Keen starts at the memorial at about 210m beside the Bridge of Muick near Ballater and runs as a private road past Ballintober and then as a rough track up the north slope of Cairn Leuchan ('loochan) on the east side of Glen Muick. On Cairn Leuchan you are on the edge of a huge sweep of rolling peaty high moorland and whalebacked hills. A bulldozed track goes south downhill from Cairn Leuchan to cross the headwaters of Tanar towards Mount Keen. Another bulldozed track heads south-west of Cairn Leuchan along the watershed almost on to Fasheilach and down Druim Cholzie to the burn south-west of the Linn of Muick.

Broad Cairn (998m)
Cairn Bannoch (1012m)

These two Munros are easily climbed as a pair. Broad Cairn is a heathery, stony, granite hill, strikingly different from the green grassier hills of Callater and Glen Doll on the more fertile schists away to the west and south. The easiest way to its conical summit is from Loch Muick, via the bulldozed track from Spittal of Glen-muick along the east side of the loch and up to Allan's Hut at 700m. The track continues up to 860m and a path carries on most of the way to the top (from the Spittal 9½ kilometres, 620m ascent).

The most interesting route to the Broad Cairn goes by the Dubh Loch. To the west of Glas-allt-Shiel a path goes along Loch Muick, then past the rocky shelves and pools of Allt an Dubh-loch up to the Dubh Loch at 638m (3 kilometres, 240m ascent). As you ascend this path, you pass the Stulan (Gaelic Steallan, 'styoolan) or little cataract, a burn that tumbles down from the hidden Loch Buidhe, lying high above and behind a precipitous face to the north. On the south side, beyond high clumps of birch, some jagged spurs, bluffs and slabs lead up to the stony cone of the Broad Cairn, but the finest feature by far stands north-west of this, where a huge slabby wall of granite cliff rears abruptly above the Dubh Loch. Dubh Loch ('doo loch) or black loch is a good name, as this high wall facing north-east keeps out much of the sun from the loch. Queen Victoria's son the Duke of Edinburgh once swam out into the dark loch after a wounded stag and killed it in the cold water.

Morven seen from the east across the Muir of Dinnet

Broad Cairn from Glas-allt-Shiel

The great wall above the loch is Creag an Dubh Loch or, as local folk call it, the Craigs o the Dubh Loch; hence the correct Gaelic spelling should perhaps be Creagan Dubh-loch. With a vertical height of 270m at one point, and most of the 1½ kilometre line of cliff rising for around 200m, here stands the highest continuous rock face in the Cairngorms and one of the highest in Britain. The north slope above the Dubh Loch also looks striking, with a big sunny wall of undercut slabs called Eagle's Rock (from Gaelic Creag na h-Iolaire) lying to the south-west of a 1051m top, and a fine waterfall leading to the plateau of the White Mounth behind. The waterfall's local name is The Piss o the Coire Boidheach. The west half of Creag an Dubh Loch is split by the wide scree shoot of Central Gully, locally called the Black Spout (pronounced spoot). It slants up to the plateau and for a walker makes a fine approach to the top, with no difficulty if you are used to crossing the bouldery screes so common in the Cairngorms. The right-hand side of the gully consists of a spectacular wall of steep, smooth and slabby rock, where some of the hardest climbs have been pioneered.

From the Dubh Loch you can walk easily into the upper basin of Coire Uilleim Mhoir or muckle Willie's corrie which lies to the west of the big cliffs. Easy walking then follows to the top of Broad Cairn (from Glas-allt-Shiel 7½ kilometres, 600m ascent). From Coire Uilleim Mhoir, a gentle climb leads south on to the green top of Cairn Bannoch, 2½ kilometres from the east end of the Dubh Loch (370m ascent). Its name comes from Carn Beannach (kairn'byanich) or peaked hill. Once there, you are on a plateau of crisp herbage leading easily for nearly one kilometre west to the 1000m Fafernie (fi'fernie), or east-south-east for 2 kilometres to Broad Cairn past the 983m top above the cliffs of Creag an Dubh Loch. This high well-vegetated plateau, with excellent walking on springy turf, runs for miles south-west to Glas Maol and south-east to the hills on the south side of Glen Doll.

Brown Cow Hill (829m)

The vast moors of the upper Gairn are dominated by the great brown heathery whaleback of A' Bho Dhonn or the Brown Cow, locally the Broon Coo with no 'Hill' as on the OS map. A snow wreath lasts far into the summer on its south face, and local folk call it the Broon Coo's White Calf. The hill - a Corbett - has a big summit plateau with short, wind-clipped vegetation. The finest approach is from Gairnshiel via Corndavon Lodge, but the shortest route leaves the A939 road near Cockbridge Farm and goes up a vehicle track which ends at 630m, south of Carn Oighreag. From here, easy slopes lead south-west to the summit and its plateau (6½ kilometres, 430m ascent). Beyond to the west stands Meikle Geal Charn ('muckle'geliharn), where fine views open out across Glen Builg to Ben Avon. One can easily descend from there to a vehicle track which runs down to Delnadamph and so back to the public road at the Cock Bridge.

WALKING IN THE GLENS

Glen Gairn.   One of the longest glens in the Cairngorms from its source south-west of Ben Avon to its exit at Ballater, Glen Gairn is beautiful, varied and contains many fine lower hills, moors and scrubby woods rich in wildlife. It now looks sadly depopulated, and the many ruins of old farms and shielings give the glen some of its lonely atmosphere. Narrow in its lower reaches, with many birch woods, it widens higher up into a broad glen among open moors and gently sloping far hills.

The old drove road called the Glas-choille ('glas-chil or green wood), now a public road, runs from Gairnshiel up the Shenval brae to Strath Don. A continuation of it to the south of Gairnshiel, the Sron Ghearraig (stron'yarik), goes from Braena-loin up the hill nose and over the top to Crathie. On the Gairn side of the Sron Ghearraig pass there stands an old cairn on the Strone, Meggie McAndrew's Cairn, where a young woman died in a snowstorm, returning to the Newton of Crathie. Sheep drovers still used the route from Tomintoul past Loch Builg to Corndavon and Crathie as recently as the early 1900s, often stopping for the night at Blairglass farm. Other fine old drove roads passing from upper Gairn to Don are the Camock from Gairn at Easter Sleach to the north over Tom Odhar to the A939 west of Corgarff (8 kilometres, 290m climb), and the Ca from the Gairn at Tullochmacarrick to Delavine and Corgarff (8 kilometres, 270m climb). From near the highest point on the Sron Ghearraig, a vehicle track climbs to the 743m top of Geallaig ('gyaalik, no 'Hill' as on the maps), a fine viewpoint. Its south-east slopes, which now support natural young pine woods, make an interesting descent to Bridge of Gairn.

Glen Muick. This fine glen, locally called glin'mek ('e' as in her) is narrow and wooded with old birch and young plantations lower down. Beyond the fine fall at the Linn of Muick, where a salmon ladder allows fish to get up, it becomes wider and more open. A public road runs up the east side to a car park just before the Spittal of Glenmuick at 411m. Walkers and cyclists, but not cars, are permitted beyond here. In ancient times, the Spittal was a hospice for travellers crossing the Capel Mount (Chapter 13). Beside the house at the Spittal, the rough road to Allt-na-giubhsaich and Lochnagar turns sharply right. Straight ahead, a dirt road continues for 1½ kilometres to Loch Muick. On the way to the loch the Capel Mount track over to Clova slants uphill to the left, a former path which is now a bulldozed track.

Ahead, another bulldozed track which obliterated yet another fine old path now skirts along the lochside through fine groves of birch, crosses the Black Burn, and zigzags up to the plateau beyond. It then runs along the plateau, in places almost on the edge of the steep drop to Loch Muick. This road goes over the col south of Corrie Chash, beside Allan's Hut at 7½ kilometres from the Spittal of Glenmuick; beyond, a path continues, dropping south down the Style Burn to Bachnagairn. However, instead of using this bulldozed track, a better way for the walker is to take the old path that starts at the Black Burn and then goes along Loch Muick. At the top of the loch, 6 kilometres from the car park at the Spittal, one branch turns round and over to Glas-allt-Shiel. The other goes in a long slanting climb up the Diagonal Path to meet the bulldozed track on the plateau.

Loch Muick at 400m is a fine sheet of water lying in a narrow trench between the hills. Steep slopes with some crags rise from the lochside to the plateaux above, and in this respect it has something of the character of Gaick. In places the ravines and screes run right into the water. Loch Muick consists of a long, broad basin with water up to 83m deep, held back at its north end by a barrier of glacial gravel which is

Creag an Dubh Loch from the Dubh Loch

Climbers on Cougar, Creag an Dubh Loch

topped by a thick blanket of peat. Covering 220 hectares, 3½ kilometres long and up to 800m wide, with an average width about 600-700 metres, Loch Muick excels as the biggest loch of the Cairngorms and the Mounth, and also one of the most beautiful ones. Glas-allt-Shiel, a private lodge 4 kilometres from Allt-na-giubhsaich and 6 kilometres from the car park at the Spittal, was built by Queen Victoria in 1869. It is sheltered by a pine plantation, with a very high stone wall that kept out the deer when the trees were young. The Shiel stands on ground thrown into the loch by the Glas Allt or green burn which bursts tempestuously from a ravine behind. Queen Victoria used to like to spend a night or two here in Qctober, preferably when the hills were white with the first snow of winter. Glas-allt-Shiel has undoubtedly one of the most spectacular situations of any lodge in the Highlands. From the Shiel a road runs all the way down the west side of Glen Muick past Inchnabobart to the public road near Birkhall.

The first pitch of Theseus Grooves

CLIMBING

Creag an Dubh Loch forms the highest and longest continuous wall of rock within the area described in this book. As this cliff faces north-east and the granite is steep and smooth, the climbing is mostly hard. In recent years it and the Loch Avon cliffs have become the main centres for exploration of new hard climbs. Yet the first pioneer, G.R.Symmers, came here only in the late 1920s, and not much was done until the early 1950s. As Creag an Dubh Loch is not a high-altitude cliff, it is (by Cairngorms standards) a warm and sunny crag, in summer at least, and is primarily a summer rather than winter climbing ground.

The very steep western section is separated from the highest wall of cliff by the wide boulder-filled *Central Gully*, which slants back at an angle and makes an easy route to the plateau, providing magnificent views of the cliffs. The high precipice to its left carries an impressive curving black couloir going from top to bottom, the *Labyrinth Groove*, which offers a very hard winter route (Grade V). To its left again and high up lies an obvious hanging green hollow called the *Hanging Garden* (an excellent snow and ice climb in winter), with the vegetated Broad Terrace leading from it across and then slanting down to the foot of South-East Gully to its left. *Labyrinth Direct*, following the Labyrinth couloir throughout, makes a grand Grade V ice climb, 'one of the most demanding in the Cairngorms, and with negligble protection' (Climbers' Guide). Above Broad Terrace towers the very steep Broad Terrace Wall, one of the most imposing cliffs in the Cairngorms. The climb of *Culloden* (E3) goes up a series of overhangs in the centre of the face and excels as an outstanding hard ascent. The *Sword of Damocles* (E1) is a superb corner line on the left of this wall, up a large rock fault which looks prominent even from Loch Muick. Other climbs on this face are all very hard. The 135m *Flodden* (E5), starting to the left of Culloden and slanting leftwards across the face, took two days on the first ascent.

Further to the west of Labyrinth, towards Central Gully, stretches a huge wall of smooth slabs called the Central Slabs. The VS *Dinosaur*, first climbed in 1964, starts on the left side of the lowest slabs and goes up by slabs and cracks on fine clean rock. The ascent of *Blue Max* (HVS) in 1967 forced a more direct line up the slabs, starting just to the right of Dinosaur. Another route here, the *Dragon Slayer* (E4), passes up a stepped series of corners just to the right of and at a few places actually on Blue Max, taking a central line through the main overlap. The most popular climbs are the classic *Black Mamba* (VS) to the right of Dragon Slayer, Blue Max, and a combination of the lower half of Dinosaur with the top half of *Pink Elephant* (VS), so called from the pink streak and groove which the lower part of the route follows on the left of the Central Slabs. The *White Elephant* is a winter ascent of Pink Elephant, and gives a superb ice route (Grade V).

To the west of Central Gully rises Central Gully Wall, with a massive wide slabby face on the centre and right, a narrower overlapping wall above the bottom of Central Gully, and a series of steep aretes on crags starting further up the gully. High on these uppermost cliffs rises the short climb of *Sabre Edge* (Hard Severe). *Vertigo Wall* (VS) goes up a recessed scoop in the higher and wider 160m wall rising from further down Central Gully, and recognisable by its scar from a rockfall. *The Giant* (E3), which starts about 30m down Central Gully from Vertigo Wall, 'climbs the lowest of the three great corner systems, an impressive slash in the fiercest section of the wall' (Climbers' Guide). Other magnificent routes are *The Naked Ape* (E5) up the big arete to the right of the Giant, and *Cougar* (E2) starting at the right side of the wall and curving left through the overlapping roofs above. Between Vertigo Wall and The Giant, another excellent climb is *Goliath* (HVS).

The huge overlapping slabs rising above the bottom of Central Gully were first climbed in 1958, up *Waterkelpie Wall* (E1), which starts from the lowest rocks to the right of the foot of Central Gully and swerves intricately up to the cliff top. The outstanding breakthrough of the 1950s was *The Mousetrap,* a VS exposed route with entirely free climbing from the foot of Central Gully directly to the plateau. The Mousetrap is one of the best climbs of its grade in the whole massif; sustained but at no point very hard, it goes right to the top of the cliff on grand rock. Since then, several magnificent climbs have been made on the Central Gully slabs, such as *King Rat* (El) and *Predator* (HVS). King Rat goes up a series of cracks straight up the frontal face to the left of Waterkelpie Wall and to the right of The Mousetrap. Creag an Dubh Loch has become justly famed for its many excellent hard rock climbs on clean, sound, steep granite up a massive slabby face. To the right of the slabs, beyond the left-tilting False Gully, *Falseface* (E2) is a fine climb up the wall. Beyond North-West Gully a stretch of pink slabs gives short but good climbs, varying from HVS to E3.

On the opposite side of the Dubh Loch soars Eagle's Rock, a steep slabby mass of granite. Ignored in earlier years, it nevertheless sports up to 150m of clean, south-facing rock. Hard summer routes (mostly VS or harder) have been made. There are some fine winter routes on ice, including up the frozen waterfall. As the wall faces south it thaws early, but in hard frost gives excellent ice climbing with some impressive icefalls.

On the north side of the Pass of Ballater, Creag an t-Seabhaig offers fine, though short climbs on a steep rock wall in the midst of beautiful scenery. There are many routes of all grades of difficulty up to E6 on rough, pink granite. The crag faces south above the road through the pass and is very sheltered behind the bulk of Craigen-darroch to the south and among pine trees growing all around. See the SMC Climbers' Guide *North-East Outcrops,* to be published in 1993, for more detail.

SKIING

This area generally gets good snowfalls, so ski touring can be superb in most winters. The hills are suited to light Nordic skis, but ski-mountaineering techniques includ-ing ice axe and crampons may well be needed on steeper ground such as the splendid runs off Cairn Bannoch or from the Broad Cairn down to the Dubh Loch or Corrie Chash. Good places for descents on other hills are down the east side of Morven towards Groddie, and from Cairn Leuchan into the Pollagach Burn.

FURTHER READING

A.Bremner *The Vat (Burn of the Vat).* CCJ 8, 85.

G.Duncan *The Broad Cairn range* (Guide Book article) SMCJ 8, 49.

CHAPTER 12

Dark Lochnagar

Lochnagar	1155m	244 861
Carn a' Choire Bhoidheach	1118m	227 846
Carn an t-Sagairt Mor	l047m	208 843
Meikle Pap	980m	260 861
Conachcraig	865m	285 872

ACCESS, PUBLIC TRANSPORT, ACCOMMODATION AND BOTHIES
Lochnagar is best approached from the public roads on Deeside to Spittal of Glenmuick, Balmoral village south of Crathie, Invercauld Bridge east of Braemar, and Auchallater south of Braemar. See Chapters 2 and 11 for more detail, and Chapter 11 for bothies. In addition, there is a bothy at Gelder Shiel at 257 900. A bivouac at 252 864 under a boulder in the north-east corrie holds three people.

MAPS
Ordnance Survey 1:50,000 Sheets 43 and 44

One of the grandest hills in Scotland, Lochnagar at once surpasses all other hills in North-east Scotland for its variety and its fine setting. Look at it from east of Ballater on a spring day, or from the Old Bridge of Dee east of Braemar. It soars far above a complex mass of lower hills, wooded slopes and glens. It has so many tops that it forms a small hill range rather than a single big hill. Behind its Ballater face, the vast plateau of the White Mounth stretches for miles to the west and south. It runs out to the great walls of granite above the Dubh Loch and the fine snowy Coire Loch nan Eun above the grand pine forest of Ballochbuie. Best of all, the great cliffs of the cold granite wall in its north-east corrie - the Corrie of Lochnagar - sparkle with snow and ice far into the spring.

GEOLOGY, LANDFORMS AND WILDLIFE

The virgin rock is a greyish-pink granite, as one can see after a fresh rockfall, but gradually darkens because of lichen growth. On the lower hills of Balmoral Forest to the north of Lochnagar, granite boulders are unusually abundant for such low altitudes. The ravine of Clais Rathadan on the way up from Allt-na-giubhsaich is a very good example of a dry defile once cut by a powerful glacial meltwater river. Snow occasionally lies all the year round in Coire Loch nan Eun of the White Mounth but not in most years. Yet an old legend says:

> When ye White Mounth frae snow is clear
> Ye day of doom is drawing near

suggesting a colder climate than today.

Because of the influence of the schist around the main mass of Lochnagar granite, the hill has a more fertile soil than ground on the pure granite of the Cairngorms. Vegetation is slightly richer, and hill birds and mammals more abundant. Some rare arctic-alpine plants grow on damp shady places in the two north-facing corries, such as blue sow thistle, Highland cudweed and brook saxifrage, and rare sedges on the summit plateau. Big tracts of high alpine grassland and gravelly barrens occur, and the mountain azalea thrives more commonly here than on most Scottish hills, its pink flowers making a bright show in June on bare exposed ground. Lochnagar is one of the best hills in Scotland for abundance of ptarmigan, which often perch and take off on song flights from pinnacles on the buttresses.

Ballochbuie Forest contains the largest continuous block of very old pines in the Highlands; Abernethy covers a bigger area but consists mostly of much younger trees. Unlike the natural forests of Rothiemurchus, Glen More and Abernethy of Spey, it has not been felled in the last 150 years and no big fire has burned in this century. However, the forest has been slowly dying because red deer have eaten all young seedlings for the last century. In recent decades Balmoral Estate have fenced off several areas where pines are regenerating well, for instance on the hillside at the north-west corner, to the west of Craig Doin, and a big tract south of the woods of Garmaddie. A 7½-kilometre deer fence was erected in 1992, with stiles at path crossing points.

ESTATES

Most of Lochnagar belongs to Balmoral Estate (bil'more-il). Invercauld has the Callater side all the way up to Carn an t-Sagairt Mor. Glen Girnock and the moor above Lochnagar Distillery are on Abergeldie Estate.

HISTORY

Many artists have been fascinated by the beautiful shapes of Lochnagar, like G.F.Robson who, in his *Scenery of the Grampian Mountains* (1814), gave three etchings of it, and John Phillip who painted Lochnagar as a background in his portrait of the Prince Consort. More famous is Byron's verse, later set to music and ending with the stirring lines:

> England! thy beauties are tame and domestic
> To one who has roved o'er the mountains afar:
> Oh for the crags that are wild and majestic!
> The steep frowning glories of dark Lochnagar!

When a boy of 15, Byron climbed Lochnagar from Invercauld by the Garbh Allt, accompanied by a gillie (see *Byron and Deeside: the facts and the legends,* by J.D.Symon 1924, Deeside Fld 2). Queen Victoria, who loved the hills of upper Deeside, often wrote about Lochnagar in her *Leaves from the Journal of our Life in the Highlands,* and in 1878 she bought Ballochbuie Forest which had been about to be felled. She commemorated its saving by having a cairn built on Craig Doin (pronounced dein) overlooking the beautiful forest, with an inscription recording the purchase and ending 'The Bonniest Plaid in Scotland', from the old legend that McGregor, the last laird of Ballochbuie, had sold it to Farquharson of Invercauld for a tartan plaid. She also had cairns built on several other low hills between Ballochbuie and Crathie in memory of members of her family, the biggest being the large pyramid to Prince Albert on Creag Lurachain south of Crathie. The track at the head of Feith Laoigh to the west of Gelder Shiel goes to the Prince's Stone, which marks the spot where the Prince Consort once spent a night in the open. In those days, when most people spoke Gaelic on upper Deeside, Gelder Shiel was called Ruighe na Ban-righ or shiel of the Queen. Victoria fostered Highland piping at Balmoral, and the tradition lived on, as some of the finest pibroch pipers of Scotland in recent decades have been Balmoral deer stalkers.

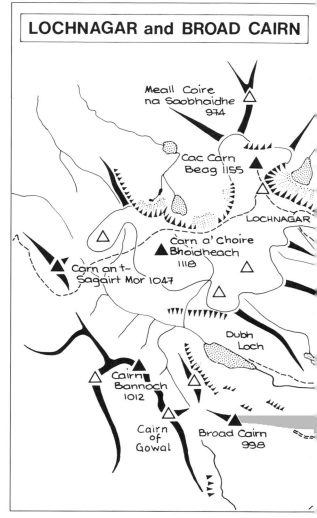

NAMES

The name Lochnagar properly belongs to the small loch at the foot of the north-east corrie, which is marked L. Garr in the map in Blaeu's *Atlas* (1654). A little to the south of L. Garr, the Atlas shows a hill Ben Chichnes. The same name in the forms Benchichins or Binchinnan appears in other early accounts, referring to the range between Aberdeenshire and Angus. Clearly it is an anglicised version of the Gaelic

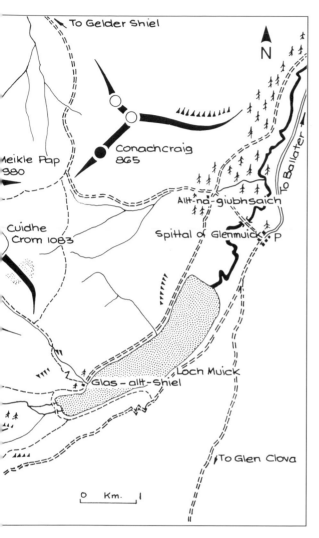

To Gelder Shiel

N

Conachcraig 865

Meikle Pap 980

Cuidhe Crom 1083

Allt-na-giubhsaich

Spittal of Glenmuick P

To Ballater

Loch Muick

Glas-allt-Shiel

To Glen Clova

0   Km.   1

Beinn Chiochan or hill of paps. This tallies with the names the Meikle Pap and the Little Pap which still survive. In 1771 Pennant mentions Laghin y Gair, and much later Byron wrote his well known poem *Lachin y Gair*. The name Lochnagar comes from Lochan na Gaire or the lochan of the noisy sound. Some names of individual tops are confusing on the OS map, which absurdly gives Cac Carn Beag or little shit cairn for the summit, and Cac Carn Mor for the 1150m top on the plateau. The name for the summit should be Cadha Chuirn Mor or big steep of the stony hill, whereas Cadha Chuirn Beag is the little point to the west-north-west at 241 863, so prominent in the view from Ballater or Crathie. The big plateau to the south-west is the White Mounth (pronounced munth), in Gaelic formerly Am Monadh Geal.

THE HILLS

Lochnagar *(lochan of the noisy sound)* (1155m)

The usual route from Ballater starts at the Spittal of Glen Muick and from Braemar at Auchallater, but to see the hill best you should climb one way and go down the other, by a path all the way. The estates allow free access to the top by these routes, although neither is a right of way.

From Glen Muick. For roads up Glen Muick, see Chapter 11. A car park lies just north-east of the Spittal of Glenmuick (411m). From the car park a rough private road goes 1½ kilometres north-west to Allt-na-giubhsaich, a shooting lodge in a plantation. Distance: from Allt-na-giubhsaich to summit 7½ kilometres, ascent 800m. The name here comes from the nearby burn of Allt na Giubhsaich or stream of the pine wood. The Lochnagar path starts at the bridge over the burn and goes up its south bank to join a bulldozed track which goes from the lodge up the south bank and later crosses to the north bank on the line of the old path. From here you look up to the bouldery 956m cone of the Little Pap, formerly Cioch Bheag. To the

Lochnagar

right it leads on to the big flat mass of the Cuidhe Crom (kooee'krome) or crooked wreath, named after a snow field which lies late into the summer on the steep grassy face north of the 1083m top. Further to the right rises the prominent big cone of the Meikle Pap (locally the Muckle Pap, and formerly A' Chioch Mhor). The track curves above the curious gorge of Clais Rathadan (locally klash'vrotan), and then continues further to a col at 678m where you look down Glen Gelder and over to Ben Avon. Here the bulldozed track carries on north to Gelder and the Lochnagar path turns west uphill.

The path heads towards the gap between the Meikle Pap and Cuidhe Crom, passing the Fox Cairn Well, locally called the Foxes' Well. Just before the gap ahead, the path starts to zigzag leftwards up a steeper slope called the Ladder. A detour here to the gap or to the Meikle Pap at 980m shows the magnificent crescent of crags in the Corrie of Lochnagar at its best, with the dark loch far below. You can walk horizontally back along the slope from the gap to regain the zigzag path of the Ladder, and so climb up to the plateau above. The route continues a little back from the cliff top past the 1045m col at the Red Spout (locally spoot), a wide open scoop of reddish gravel where you can easily descend to the loch in late summer. The path now rises to the higher plateau of Cac Carn Mor at a cairn on a small tor at 1150m, where the path from Callater comes in on the left. On the way along the high plateau just before Cac Carn Mor, you will enjoy diverging to the right, to wander along the

The central part of Lochnagar's corrie between Douglas-Gibson and Raeburn's gullies

cliff top. The plateau projects out in a few places which give magnificent views down and along the cliffs on either side. The old name for these grand cliffs was Creagan Lochan na Gaire or crags of Lochnagar. You look across to the Black Spout (locally spoot), largest gully in the corrie, which carries a snow cornice in spring but in late summer becomes an easy wide shoot of scree. At their highest the cliffs fall 210m, and screes run steeply below to the loch at about 785m.

From the cairn at Cac Carn Mor a small dip follows to the head of the Black Spout and then a short stroll over flattish ground up to the 1155m summit at Cac Carn Beag, which protrudes as a great mass of granite weathered into gigantic blocks. On a flat slab close to the highest point stands the indicator built by the Cairngorm Club in 1924. It shows in the north the Caithness hills, in the east Girdleness Lighthouse at Aberdeen harbour, in the west Ben Nevis (with binoculars you can easily see the Great Tower on Tower Ridge), and in the south Ben Lomond, the Pentland Hills and Lammermuirs, and Cheviot on the English border 174 kilometres away.

From Callater. Distance: from Loch Callater to the summit 10 kilometres, ascent 760m. You can walk or cycle the 5 kilometres on the private road up to Loch Callater (see Chapter 10). The Lochnagar path starts up the hillside just before the lodge beside Loch Callater at about 500m, and then slants along Creag an Loch, with attractive views down to Loch Callater and the fine corries higher up. From the neck between Creag an Loch and the 1047m Carn an t-Sagairt Mor (kairn tagart'more) or

The view south-west from Lochnagar towards The Stuic above Loch nan Eun

big hill of the priest, the path slants uphill along the south side of the rounded Carn an t-Sagairt Mor and then drops slightly into the green basin at the headwaters of Allt an Dubh Loch. You now climb easily onto the plateau of the White Mounth above 1000m, and a stroll just north of here takes you to the 1093m point of The Stuic (styook, from Gaelic stuc, a projecting hill). This rocky buttress almost divides into two parts the wide western Coire Loch nan Eun (nan'yain) or corrie of loch of the birds. To the south of the path here rises the 1118m Carn a' Choire Bhoidheach (kairna kor'booich) or hill of the beautiful corrie, the highest point of the White Mounth. You now continue along the grand high plateau and finally climb 100m of height to Cac Carn Mor. There you should go east to the cliffs to enjoy the magnificent view which comes suddenly and contrasts with the long walk over the flattish plateau.

As Carn an t-Sagairt Mor and Carn a' Choire Bhoidheach rise close to the Loch Callater path up Lochnagar (above paragraph), they can easily be climbed from that path, either by themselves or en route to Lochnagar. The shortest way to Carn an t-Sagairt Mor is to leave the path at 203 846 where it crosses an old broken-down stone dyke, and then climb alongside the dyke for 600 metres to the top. Carn an t-Sagairt Mor is a big rounded hill with many boulders, rising to a flat top which gives fine views into Glen Callater and over Ballochbuie Forest to the Cairngorms. Carn a' Choire Bhoidheach rises gently about 300 metres south of a 1083m col on the path to the north of it. This smooth top stands at the west end of a big plateau with spacious wide corries. It is also easy to reach Carn an t-Sagairt Mor and Carn a' Choire Bhoidheach from Ballochbuie Forest via the Feindallacher Burn and the Smugglers' Shank (see below).

From Glas-allt-Shiel. Distance: from car park at the Spittal of Glenmuick to Glas allt-Shiel 6 kilometres, to summit of Lochnagar 11 kilometres, ascent 780m. One of the best routes to Lochnagar is by the path that zigzags up the Glas Allt or green burn behind the lodge at Glas-allt-Shiel. Giving grand views, it takes you up a fine steep gorge with broken rocks where the Glas Allt thunders down in foaming falls towards dark Loch Muick. You come out higher up on a peaty plateau at 600m; half a kilometre beyond, the Cross Path turns right, across the burn, and leads above the Monelpie Moss to meet the Allt-na-giubhsaich path between the Meikle Pap and Conachcraig. Your path to Lochnagar summit goes between the Little Pap and Creag a' Ghlais Uillt, straight up the Glas Allt to the top.

Other routes. Allt-na-giubhsaich, Callater and Glas Allt are routes with obvious paths. Other routes such as the one described below make finer ascents, though they lack paths in places and thus are suitable only for those with more experience; ask for permission from the stalkers, as deer stalking may be in progress. For courtesy you should avoid these other routes when the royal family is at Balmoral, usually from mid-August to early October.

From Ballochbuie Forest. Distance: from Old Bridge of Dee (leave cars at the end of the Keiloch road) to the top by Blackshiel Burn 8½ kilometres with ascent of 840m, by Carn an t-Sagairt Beag and The Stuic 11 kilometres. This is one of the most varied approaches. The forest roads, which lead through beautiful natural pine forest, were carefully made in Victorian times; they make a contrast with the ugly bulldozed roads now torn out on the hills. The special character of Ballochbuie, which makes it one of the finest although not the largest area of natural pine wood in Scotland, lies in its many glens and shoulders, some quite steep, where the carpet of pines rises up in places on to the hill crags themselves. Only when you walk right through it do you become fully aware of the rich variety of the forest and its seemingly greater size.

Starting from the west end of the Invercauld Bridge at 185 910, a private road runs past the south end of the Old Bridge of Dee to a cross roads at 188 907. Go straight across, and then straight across the next cross roads at 194 899 by a road that goes to the Falls of Garbh Allt ('garra-walt) or rough burn. An iron bridge spans the Falls of Garbh Allt. Here you will enjoy a wonderful view north down the roaring stream, framed by pine forest, to the Invercauld flats of Dee and beyond to snowy Beinn a' Bhuird.

From the Falls, go back to the road and up it for a short distance to 197 895. Here a bulldozed track starts uphill to the left, snaking far up the Feindallacher Burn (Feith an t-Salachair, fain'dallacher) to about 600m, near where Allt a' Choire Dhuibh flows in. From there you climb easily by a path running up the Smugglers' Shank to 930m,

High up on Eagle Ridge, looking down to the Lochnagar loch

and then breast the shoulder between the two burns on to the 1044m Carn an t-Sagairt Beag. A stroll follows along the plateau to the edge of the cliff and The Stuic.

From Gelder. Distance: from 264 942 at Easter Balmoral to Gelder Shiel 5 kilometres, to the summit by the Lochnagar Burn 10 kilometres. The finest route for seeing the Corrie of Lochnagar starts from Gelder Shiel. At Easter Balmoral south of Crathie, on the south side of Dee, leave your car beside the gravel road east of the shop, and then walk up the private road leading uphill from the shop. It passes through the steep-sided gap of Dubh-chlais ('doo-chlash or dark furrow) between two wooded hills, and then up the moor of Glen Gelder. About one kilometre before the Shiel, a bulldozed track goes straight ahead to 680m altitude, joining on to the one coming from Allt-na-giubhsaich in Glen Muick on the far side of the col. However, the best approach from Gelder is to walk up the Lochnagar Burn to the loch, a route which brings the grand corrie ever nearer and more spectacular. You can then reach the top by the scree shoot of the Black Spout, or by the easy bouldery ridge of the Sneck o Lochnagar just west of the corrie cliffs. Avoid the slope further west, immediately to the north and north-east of the summit, where dangerous wet slabs shelve away precipitously and a convex steep slope to the east often becomes prone to snow avalanches. If you intend to return from the summit by Ballochbuie, you should bypass this steep section by first heading half a kilometre west-north-west from the summit, and then either descend north to the 974m Meall Coire na Saobhaidhe or else go down the Blackshiel Burn or over the nearby Meall an Tionail (mil'tshainil) or lump of the gathering.

The Corrie of Lochnagar or north-east corrie has been described above. The west corrie or Coire Loch nan Eun shows a different character, less dramatic but nevertheless beautifully remote and arctic-like with its great snow fields and high blue lochans. Loch nan Eun lies at just under 900m, below the rocky promontory of The Stuic, and is the summer home for an unusually high-nesting colony of common gulls. Round the corner to the west hide two tiny lochans, the larger called Lochan na Feadaige and the smaller Lochan Tarmachan, meaning lochan of the golden plover and lochan of ptarmigan respectively. The Sandy Loch lies to the north at just over 790m. Across the plateau south-east of The Stuic stretches the high, shallow, green Coire Boidheach or beautiful corrie, a favourite haunt of hinds and their young calves in late summer. To the east of the Dubh Loch, Coire an Loch Buidhe drains into the secluded, hanging tarn of Loch Buidhe (locally Lochan Buidhe). On the north of Lochnagar, Coire na Saobhaidhe ('sivee) and further north the Glas Choire are small corries in the complex, rough terrain between the summit and Gelder Shiel.

Conachcraig (865m)
The name of this hill in Gaelic is Conachreag ('konnachraig) meaning high rocks or combination of rocks. A rough bouldery hill with small cliffs and three summits, Conachcraig rises east of Lochnagar on the west side of Glen Muick, and is so big that it often blocks some views of Lochnagar. It looks especially fine from above the Linn of Muick. The usual way to Conachcraig is from the car park near Spittal of Glenmuick, then to Allt-na-giubhsaich, and up the path through the wood on the south side of the burn to join a bulldozed track on to the moor. This continues up to a col at 700m where the Lochnagar path breaks off to the left and a fine view opens out down Glen Gelder to the eastern Cairngorms. From here it is an easy climb to the top of Conachcraig (from the car park 5 kilometres, 470m ascent). There are grand views over to Lochnagar and across Deeside to the Cairngorms.

CLIMBING

The main climbing haunt of North-east Scotland has for long been Lochnagar, where even the 1962 Climbers' Guide recorded 60 routes in the north-east corrie alone. The symmetrical cliffs of Creagan Lochnagar, rising over 200m, have two massive side walls at either end, flanking a central section of cliff. This central part stretches between Douglas-Gibson Gully (obvious on the left half of the cliff, with scree running up it far above the rock on either side) and the great scree shoot of the Black Spout on the right part. Early pioneers in 1893 were Douglas and Gibson, who climbed the Black Spout's Left-Hand Branch, and in 1895 Tough and Brown ascended the Tough-Brown Traverse. The first ascent of Raeburn's Gully was made in 1898.

To the left of the straight gash of Douglas-Gibson Gully rises Shadow Buttress B, with Polyphemus Gully on its left side. The fine winter route of *Polyphemus* (Grade IV) is one of the best gully climbs in Scotland. To its left lies the open face of Shadow Couloir where another grand winter route - *Giant's Head Chimney* (Grade IV) - goes up the right hand of the two chimneys in the couloir. Left again stands the fine winter route of *Shadow Buttress A* and then the Central Buttress which terminates the left or east end of the main wall of crag. *Douglas-Gibson Gully* itself, although unpleasant in summer, makes a magnificent Grade V winter climb. The upper wall frowns very steeply and icily, topped by one of the biggest cornices in the district. To the right of Douglas-Gibson Gully, *Eagle Ridge* (Severe) is one of the best climbs in the country, which takes a defined and sustained line up fine steep granite, at times tapering to a narrow crest; it also makes a magnificent winter route (Grade V).

Along to the right of Eagle Ridge rises *Eagle Buttress*. The next main feature is the popular winter route of *Parallel Gully A* (Grade II-III). On its right, Parallel Buttress (Severe), first climbed in 1939, offers one of the better rock climbs in the corrie and makes an excellent Grade V winter ascent. *Parallel Gully B* shows as a vertical slit further right, one of the best climbs on Lochnagar (VS, Grade V).

To the right of Parallel Buttress, the 210m Tough-Brown face swoops up as an imposing sheet of steep slabby granite. A new standard was set with *Mort* (E1) in 1967, and in 1970 by the even harder nearby *Post Mortem* (E2). From below the centre of the slabs, Mort goes up a groove on the line of a fault tending to slant slightly to the right. The nearby Post Mortem, starting at the same spot, takes a more direct line up the centre of the Tough-Brown face. Several other hard routes have been made on this magnificent face.

Immediately to the right of the Tough-Brown face rises the obvious left-slanting *Raeburn's Gully*. Although wet and loose in summer, in winter it makes a popular Grade II climb, varying in difficulty according to how deeply the snow covers the ice pitches underneath. The far wall beyond Raeburn's Gully forms the crag of *Scarface*. On the Raeburn's Gully side of it rises the extraordinary steep slit of *The Clam* (Hard Severe), a remarkable climb where boulders jam its outer walls.

The next main feature to the west is the huge mass of the Black Spout Pinnacle jutting well out from the main cliff, a fearsome 180m mass of steep slabby granite and one of the most impressive crags in Scotland. *Route 1* avoids the very hard climbing on the lower slabs by slanting back on to the Pinnacle from 50m up the Black Spout, to reach the Springboard, a platform tucked in above the slabs. This route gives beautiful views, and in winter makes a grand, hard, Grade IV ascent. The fine direct line is *Pinnacle Face*, a classic VS route which starts about 10m up the Black Spout from the lowest rocks and joins Route 1 about 30m above the Spring-board. It proved a hard Grade V winter climb. *The Link* (VS) which goes up Pinnacle Face to the Springboard and then by a major new variant on the right side of the face, ranks similar in excellence to Eagle Ridge. Further right still, *Route 2* (Severe) on the Black Spout Pinnacle starts higher up the Black Spout than Route 1 and joins it after an unusual horizontal traverse above the Springboard.

To the right of the Pinnacle, the Left-Hand Branch of the Black Spout diverges from the Black Spout about halfway up and goes straight on to the plateau. An easy gully with a huge chokestone, it featured in Tom Patey's parody:

> Of all the climbs on Lochnagar
> The Black Spout is the best by far
> While from the Ballochbuie
> You can always climb the Stuie
> But the pitch to make the experts blanch
> Is the chokestone in the Left-Hand Branch!

Between the Left-Hand Branch and the Black Spout itself soars the bold buttress of *The Stack,* a popular 150m climb (Hard Severe) with a fine variety of pitches on clean granite in summer, and a Grade IV icy route in winter. *The Black Spout* is a wide easy scree shoot which provides grand views of the cliffs, and in winter makes an easy Grade I snow climb at a 40° to 45° angle. In good conditions it gives a grand glissade. To its right the first buttress is *Black Spout Buttress* (Difficult) which offers a good, steep, but easy climb for a novice on granite. Further to the right, the rocky knob of the Gargoyle protrudes from the plateau rim. The ascent of *Gargoyle Direct* (Very Difficult), which finishes beside the Gargoyle, gives a good summer climb.

In Coire Loch nan Eun to the west of Lochnagar you will see fine corrie and snow scenery but only broken rocks. The jutting nose of The Stuic provides an interesting summer scramble and a Grade I way up to the plateau in winter. Under the summit of Cnapan Nathraichean north-west of Lochnagar, a stretch of bluish-grey slabs at Sleac Ghorm gives several 100m routes on fairly clean rock.

SKIING

Lochnagar is a high steep hill superb for ski-mountaineering, but good for Nordic skis when the snow is not too hard. Ballochbuie Forest makes the most beautiful approach. Excellent descents are down Allt a' Choire Dhuibh, off the White Mounth into Allt an Dubh-loch, down the Blackshiel Burn, into the upper Glas Allt, and from the Little Pap down to Allt na Giubhsaich. Glen Gelder and the Feindallacher area are very good for cross-country skiing. The White Mounth is a particularly snowy area and gives splendid touring over its vast undulating plateau, with spacious views over the hills of Angus into central Scotland. Skiing allows access to see the north-east Corrie of Lochnagar with its magnificent cliffs in prime winter condition – a glittering stupendous wall with frost feathers covering even the steepest rocks.

FURTHER READING

J.G.Michie *The Benchinnans.* CCJ 2, 34.

J.A.Parker *The horizon from Lochnagar.* CCJ 10, 359.

H.Alexander *The Lochnagar indicator: its building and unveiling.* CCJ 6, 53.

H.T.Munro *Dark Lochnagar.* SMCJ 2, 190.

G.Duncan *The Lochnagar group* (Guide Book article). SMCJ 8, 49.

A.G.Hutchison *Lochnagar (its geological history).* Deeside Fld 3, 15.

CHAPTER 13

The Hills of Angus

Driesh	947m	272 736
Mayar	928m	241 738
Ben Tirran	896m	373 747

ACCESS
The higher hills of Angus tend to run in parallel, with a line of hills between any two glens. The glens are long, generally tending to run south-east towards the North Sea. Public roads go up all the main glens. Edzell, Kirriemuir and Blairgowrie are the main centres.

PUBLIC TRANSPORT
Buses run to Edzell from Montrose, to Kirriemuir from Forfar, and to Blairgowrie from Perth.

ACCOMMODATION AND BOTHIES
There are hotels, boarding houses, and bed and breakfast places in Kirriemuir, Edzell and Blairgowrie, and a hotel at Clova in upper Glen Clova which also offers bothy accommodation for climbers. A youth hostel is at Glendoll Lodge at the top of Glen Clova. The Carn Dearg Mountaineering Club hut at 286 758 near Braedownie in Glen Clova holds 12. The Retreat in Glen Esk has a tearoom in summer. At Red Craig beside Braedownie, below the rightmost of the three main sections of cliff, is the Hole o Weems, a cave under boulders slightly left and below the South-East Crag. Jock's or Lunkard Bothy is at 234 777 beside the path of Jock's Road at 700m.

MAPS
Ordnance Survey 1:50,000 Sheet 44

From the broad flat farmlands of Strathmore and the town of Forfar you look up to a fine rampart of hills rising abruptly from the plain. Their old name was Braigh Aonghuis or upland of Angus, and Machair Aonghuis referred to the low plain below. Into the hill massifs cut several long, roughly parallel glens where the rivers flow south-east to the sea, the finest glens being Esk and Clova running into the rivers North and South Esk. Their head streams drain from the great medium-level tableland shared with Lochnagar and the Glen Clunie hills of Aberdeenshire. Glen Clova has its own special character. Such a deep trench was cut here that many crags line its sides. These crags, the steep broken slopes, the bright fertile green of the hillsides, and the farms far up the glen floor, all look very different from most glens in North-East Scotland. Visitors often remark on how Glen Clova resembles the grassy, steep craggy valleys of Argyll or the Lake District. Some of the crags come close to the road, like the spectacular Red Craig on your right just before you reach Braedownie.

GEOLOGY, LANDFORMS AND WILDLIFE

Most of Glen Clova lies over schist, with some gneiss, diorite and epidiorite, rocks that look very different from the granite of nearby Lochnagar. The Clova rock feels smoother, and has many small incut holds that climbers find more reliable than tiny holds on the granite. On the north side of the glen you will see a remarkable series of five hanging corries, two of which have fine corrie lochs at Loch Wharral and Brandy. Glen Clova itself is a great U-shaped trench with steep sides, typical of glacial cutting. The great peaty plateaux which almost encircle Glen Clova and Glen Esk form one of the biggest tracts of medium-level plateau in the Highlands.

The corries of Glen Clova, especially in Glen Doll, contain some of the best-known places for rare arctic-alpine flowers in Britain. They grow best on the fertile crags, up on ledges out of range of sheep and deer, and there the scrub of rare arctic willows is also especially fine. The district has, however, suffered much from the ravages of selfish commercial gardeners and private gardeners and collectors. The best places for rare plants - mainly the corries on the west side of Glen Doll - now form part of the Caenlochan National Nature Reserve which stretches west to Glas Maol. Because of the fertile rocks, the hills look much greener and grassier than in most of our region. Even the heathery parts are richer in other species of flowering plants. Dotterel nest on the high tablelands and dunlin on the peat bogs, and eagle, raven and peregrine on a few remote crags. After being almost extinct, wild cats have greatly increased in the Angus glens, where they are now common. On the low ground of Angus, Strathmore is one of the outstanding places in Britain for wintering wild geese, which come here in thousands. Other grand places for wild duck and geese are the Loch of Lintrathen, the marshy Loch of Kinnordy just west of Kirrie-muir, Duns Dish east of Brechin, and the fine mud-flats of Montrose Basin. Magnificent red sandstone cliffs rise north-east of Arbroath at Red Head.

ESTATES

In Glen Clova, Balmoral has Bachnagairn and the Forestry Commission Glen Doll; both are deer forest. Further down Clova at Rottal and in lower Glen Prosen stretch the grouse moors of Airlie Estate. Much of upper Prosen and the ground on the little glens west towards Glen Isla belongs to the Forestry Commission, which has planted big woods of conifers on the lower slopes. Invermark around Glen Mark and Loch Lee is also deer forest ground, along with Hunthill at the top of Glen Lethnot. Other parts of Glen Esk and Glen Lethnot are grouse moors. Hill sheep graze all the open hill ground.

HISTORY

In the 1880s the owner of Glen Doll tried to close the public path by the Tolmount to Braemar, but the Scottish Rights of Way and Recreation Society successfully fought him, and in 1887 the Court of Session upheld this historic Mounth Road. People then were used to walking straight over the hills to travel from one place to another, instead of driving far around them. On the Lair of Aldararie, a hill reaching 832m in altitude north-east of Braedownie, the local people of Glen Muick used to meet their neighbours from Glen Clova and Glen Esk every year to compete at Highland games on the green near the flat summit. Until recently, when some selfish person removed them, you could still see the stones that they used for 'putting the shot'. In 1973, Jimmy Stewart, then an 88 year-old ex-keeper on Glen Muick, told the writer how he remembered as a boy seeing people walking there to compete. It was in nearby Glen Prosen that Edward Wilson of Antarctic fame

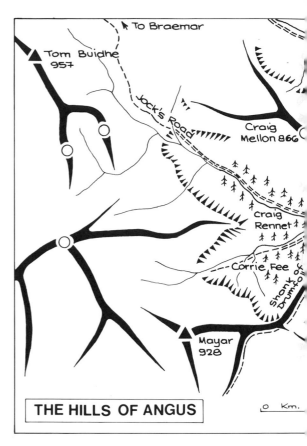

THE HILLS OF ANGUS

wrote some of his scientific works, and here Captain Scott came to discuss with him the ill-fated South Pole expedition. The district has many other interesting associations, described by Fraser (1963). Below the mouth of Glen Lethnot, the road south-east to Brechin passes over a broad ridge between two low hills called the Brown and White Caterthuns, which remain as very fine examples of hill forts from the Iron Age.

THE HILLS

Driesh *(from Dris or bramble thicket)* (947m)
Above Braedownie (bri'doonee), the sharp rocky 766m peak of The Scorrie ('skurrie, from sgor or rocky point) thrusts out boldly as an outlier of Driesh, and looks one of the finest features of Glen Clova. The glen forks at Braedownie, right to Moulzie and upper Glen Clova, left up White Water to Glen Doll, pronounced dole. Craig Mellon stands imposingly between them. If you cross White Water by the bridge at Acharn just east of Glendoll Lodge, you will find The Scorrie a fine ascent. At the

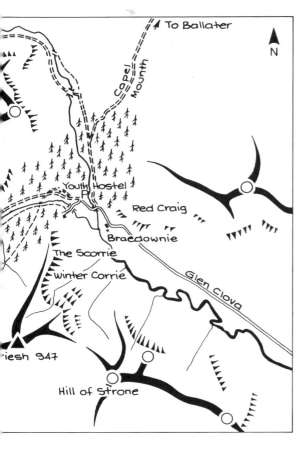

top you skirt the cliffs of Winter Corrie, which is a map error for the local name of Corrie Winter. You can stroll easily from the top of The Scorrie to Driesh (3 kilometres and 690m ascent from Acharn).

A less steep route begins by crossing the bridge half a kilometre south-south-east of Braedownie and goes easily up the open grassy Corrie Farchal between Driesh and Bassies. From the top of the corrie at the Sneck of Farchal at 703m, a fence runs west to Driesh and Mayar, and east and then east-south-east to Cairn Inks. On the Glen Prosen side a vehicle track climbs to the 633m top of Lick immediately south of Driesh, and forest roads up to 570m in altitude south-south-west of Cairn Inks. If you intend to descend from Driesh, or for that matter any of the hills ringing Glen Doll, remember to choose a descent that avoids the dense plantations. Unpleasant at any time, these are very wetting after rain and difficult in darkness.

Mayar (928m)

The 3 kilometres walk from Driesh to Mayar (locally the 'may-yar) takes only an hour as you drop a mere 140m in height between them. You can also climb Mayar directly by the Kilbo path up Corrie Kilbo, but a dense plantation covers the lower slope to about 500m. This path then climbs up to the plateau by the Shank of Drumfollow, which forms the long grassy shoulder that separates Corrie Kilbo from Corrie Fee. An even better way up is to go 1½ kilometres up the road west of Glendoll Lodge, cross the bridge over White Water, and walk up a forest road which leads towards Corrie Fee (from fiadh or deer). A path continues up the plantation to the grassy floor of this grand, extensive corrie. Immediately to the south of the fine waterfall at the top, you can reach the plateau without difficulty and so stroll over to the top of Mayar (5 kilometres from Glendoll Lodge, 650m ascent). On the Glen Prosen side, a vehicle track goes from the ruin of Kilbo at the top of the glen, past Cairn Dye and up to 830m at the fence on the watershed west of the Shank of Drumfollow.

Driesh (right) and Hill of Strone from the Capel Mounth path

From Mayar you look south into the head of Glen Prosen, west into Glen Cally and Glen Isla, and north-east to Glen Doll. A great high tableland stretches north-west and then north, so you can stroll easily to the north-west for 3 kilometres to Dun Hillocks, or for 5 kilometres to Meikle Kilrannoch and then north-east over to the Tolmount path and so back down Glen Doll.

Ben Tirran (896m)

Ben Tirran, pronounced 'turran, is the highest hill on the north side of Glen Clova, rising east of Loch Wharral. The highest point has the old name The Goet ('gote), Ben Tirran being the slightly lower lump on the Clova side to the south-west. From Clova, a path goes up for 3½ kilometres and 620m past Loch Brandy (branduibh or raven-black) to the 870m top of the Green Hill. An easy walk follows along the plateau for 3 kilometres to Ben Tirran, passing on the way the Craigs of Loch Wharral. A short and good way to Ben Tirran is by an old track heading up from Wheen, 4 kilometres below Clova, or slightly shorter by a path starting at 353 715 further up the glen. Both routes join in a path coming out near the summit by the top of a burn where there is a spectacular view down to Loch Wharral at 625m (4 kilometres, 650m ascent).

Once on top, away from the steep glen side, you are standing on a long plateau parallel to the glen, with many tops that rise as mere bumps. To the east and

Loch Brandy, Glen Clova

north-east you will see a great contrast; here the plateau shelves very gradually for miles into remote peaty uplands with meandering streams and twisting lower glens, a difficult country to navigate in when mist and snowstorm conceal the few land-marks. If you start from Ben Tirran or the Green Hill, you can walk easily along this plateau into the wide open valley of Water of Unich ('yoonich) away to the north and north-east, and down to Loch Lee and Glen Esk. The plateau also rolls far to the east across vast high peaty moors into the gentle upper valley of the Water of Saughs and over to Glen Effock. Distance: from the Green Hill to Unich stables 3½ kilometres, to Inchgrundle west of Loch Lee 8 kilometres either by the stables and the Shank of Inchgrundle or else by White Hill, Muckle Cairn and Skuiley; to Loch Lee Kirk at the public road end 12 kilometres.

WALKING

The corries of Glen Clova have great variety and more interest than some of the hills around them. On the north side, Loch Wharral and Loch Brandy are remarkably big corrie lochs in wild cirques with broken crags behind. Further west, the Corrie of Clova forms a fine bowl with faces of broken rock, and round the next corner to the west of Ben Reid, so does the similar Corrie Bonhard (Coire Bun na h-Airde, bon'hard) or foot of the height. On the south side, you will find Winter Corrie well worth a visit. A good way goes straight up the Gourock Burn that leads into its precipitous screes and dark broken rocks. Corrie Fee to the west is the finest of Clova's corries, with beautiful green meadows, waterfalls and long stretches of crags. On the north-west side these end in the bold face of Craig Rennet (745m), round the corner from which the crags of The Dounalt stretch westwards to the next burn. Beyond, the long line of crags continues by Craig Maud (kraig'mad), ending beside the Jock's Road path. At Bachnagairn, one of the most beautiful spots in the area, broken crags lie above the green West Corrie, opposite to the steep cliff of Juanjorge which soars abruptly on the north side. The improbably Mediterranean-looking map spelling seems an obvious anglicisation, and one pronounces it gin'george as in English gin and George.

Glen Esk excels as the loveliest glen of Angus and has some grand wild country for hillwalkers. Its long twisting course surpasses most Highland glens in variety, with fine old birch woods, bright green bracken, open heathery hills, river shingles and linns, and varied hill farms. Higher up stretch vast plateaux with peaty moors, wild glens with rugged cliffs, and high stony hills. At the foot of the glen, above Gannochy Bridge, you leave behind the flat lowland of Edzell and very abruptly enter Highland country. Walk west of the road at 589 728 and turn south, to see one of the finest river gorges in North-east Scotland, where the North Esk hurries through a long, magnificently wooded ravine.

At the top of Glen Esk, beyond the public road end at 261m beside Loch Lee Kirk, private roads continue to the north-west up Glen Mark and westwards past the ruined old Castle of Invermark to Loch Lee and Glen Lee. Both glens are steep and craggy, the 687m Craig Maskeldie being a particularly fine sharp peak as seen from Loch Lee. Immediately west of the Craig lies a fine gorge at the Falls of Unich, where a path takes you up on to the plateau at Falls of Damff, 7½ kilometres from Loch Lee Kirk. You can also reach the plateau from the house of Inchgrundle (Innis Grunndaile or meadow of good foundation), by a bulldozed track which goes up the Shank of Inchgrundle. It continues on the line of the old footpath to the Water of Unich about half-way between the Falls of Damff (damh or stag) and the ruined Unich stables. From Inchgrundle a path also climbs by Skuiley further to the east, right to the top of the 826m Muckle Cairn, which in turn stands 3½ kilometres east-north-east of the Green Hill (for continuation to Clova see above).

The private road to the stables at the top of Glen Lee continues as a bulldozed track to 725m on to the Muckle Cairn to the north-west, which is a different hill from the higher Muckle Cairn south-west of Inchgrundle. A private road also runs up Glen Mark to the cottage at 320m at the top, from which a vehicle track goes west up the glen to just past the lochan of Carlochy (kar'lochie). Upper Glen Mark is a lovely green glen with beautiful pools and rapids, surrounded by steep hillsides and crags, the Craig of Doune being especially imposing. Balnamoon's Cave lies at 396 833 on the south side of the Water of Mark, among rocks about 20m in height above the river; an old Jacobite's shelter, it is grassy on top, with a narrow vertical door and with its sides built up by stones. From either the upper Mark or Lee, you can

The Water of Unich at the head of Glen Lee

easily walk over to Glen Muick. Distances: from public road at Loch Lee Kirk at 445 803 to Lee stables 8½ kilometres, by Muckle Cairn and Creag na Slowrie to Spittal of Glenmuick 16 kilometres, 500m ascent. From Loch Lee Kirk to Glenmark Cottage 4 kilometres, via Glen Mark and the Burn of Fasheilach to the Glen Muick public road at 328 889 by a bulldozed track going down from Druim Cholzie 17 kilometres, 400m ascent. There are endless other possibilities for hillwalkers keen on exploring for themselves.

Between Glen Esk and Glen Clova, Glen Lethnot (Lethnocht or naked-sided) and its West Water form a long narrow valley twisting up into hilly grouse moors. The public road ends at Hunthill Lodge, but beyond the lodge a vehicle track runs far up the remote Water of Saughs ('sachs, north-east Scots for willows). At the top of the Water of Saughs you are on an undulating high plateau with Ben Tirran to the south-west, whereas to the north-east the secluded Glen Effock falls steeply with several broken crags to Glen Esk. Distances: from the public road end near Hunthill by the vehicle track to the Shank of Donald Young 5½ kilometres, to Ben Tirran 11 kilometres, 600m ascent. From Hunthill by the track up Water of Saughs to the Shieling of Saughs 9 kilometres, to the Green Hill via White Hill 14 kilometres. From 492 729 in Glen Lethnot north by the Whisky Road over the Clash (Gaelic clais or furrow) of Wirren to Tarfside 7½ kilometres, 200m ascent.

The next glen to the west of Lethnot is Glen Ogil behind Noranside, a short little glen with planted woods, a reservoir and rolling grouse moors. Next, after the short Glen Moy you come to Glen Clova, and almost immediately to the west of its entrance at the beech woods of Cortachy ('kortachie), the long Glen Prosen also opens out to the plain. The attractive lower part of Glen Prosen has natural birch woods, and higher up becomes open and wilder where it drains the south sides of the Mayar and Driesh. Glen Isla, westernmost of the Angus glens, is described in Chapter 10.

THE MOUNTH ROADS

Two well-known Mounth roads go over the hills from Glen Clova to Deeside, the Capel Mount to Ballater and the Tolmount to Braemar (for the Mounth roads from Glen Esk to Deeside, see next chapter). The Tolmount has the more rugged scenery of the two and is also a much higher and longer route than the Capel Mount.

Capel Mounth. Pronounced the 'kaipil'munth, this name comes from Monadh Chapull or mounth of horses. Distance: from public road end near Braedownie to county boundary 4 kilometres, to car park at Spittal of Glenmuick 10 kilometres, total ascent 500m but only 350m if you start at the Spittal. At the bridge north of Braedownie you come to the end of the public road at about 260m. A private road continues to Moulzie (Muillidh, 'moolee or mill place). About one kilometre up, the Capel track slants through a plantation to the right and then zigzags up the open hillside above to the plateau. The next 4½ kilometres of peaty plateau are marked by posts, with the highest point at about 695m, and the path changes to a bulldozed track for the descent to the public road near the Spittal of Glenmuick at 411m. A finer route, 5 kilometres longer, goes well up the South Esk to Bachnagairn in its magnificent setting of larches and green meadows surrounded by high crags and waterfalls (footbridges north of Moulzie). From here a path climbs north to the plateau at 700m beside Allan's Hut, and then continues as a bulldozed track zigzagging down to Loch Muick across the Black Burn. You can also vary this descent by taking the Diagonal Path down to the head of Loch Muick (see Chapter 11).

The Tolmount. For the meaning of this name see Chapter 10. Distance: from the public road end past Braedownie to the end of the bulldozed road in Glen Doll 5 kilometres, to county boundary 9 kilometres, to Loch Callater Lodge 15 kilometres, to Auchallater 20 kilometres, total ascent 690m but only 570m if you start at Auchallater. This route begins in Glen Doll, where you can walk along the road past the youth hostel at Glendoll Lodge and then up a bulldozed road which runs well up the glen to 560m. At the road end you stand in a very fine secluded spot, with craggy faces and steep hillsides rising all around. Straight ahead, the main stream comes down a narrow ravine, steep and rocky, but for a climber worth scrambling up. The path now slants to the right up the hill, avoiding the ravine and going above the smaller stream to the north of it. This steep part is called Jock's Road, said to be named after a John Winters (CCJ 12, 220). The path climbs past Jock's Bothy and around Cairn Lunkard above it to the plateau north of the main stream, and then

Craig Rennet and the north-west wall of Corrie Fee

goes gently upwards to the highest point at just over 910m, on the Crow ('kra) Craigies. Passing through the shallow dip at 883m to the east of Tolmount, beside a broken fence, it then descends fairly steeply into Coire Breac towards Glen Callater, down grass amongst scattered broken rocks. You now pass the fine Coire Loch Kander on the west side of the glen, and go along the east side of Loch Callater at about 500m to Loch Callater Lodge, where a private road leads to the locked gate at Auchallater on the public road up Glen Clunie near Braemar. Walkers unaccustomed to navigating in mist and snow should avoid the Tolmount in winter as the path crosses a big tract of exposed high plateau with very few landmarks, where several people have succumbed in storms. However, for the experienced hillwalker the Tolmount in snow makes one of the finest winter crossings of the Mounth.

The Sidlaw Hills
This range north and west of Dundee (known to local folk as the 'seedleez) is more interesting than its low height might suggest. Many outcrops of volcanic rock give a knobbly appearance to some of the hills, especially at the west end near Dunsinane. The Sidlaws offer very fine views of the Mounth to the north across the wide lowland of Strathmore. Several good paths and tracks onto and across the hills from either side give good walking routes.

Cross-country tracks on lower hills
There are many walking routes on the lower hills and moors. One old route starts
from near Little Foster in upper Glen Isla, goes north of Auchintaple Loch and east
to the col between Bada Crionard and Craigie Law, next by a forest road across Glen
Finlet to Glenmarkie Lodge, then by an old track crossing Glen Taitney and Glen
Damff to the Moss of Glanny and Glenhead Lodge, and finally south of the Hill of
Strone to Cormuir in Glen Prosen.

An old right of way runs uphill from Clova by Loch Brandy to the Green Hill,
Inchgrundle and Invermark in Glen Esk (see Ben Tirran, above). Another old route
runs north from Glen Ogil up past the east side of Mount Sned to Waterhead in Glen
Lethnot. A continuation is the Whisky Road from Tillybardine in Glen Lethnot north
to Tarfside.

CLIMBING

In Glen Clova, Red Craig beside Braedownie has for long been popular for climbing
on a clean dry face of diorite rock, with many short routes which vary in standard
from Moderate to VS and harder. Further west rises the conical rocky mass of the
Downie where many short hard routes up to E6 have been climbed. The Climbers'
Guide *North-East Outcrops* describes the climbs on Red Craig and the Doonie in
detail.

Corrie Fee extends far as a grand wild cirque with crags of schist and epidiorite
or hornblende gneiss, but much of its rock is too broken and vegetated for fine
summer climbing; however, in snow and ice the gullies and buttresses give the
longest and best winter climbs in Glen Clova. On the south face of the corrie, the left
part of the main, Central Buttress ends near an obvious gully called *Look C Gully*, a
summer stream which becomes a fine winter ice route. On its left the next obvious
trough forms *B Gully*, another watercourse that gives a good winter climb on ice. On
the north wall of Corrie Fee stands the impressive 210m crag of Craig Rennet, but
its rocks are ill-defined and broken, as are the schist cliffs of Winter Corrie and those
at Loch Brandy and the other corries on the north side of Glen Clova. However,
under snow and ice the gullies give sporting climbing of Grade I-III standard,
reaching 200m on the Scorrie Buttress of Winter Corrie.

About 2 kilometres to the west-north-west of Bachnagairn a sheet of rock outcrops on Craig of Gowal (locally the Craig o the Gowal); although it lies back at a
low angle, its central part has given a long route, *The Gowk* (HVS) on clean granite
slabs.

In Glen Esk, Craig Maskeldie makes an interesting route to the plateau in winter
when snow and ice cover the considerable amount of vegetation. Other rocks,
although looking impressive at a distance, turn out to be broken, rather short and
fairly heavily vegetated in summer. Try to avoid these small broken crags in all the
Angus glens in spring and summer, as they are the nesting places of scarce and
much-persecuted birds of prey.

SKIING

Green Hill near Milton of Clova has long been popular for skiing, but in good snow conditions the entire area is excellent for short or long ski tours. Nordic skis are good for long routes over the plateaux, but the steep slopes of the main glens and corries often give heavier skis an advantage for good quick descents. Many hills not described in this chapter, such as Cat Law near Kirriemuir, the Wirren near Edzell, and the hills around Tarfside, give excellent touring when there is good cover. The forest roads in Glen Clova, Glen Prosen and other glens are useful lines of ascent and descent to get through the dense conifer plantations.

FURTHER READING

H.T.Munro *The Braes of Angus* (Guide Book article). SMCJ 8, 125.

J.Scrimgeour *The Glen Doll Right of Way Case.* CCJ 12.

Guide to the district of Glen Clova. Grampian CJ 1937, 14.

D.Fraser (1963) *Guide to the Glens of Angus and Mearns.* Standard Press, Montrose.

CHAPTER 14

Lower Deeside and the Mearns

Cairn Mon Earn	378m	782 919
Kerloch	534m	697 878
Clachnaben	589m	614 865
Mount Battock	778m	549 844
Mount Keen	939m	409 869
Scolty	299m	678 939
Hill of Fare	471m	672 028
Mortlich	381m	535 017

ACCESS
The best access is from public roads in lower Deeside. The public roads up Glen Tanar and up Glen Dye to the Cairn o' Mount are fine scenic routes as well as giving good access to some of the main hills.

PUBLIC TRANSPORT
Air, rail and bus services come from the south and north to Aberdeen, and buses go from Aberdeen to Ballater via Banchory and Aboyne, and also via Tarland.

ACCOMMODATION AND BOTHIES
There are many hotels, boarding houses and bed and breakfast places at villages and in the rural areas, youth hostels at Aberdeen and Ballater, and many caravan and camp sites. Bothy at Charr at 616 831 in Glen Dye. The bothy at the Shiel of Glentanar at 401 894 burned down in June 1992.

MAPS
Ordnance Survey 1:50,000 Sheets 37, 38, 44 and 45

This chapter describes the hills of lower Deeside from Aberdeen to Dinnet, including the east end of the Mounth and its southern braes that fall towards the Mearns and the wild North Sea cliffs of Kincardineshire. As you come north by road or rail through fertile Strathmore and the Howe of the Mearns (from Maoirne or Stewartry), the Mounth gradually hems you in against the North Sea until before Aberdeen you have to rise over its eastern extremity of peaty moorland near the cliffs of Nigg. The commercial air flights to Aberdeen from the south pass low over the area and give a good appreciation of the vast extent of its rolling, brown moors and hills, which are tinged a powdery pink in August and September from the myriad heather flowers. Although it lies so near the towns, much of this hill country is less visited by people than any other part of Deeside.

GEOLOGY, LANDFORMS AND WILDLIFE

This part of the Mounth consists mainly of pink granite in an extensive mass stretching from Mount Keen to Glen Dye and Cairn Mon Earn; the Hill of Fare forms another, smaller mass of pink granite. The ground near Aberdeen lies over grey granite, where the colossal 150m hole of Rubislaw Quarry reaches well below sea level, having until 1972 produced the rock for most buildings in Aberdeen. Gneiss occurs on the fine sea-cliffs at Souter Head and Nigg, whereas south of Stonehaven the fantastic vertical cliffs of Fowlsheugh are composed of conglomerate. Many glacial deposits have formed hillocks and valley ridges, such as you will see to the south-east of Strachan ('straan). Meltwater rivers from glaciers cut the fine dry ravines at the Slug, Mount Shade, and the remarkable 1½ kilometre-long gorge at the Slack of Birnie east of the Cairn o' Mount.

The hill ground supports some of the most extensive stands of uniform heather sward in Scotland; heather thrives in the dry climate here and on the well drained granite soil. A vast low moorland bog once covered most of the ground south of Aberdeen and good patches of it still remain at Red Moss near Netherley (nether'lei) and also nearer Aberdeen. Glen Tanar holds one of the largest stretches of natural pine forest in Scotland and moreover one of the few where the young trees are regenerating well. New natural woods of young pine have grown up on heather moorland at Forest of Birse, Glen Tanar, Finzean ('fingin) and Kerloch, more exten- sively than anywhere else in Scotland. Near St Cyrus, many southern species of plants grow on and below the unusually fertile, sheltered and partly-inland sea-cliffs of andesitic lava. For wild animals, naturalists find the notable features to be the pine-forest insects and birds of Glen Tanar, the richness of moorland birds, and the very densely populated sea-bird colonies at Fowlsheugh (fowls'hyooch).

ESTATES

There are many small ones. The larger ones that cover most of the hill country include Fasque Estate for Glen Dye (locally the Glen o Dye), Dunecht Estate for Birse and the Hill of Fare, and the separate estates of Glen Muick, Glen Tanar, and Ballogie which lies east of Glen Tanar.

HISTORY

The area is rich in ancient remains. Below Kerloch you will see fine circles of standing stones near Garrol Hill and West Mulloch. Nearer Stonehaven, beside Auquhollie up from Rickarton, a standing stone bears an Ogam (ancient Celtic alphabet) inscription; nearby are a few circles of standing stones, and further east the site of an old Roman camp at Raedykes. In the wood east of Raemoir by the B977 road stands a stone monument erected by the Deeside Field Club, commemorating the Battle of Corrichie (korr'eechee) which was fought higher on the Hill of Fare in 1562. At Corrichie the army of Mary Queen of Scots, led by the Earl of Moray, routed the Earl of Huntly in one of the many religious squabbles of the times. In the Mearns the kirk of Auchenblae is dedicated to St Palladius whose name appears again in Paldy Fair, a market that used to be held on the moor across from Glenfarquhar Lodge.

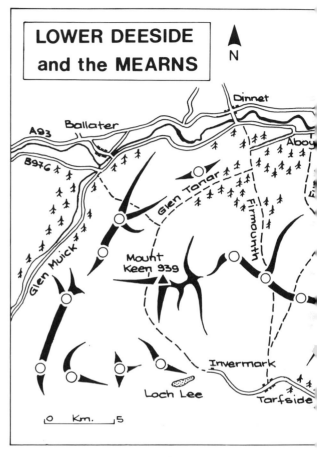

The Drumlithie-Glenbervie area was an ancestral ground of the poet Robert Burns, whose father was born there and later moved to Ayrshire. On farmland at Arbuthnott, J.L.Mitchell, who later wrote under the pen name Lewis Grassick Gibbon, spent his childhood. His fine descriptions in *Sunset Song* and *Cloud Howe*, the first two books of the classic trio forming *A Scots Quair*, are important reading for anyone wishing to understand the upland folk and their countryside in the area described in Chapters 14 and 15. Banchory was the birthplace of Scott Skinner the 'Strathspey King' who composed and played fine reels on the violin, and the town has one of the best-known group of Strathspey fiddlers in Scotland. From Banchory the unusual granite tor on Clachnaben looks very prominent to the south-west. The old local legend to explain it was that, in the midst of a row with his wife, the Devil tore up the rock from the valley and flung it to the top of the hill where it crushed and killed her.

THE HILLS

Cairn Mon Earn (378m)

As you go inland west from Aberdeen, this is the first obvious hill in the Mounth south of the Dee. A gently rising, boulder-studded cone, it stands close above the Slug Road from Stonehaven to Banchory. The lower slopes have been afforested, but opposite a lay-by on the public road at 779 911 you can go through a gap in the plantation and so for one kilometre up to the top. A more gradual route (3½

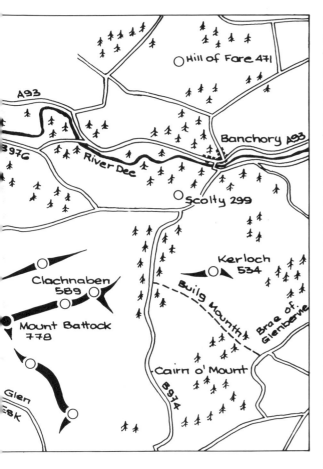

kilometres, 180m ascent) goes by the gravel road which starts at 780 909 and winds round to the Aberdeen side on the way up to the top and its radio aerials. The coast, lowlands and Deeside look very fine from here, and you can see as far as Garbh Choire Mor and Sgor an Lochain Uaine of the Cairngorms, a particularly well-hidden spot which is invisible in nearly all distant views.

Kerloch (534m)

Local people pronounce the name ker'loch. This hill gives grand views down into Deeside and south over lowlands to the North Sea. The easiest way up starts from the Strachan-Stonehaven road at 699 916, from where a vehicle track goes south for most of the way to the top (4½ kilometres, 410m ascent). An interesting descent takes you on the west side to the old Bridge of Bogendreip in Glen Dye, down through a fine, natural young pine wood, but most of the upper slopes were ploughed for tree planting in the 1980s.

Clachnaben (589m)

Locally called Clochna'bain, the name comes from Clach na Beinne or stone of the hill. With Bennachie it ranks as one of the most familiar hills in north-east Scotland, hence the couplet:

Clochnaben and Bennachie
Are twa landmarks frae the sea

Clachnaben is well known because of the great granite rock which sticks up for about 30m like a gigantic wart on its east side near the hilltop. The main route is from the public road at 649 867 in Glen Dye. A track leads west-south-west along the edge of the wood, then descends to cross the Mill Burn, and heads west to end in a wood further up. A path from here strikes uphill to Clachnaben (4 kilometres from the public road, 530m ascent). An electrified deer fence now runs along east and west of Clachnaben, but stiles in a few places allow access past it. On descent it is well worth diverging by Mount Shade to see the Devil's Bite, the dry rocky gap cut by

Clachnaben from Glen Dye

past glacial meltwater. Another route to Clachnaben comes from the north by a path which leads up the Burn of Greendams to the top (5 kilometres, 440m ascent).

Mount Battock (778m)

Called mun'batak locally, this shapely hill with its domed top stands high over Feughside and Glen Dye. A good approach comes in from 542 907 on the public road beside Burnfoot in the upper Feugh (fyooch). On the way to Burnfoot, you should stop just west of Woodend to see the fine naturally regenerating pine woods there. From Burnfoot, a gradual climb up the moor takes you east of Cock Hill and past the remote Loch Tennet to the stony and mossy top (6½ kilometres, 630m ascent). Mount Battock is notable as the furthest east hill in Scotland where ptarmigan nest.

You can also climb Mount Battock from Glen Esk, an approach that gives grand views on the way up. North of Millden a rough road leads to the old farm of Blackhills, from where you can climb easily north over Allrey ('alarie) or north-west by Mount Een (munth'een) to the top (6 kilometres, 640m ascent).

There are several vehicle tracks around Mount Battock. One goes from Mill of Aucheen in Glen Esk up the Hill of Turret to about 460m on Hill of Fingray, 5 kilometres south-east of the summit. Another starts to the west of Charr Cottage in Glen Dye, which you can reach easily by leaving the B974 road at 647 845 below Spital Cottage, and following a gravel road up to Charr ('tshar). Beyond Charr the

Looking east from Creag an Dubh Loch across Loch Muick to Mount Keen

track climbs to about 640m, west of the Hill of Badymicks and just over one kilometre from the top (total distance 11 kilometres, 560m ascent).

Mount Keen *(monadh or hill, keen of uncertain meaning, pronounced mun'keen)* (939m) To see this shapely cone at its best, and one of the finer views of Scotland, go to Tillypronie on the Dinnet-Strath Don road; from here it soars magnificently above the woods and farms in the great bowl of the Howe o Cromar. The Mounth road from Ballater to Invermark (see below) goes over its high west shoulder by a wild, open route. A more varied way comes in from Glen Tanar to the south-west of Aboyne, by the public road to a car park at about 180m altitude beside Glen Tanar House. From there a rough road runs beyond Etnach to the Shiel of Glentanar which was burned down in 1992 (11 kilometres, 180m ascent). The road is a right of way for walkers and cyclists but a locked gate keeps out cars. It leads through fine natural pine forest. From just before the Shiel, a bulldozed track goes left to climb on the old Mounth route to 530m; beyond, the old Mounth path continues and another path forks left to Mount Keen's stony granite summit (3 kilometres from the glen road east of the Shiel, 560m ascent). On the way up you bypass the damp rocky corrie called the 'korlach (not Corrach as on the maps), low on the north side of Mount Keen.

It is easy walking for 2 kilometres east from Mount Keen to the 887m Braid Cairn (200m ascent), locally called The Braid Cairns. Although looking a rounded dome from Cromar, Braid Cairn is a long sprawling lump of a hill when seen from Glen Esk and Laurencekirk. It rises high above the vast peaty plateaux, locally called the Leg o Moss, which stretch south-east over the Hill of Saughs towards Tarfside and form one of the more notable tracts of wild country in the area. From the Braid Cairn, grand walking on dry, wind scoured dwarf heather takes you along the line of tops east to Mount Battock. These tops, bounding the great basin north of Tarfside, form the Glen Esk skyline which the local glen folk call The Riggin, Scots for the hill ridge. One of the best ways of climbing Mount Keen starts in Glen Esk; you go up Glen Mark, take the Mounth route (see below) up a bulldozed track to 670m, and then walk by a path to the top.

Scolty *(from sgoltaidh or splitting)* (299m)

With its prominent tower and conical shape, Scolty is one of the best-known and easily recognised hills of lower Deeside. It rises close above the town of Banchory (Beannchraigh, 'bangchree, or place of river bends or peaks). On the Auchattie public road at 692 950, a forest road goes right. It leads to a path up through the woods to the upper heather moor and so to the top (2 kilometres, 220m ascent), where the view is very fine for such a low hill. The big plantations of Blackhall stretch north to the River Dee and west to the Commonty and the Shooting Greens on the road from Potarch to Feughside. A forest trail starts at 633 943 on that road, which was once an important cattle-droving route on the way south to the Cairn o' Mount.

Hill of Fare *(from faire or horizon ridge)* (471m)

Standing isolated from the farmlands north of Banchory, this flat-topped hill contains a remarkably big area of moorland plateau and sends a number of shoulders far out to enclose little wooded glens. For its low height it forms an unusually complex hill, almost a miniature hill range, and gives fine spacious views. The road to the Hill of Fare from Banchory goes through a marshy depression with reeds and willows near the house of Lochhead. This reminds us that, before the land was intensively drained, the Loch of Leys (leiz) once stretched far to the east of here, joining up with the Loch of Park in a great wetland of loch and marsh. Many tracks now lead on to the Hill of Fare. From 685 993 west of the T-junction of roads at Raemoir (ri'more), an interesting route goes north up past the old castle at Cluny, then by a hill road which winds through some old trees skirting Craigrath, and so to the wide plateau on top (6½ kilometres, 380m ascent). Another good way up comes from the north side at 703 058, past the old castle of Midmar and Craigshannoch above the Gormack Burn (Gormag or little blue one) by forest roads, then by an old peat track to Tornamean and so to the summit (5 kilometres). To the north-east of the Hill of Fare, the little hill of the Barmekin ('barmikin) near Echt gives a grand view of the low country and carries an ancient circular fort on its summit.

Mortlich *(Mor-thulaich, 'more-tlich or big hillock)* (381m)

This is the conical hill rising north of Aboyne (a'bein). An interesting approach starts up the road east of the Loch of Aboyne, past a fine old churchyard to the grassy slopes of Queen's Hill, and so to the top (2 kilometres, 240m ascent) with its big cairn, where you will see a fine view of Deeside and Glen Tanar. To the east lies Auchlossan, once a loch, then drained, and later a loch and marsh in the 1960s until it was drained for agriculture in 1972.

Mortlich is the south-east extremity of a curving band of hills that enclose the wide fertile bowl of the Howe o Cromar (how-a-kro'mar). North of Mortlich rises the slightly higher Craiglich (kraig'lick), easily reached in one kilometre (180m climb) from the A974 road at 526 063 at the gap called the Slack of Tillylodge, where you get a magnificent view up Deeside. On the other side of the Slack rises the higher hill of Pressendye (praissin'dei). A public road runs from Tarland ('tarlan) to 465 074 beside the Davoch (locally the 'dach), from which a track climbs to a saddle west of the summit. The track is part of an old drove road from 468 134 near Towie on Donside to the Davoch (8 kilometres, 330m ascent). At the Davoch, the old drove road called the Lazy Well Road comes in from 425 109 near Boultenstone (6 kilometres, 100m ascent). Between the two runs a third drove road starting from Culfork at 455 114 on Donside, with another variant at Mill of Culfork, and then over Green Hill to the Davoch. The ridge between Lazy Well and Pressendye is called Maalie'waat by local folk, probably from Gaelic but absurdly anglicised in the OS Pathfinder map to Molly Watt's Hill.

THE MOUNTH ROADS

Many paths, once called roads as they were the best roads then available over the hills, lead across this eastern part of the Mounth. Between the coast and Glen Muick near Ballater, there are ten main Mounth roads. Most of them have variants spreading out fan-like at either end towards different settlements on the low ground.

During his attempts to conquer Scotland, Edward I and the English army went north to Aberdeen in 1296; he probably took the Cryne Corse Mounth, as he stopped at Glen Bervie and Durris. By the track from Glen Tanar over Belrorie to Dinnet stands a memorial stone put up by Sir W.C.Brooks who was a former owner of Glen Tanar; its inscription says that Edward also crossed the Firmounth but this is doubtful. Until the 1870s some families farmed upper Glen Tanar, but when Brooks bought the glen he cleared them all out. He erected the imposing tower beside the Bridge o' Ess at the end of the glen road beside the South Deeside Road, which erroneously may suggest that the road to Glen Tanar House is private. Brooks also erected the many curious memorials, quartz pillars and wells that are so much a feature of the Glen Tanar area, as well as many houses of warm red granite and unusual design for the district.

Drovers from Tomintoul once used the Mounth Road over Mount Keen frequently on their way to Trinity ('tarantie) Fair at Brechin. Walking by the Lecht to Don, they then crossed by the Glas-choille and Glen Fenzie to Glen Gairn, over the Mounth Keen to Invermark, and next from Tarfside over the Clash of Wirren to the West Water and Brechin. Many people travelled by the Firmounth while carrying timber and resinous torches from Glen Tanar to the south, and all the Mounth roads

Langlauf on Clachnaben

from the Capel to the Forest of Birse were in heavy use till the mid-1800s for taking illicit home-still whisky to Dundee and Perth.

Near the top of the Firmounth flows St Colm's Well, one of the many places in north-east Scotland visited by that early Christian missionary. The Tinker's Cairn near the well marks where a tinker murdered his wife. At the trial in Aberdeen, one witness was a Tarfside woman at whose house the couple had called on their way over the Firmounth. The man denied he had ever been there, but when the witness said she had given them a drink of milk, he exclaimed indignantly that it was only whey, a fatal remark!

The Mounth ends in the tiny hills behind Kincorth, above the south suburbs of Aberdeen (aiber'deen). Some Aberdeen town folk call them 'the Gramps', which is the only common use of 'Grampians' that the writer has come across in the whole region. Just west of Loirston ('loriston) Loch to the south of Aberdeen, the Blue Hill gives very fine views up to the Cairngorms and carries a hill indicator. Another indicator stands on the low heathery rise of the 265m Brimmond ('brimon, with no 'Hill' as on the maps), to the south-west of Aberdeen Airport; it has now been disfigured by a bulldozed road from the north and by radio aerials.

There are many fine views of the higher hills from the farmlands of lower Deeside. Just east of Durris off the south Deeside road, the side roads to Ashentilly and Denside give magnificent panoramas; you can see most of the Cairngorms including Cairn Toul, and a complex multitude of lower hills round to Bennachie and Buchan. About 400m up the Slug Road from the Dee bridge at Crathes, you will notice a very fine view of Ben Avon and Beinn a' Bhuird; you look right into Coire an Dubh Lochain of Beinn a' Bhuird, a corrie remarkably well hidden from most places. A fine far view of Ben Avon is from the roadside at Garrol Hill east of Strachan. In the low country of the Mearns, Garvock Hill between Laurencekirk and St Cyrus offers very good views over to the long line of the Mounth.

The Causey Mounth. This went from Aberdeen to Stonehaven over what was then a stretch of moors, bogs, stony ridges and peat mosses. The name Causey comes from Causeway, locally pronounced 'cassie. Although much of this ground has been turned into farmland, fragments of these lowland moors and bogs still remain, the soil is poor, and here the east end of the Mounth presses close to the North Sea. Most of the Causey Mounth path has been obliterated, but small sections still exist.

The Elsick Mounth. This went from Peterculter to Stonehaven along a higher route and further to the west than the Causey Mounth. Farming and new roads have destroyed much of it, but a substantial part still survives. Starting at 807 941, up from Durris on Deeside, it goes through a forest to come out on the hill of Bawdy Craig, and then descends on Rickarton moor to a public road near the farm of East Auquhollie.

The Slug Road. From Gaelic slug or gullet. The Slug Road is now the public road from Banchory and Durris to Stonehaven, cutting east of the rocky gullet that gives this Mounth road its name.

The Cryne Corse Mounth. Probably from Crion Crasg or little crossing. This Mounth road goes from Durris to Drumlithie on a line just west of the Slug. Distance: 8 kilometres from the Slug Road to 764 841, ascent 230m. Go to 762 916 on the Slug Road, where a private road runs uphill through dense forest towards a television mast. The original path was bulldozed to make way for the road. The mast rises for 300m from the shallow basin east of Mongour (from gabhar or goat), and is a familiar landmark, especially at night when its red lights are visible a long way off. From 765 904 you hold to the left past Red Beard's Well, and then by a track which descends towards the afforested valley of Cowie Water (collaigh or hazelly). You can follow forest roads across the valley and up the other side to the old track leading to the Brae of Glenbervie.

The Stock Mounth. Pronounced 'stoke munth, from Strachan to Glen Bervie. Distance: 10 kilometres from 699 916 to 759 838, ascent 260m. Several tracks from Pitreadie, Moss-side, Midtown and Garrol Hill join at Tod's Stone (tod'steen, Scots tod means fox) at 715 881 on the east flank of Kerloch. Here you follow the old Mounth road into the peaty basin at the head of the Sheeoch Burn (sithich or fairy), then into the head of Cowie Water and up to Leachie Hill where the track descends to the Brae of Glenbervie. The slopes of Cowie Water are now afforested but you can travel by forest roads.

The Builg Mounth. Pronounced 'boolig munth, from Glen Dye to Glen Bervie. Distance: 11 kilometres from 652 873 to 736 819, ascent 200m. The Builg Mounth starts from south of Scolly's Cross in Glen Dye, crosses the Water of Dye by a footbridge west of Heatheryhaugh, and then climbs up the Builg Burn south of Kerloch. Over the top, it goes down the shoulder of The Builg and into the head-waters of the Bervie Burn (bearbha or boiling). There you should take the forest road as the plantations in this glen are huge and thick.

In 1991, Kincardine and Deeside District Council and the Forestry Commission agreed to clear trees and branches from the afforested parts of all the Mounth tracks from Elsick west to Builg.

The Cairn o' Mount. Locally the Cairn o Munth or often just The Cairn, it is now the public road from Banchory to Fettercairn and Brechin. Although reaching only about 450m, it runs across an exposed plateau and often becomes snow-blocked. One of the most important of the Mounth roads, it had the beautiful old Bridge of Dye as early as about 1680, and also a spital (Gaelic spideal or hospice) at either end of the high moorland section; one stood at the foot of Spital Burn in Glen Dye and the other uphill from Clatterin Brig in Glen Saugh. In earlier times the Cairn o' Mount was also often used by armed forces on the march.

The top of the Cairn o' Mount is one of the best viewpoints from any road in Scotland. Here you stand right on the edge of the main Highland fault and look steeply down to the uniform sweep of flat green farmlands to the south, whereas to the north and west you see a complex jumble of brown heathery hills and glens inside the outer boundary of the Highland rocks. This contrast, as you reach the summit of the road, comes as a great and sudden surprise. To the east, north and west, vast peaty heather moors stretch out to rolling hills, giving an unusual sense of wide, open space. Snowy Lochnagar, rising beyond the great high plateau of the Glen Esk hills, looks like a peak rising from an undulating subarctic tundra, as in Dovre Fjell or Iceland. To the south, a huge expanse of fertile low farmland in the Mearns and Strathmore sweeps far down to central Scotland and out to the North Sea, often glittering in the sun. On a good day you can see the Firth of Tay beyond the Sidlaw Hills, the Bell Rock lighthouse, the east tips of Fife beside Tentsmuir and St Andrews, the Fife hills of Falkland and Lomond, and the Ochil Hills and Earn valley. On the clearest days you can see beyond Fife to the Firth of Forth, the Isle of May, the Lammermuir Hills beyond Edinburgh, and the Scottish coast as far as St Abbs Head not far from the English border.

At the south end of the Cairn o' Mount the road drops steeply to Clatterin Brig. The big house on the hill to the east is Glensaugh Lodge (sach, from north-east Scots for willow), a research farm. Shutting off Glen Saugh from the Howe o' the Mearns rises the bulky brown Strathfinella Hill. The road to Auchenblae runs past Loch Saugh, one of the extremely few lochs in Kincardineshire. It continues on through Strath Finella ('finla) and the Glen of Drumtochty, which are steep-sided and thickly wooded with tall trees. The scenery is quite unlike the open sweeps of farmland and hills so characteristic of the Mearns.

The Birse Mounth. This runs from Birse (berss, 'e' as in her, from am preas or the thicket) east of Aboyne, to Tarfside. Distance: from 536 966 at Birse to Glencat 3½ kilometres, to the Feugh road below Ballochan 6½ kilometres, to county boundary 12 kilometres, to Shinfur 16 kilometres, to Tarfside 19 kilometres, total ascent 700m. The Birse Mounth goes over the low hill to Glencat, and over the next low hill to Birse Castle and Ballochan (ba'lochan) which stand at the west end of the public road up Feughside from Strachan. At Ballochan the valley of Feugh leads south, and the route now runs up the west side of the stream, coming out past the gap at the Sloch to the col between Tampie and Mudlee Bracks. A fine view opens out here into the great circular basin of Glen Tennet and Tarf, round to the hill of the Rowan with its monument. The track now descends south to the unoccupied farms of Glen Tennet and down to Tarfside.

The Fungle ('fung-gil). This goes from Aboyne to Tarfside in Glen Esk. Distance: from Birsemore to Ballochan 8 kilometres, to county boundary 13 kilometres, to Shinfur 17 kilometres, to Tarfside 20 kilometres, total ascent 690m. At a signpost at 524 977 on the South Deeside Road (B976) south of the Dee bridge at Aboyne, a track heads uphill to the south-west. About 2 kilometres up from Birsemore you come to the seat at the fine viewpoint of 'Rest-and-be-thankful', above a grand, steeply wooded little glen. The route then passes the cottage of The Guard, goes on to a moor with good natural regeneration of young pines, and later joins a rough road that comes in from the farm of Newmill to the north-east. At about 425m you cross a flat shoulder before descending to Ballochan at the head of the Water of Feugh. From here the route to Tarfside is the same as by the Birse Mounth (see above).

The Firmounth, in Gaelic *Am Monadh Giuthais.* This is one of the most varied of the Mounth Roads crossing from Deeside to Tarfside. Distance: from 472 982 on the public road near Dinnet to Millfield 2 kilometres, to county boundary 12 kilometres, to Shinfur 18 kilometres, to Tarfside 21 kilometres, total ascent 690m. The old road starts at Dinnet and passes over Belrorie Hill to the Tanar bridge above Millfield, a place which is now on the public road up Glen Tanar from Bridge o' Ess. Just south of the bridge above Millfield lies a meadow where the landowner Brooks cleared out the unfortunate farmer and erected a private chapel. The road now curves uphill above the Burn of Skinna (sken'aaie); do not take the other road far up beside the river. You next enter a great bowl of magnificent pine-juniper forest, and then climb on to the open hill of Craigmahandle (kraigma'hanil) and beyond to the plateau. Passing St Colm's Well, the route goes right over the 723m top of Tampie and then drops down a vehicle track to Shinfur and Tarfside.

The Mounth Keen (the munth 'keen). This fine crossing goes from Ballater to Invermark in Glen Esk. Distance: from the mouth of Glen Muick to the Pollagach Burn 4½ kilometres, to the Water of Tanar 8½ kilometres, to county boundary 11½ kilometres, to Glenmark cottage 15½ kilometres, to public road at Invermark 19½ kilometres, total ascent 840m. You leave the public road at 366 947 at the Bridge of Muick. Turn left here up the dirt road that starts at the memorial at about 210m, go past Balintober, and then at the next junction keep uphill into the larch wood.

The old path, now a bulldozed track, passes at about 585m between Cairn Leuchan and Craig Vallich. From here, take the vehicle track leading into the peaty head-waters of the open basin of the Pollagach ('poolich') Burn. The old footpath leaves this track at 384 922 to head east-south-east (indistinct) to 394 917 at the fence on the ridge beyond, where you can see into Glen Tanar and the path becomes clearer. After crossing the Water of Tanar at a footbridge at 406 896, you climb on a vehicle track to 530m and continue beyond by a path up to about 770m that skirts to the west of the upper cone of Mount Keen. The route next leads gently downhill along a path, becoming a bulldozed track at 670m, and then steepens to zigzag down the steep slope called The Ladder to the cottage of Glenmark at 320m. Below the cottage a

Climbing on the sea-cliffs of the North-East at Longhaven

stone memorial over a well commemorates Queen Victoria's crossing of the Mounth here in 1861. On the last and very fine part of the route, you walk down the east side of rocky Glen Mark to the public road at 445 803 at Invermark.

CLIMBING

You can scramble on small broken rocks in many places, but there are no good high natural crags inland. The tor on Clachnaben is of steep, fairly holdless rough granite, giving chimney routes as well as miniature ridges and some crack and face climbs on the wall. Several disused quarries offer short, hard climbs on granite. Now that the Rubislaw Quarry at Aberdeen has gone out of use, its 150m walls of grey granite have become more stable and offer several hard rock climbs. Water fills the floor of this and several other old quarries. The smaller cliffs on the coast at Souter Head and Cove to the south of Aberdeen have long been a popular climbing ground, giving good short routes of all grades of difficulty on excellent clean gneiss. For a short distance from about Cove Bay south to Clashrodney, a section of higher granite cliffs offers the grand climbs at South Cove. Beyond South Cove, excellent climbs are at Craig Stirling ('stirlin, local Scots for starling) about 13 kilometres south of Aberdeen, and in the Findon area. The cliffs have been fairly well explored for climbing as far as the Newtonhill area, with some routes done as far as Muchalls. The Climbers' Guide *North-East Outcrops* gives full details. The many sea-cliffs further south consist mainly of altered grits on the wild indented coast from south of Cove to Stonehaven, and sandstones and conglomerate from Stonehaven to St Cyrus.

SKIING

The area lies in a snowy part of Scotland and offers excellent ski touring when there is good snow cover. Often there are so few rocks that the entire landscape becomes snow-covered, giving an impression of being on an ice-cap. In Glen Tanar, Forest of Birse, Pressendye and many other places there is another unusual characteristic, of skiing over moorland dotted with naturally regenerating pines, just like parts of Lapland. Hills such as Kerloch and Cairn Mon Earn are near enough to the sea to get milder temperatures, and so are seldom in good skiing condition. However, Clachnaben, Mount Battock and other hills further inland tend to get heavier snow cover. Some formerly very good ski-touring areas accessible to the towns have unfortunately been afforested, so access there is now confined to monotonous routes along forest roads with impenetrable coniferous walls on either side.

FURTHER READING - HISTORICAL

A.Cruickshank & A.Copland *The Blue Hill*. CCJ 1, 29.

A.Copland *The Brimmond Hill*. CCJ 1, 219.

J.Cruickshank *Mountain indicator on Brimmond*. CCJ 9. 1.

CHAPTER 15

Don and Deveronside

Bennachie	528m	663 227
Tap o' North	563m	484 293
The Buck	721m	413 234
Corryhabbie Hill	781m	281 289
Carn Mor	804m	265 183
Carn Ealasaid	792m	228 118

ACCESS, PUBLIC TRANSPORT AND ACCOMMODATION
See also Chapter 9 for the Tomintoul-Corgarff area and Chapter 14 for the Aberdeen area.
In addition, rail services go from Aberdeen to Inverness stopping at Inverurie, Insch, Huntly
and Keith, and buses likewise. A bus goes up Donside.

MAPS
Ordnance Survey 1:50,000 Sheets 28-30 and 36-38

This chapter covers a very extensive area in the valleys of the rivers Don and Deveron, and also mentions the coast. The shorter Don flows east, parallel to the Dee but north of it. Both rivers enter the sea at Aberdeen, a name which comes from Obar Dheathan or mouth of Don (Deathan, river deity). The Deveron, joined by its two main tributaries of Bogie and Black Water, flows north-east to the Moray Firth at Banff. The name Deveron, pronounced 'diverin, has come from Dubh Eireann meaning black Earn. No hill in this lower area reaches 900m but the scenery of these valleys is pleasant, the low hills show much variety, and the coast offers the finest sea-cliff scenery on Scotland's mainland east coast. Although not as grand as Deeside, Donside has fine river, hill and woodland scenery, and richer farmland, or as the old verse went:

> Ae mile o Don's worth twa o Dee,
> Except it be for fish an tree.

On Donside, Deveronside and Strath Bogie (stra'boag-ee), the many small farms give a softness to the countryside which has gone from the now uninhabited higher glens around the Cairngorms. From the farmlands of lower Aberdeenshire and Banffshire these low hills look far more prominent and are thus better known and loved by most of the people than the much bigger hills further inland.

GEOLOGY, LANDFORMS AND WILDLIFE

This area is so extensive and varied that there is space here only to mention its most outstanding features (for more details, see the Forestry Commission's booklet *Forests of North-East Scotland*). Most of the hills in Donside, Deveronside and Glen Livet lie over schists, diorites, limestones and other rocks which break down into more fertile soils than does granite. These low hills support a richer variety of plants than the low granite hills of Deeside, and also larger stocks of wild birds and mammals. Bennachie makes an exception, being an isolated mass of granite. There are striking granite tors on Bennachie and many small rocks on hills in the Cabrach. Glacial rivers have cut numerous meltwater channels, and the general lack of woodland on the big expanses of farmland on the lower ground allows one to see glacial channels, ridges, hillocks and other features very well.

On the farmlands, the vast rookeries at Hatton Castle near Turriff, at Straloch, and in other woods are the.biggest in Europe. On the coast, you will find outstanding places for wild duck and geese north of Aberdeen at the Ythan estuary and nearby Meikle Loch of Slains, and further north at the grand Loch of Strathbeg (stra'beg). The Ythan estuary is a very fine place for wading birds, and the nearby Sands of Forvie hold the biggest colony of eider ducks in Britain and great colonies of terns, as well as supporting an unusual plant community of crowberry and 'reindeer moss' lichens growing on sand dunes. You will see very large numbers of sea-birds on the wild cliffs of Troup Head, Lion's Head and Pennan Head on the Moray Firth coast.

ESTATES

Mostly small, they are too many to mention individually. All the moorland and hill ground in the area described in this chapter is grouse moor. Glen Buchat, Glen Fiddich, and Blackwater west of Cabrach are also deer forests. The Forestry Commission owns most of Bennachie and large tracts north of Morven, north-west of Rhynie and elsewhere.

HISTORY

On a hillside in upper Strath Don stands the old Castle of Corgarff. Here occurred the gruesome tragedy that features in the ballad *Edom o' Gordon*, where Margaret Forbes and her family were burned to death in 1571 during a clan feud between the Forbeses and the Gordons (see *Corgarff Castle*, by W.D.Simpson, Proc. Soc. Antiqu. Scot. 1927). Kildrummy Castle further down Donside, about 16 kilometres west of Alford, is one of the best Scottish examples of a 13th-century castle.

Bennachie used to be a commonty or common land for the use of all the people to dig their peats, quarry stones and graze their stock. Then, during the early 19th century, when the population soared and land was scarce, squatters settled on the south-east slopes and a Bennachie community grew there. The nearby lairds pushed an order through Parliament to divide up the commonty between them and to charge rent. D.G. Gordon (1973) wrote 'Known as the rape of Bennachie, it brought a poem from William Thom, the weaver poet of Inverurie. The lairds' leader was Dalrymple of Logie. Thom's lampoon described the great boon they had all enjoyed, and all their great commonty had meant to them and ends:

> Bennachie has become but a pimple,
> Upon the nose of Sir Hugh Dalrymple.'

Subsequently, many who could not pay rent on this very poor land were evicted, and the community later died out by voluntary emigration.

At the Well of the Lecht, by the roadside, an inscription from 1754 records that 'Five Companies, the 33rd Regiment, Right Hon. Lord Chas. Hay, Colonel, made the road from here to the Spey'. In spite of references to Wade at Tomintoul, this road was not constructed by Wade, who left Scotland before the 1745 rising. Up the glen to the east of the well stands a dark building, used for an ironstone and manganese mine which the York Buildings Company worked here in the 1700s; horses carried the ore in panniers to Balnagowan in Abernethy where it was smelted with charcoal from the Nethy forests.

Glen Livet and Tomintoul are Roman Catholic country in a predominantly Presbyterian region. To the south-south-east of Chapeltown, at the Scalan (Gaelic sgalan or hut), a school was run for training Catholic priests during most of the 18th century. These were years of intimidation; several times the army broke the place up, and in 1746 it was sacked on orders from the infamous Duke of Cumberland. But the college survived, later to become Blairs College in lower Deeside.

About one kilometre below the Well of the Lecht on the other side of Conglass Water ('conglass) stands a ruined cottage. Here in June 1920 occurred the Topliss affair, which was something of a sensation then in peaceful north-east Scotland. An ex-soldier called Percy Topliss had murdered a taxi driver in Hampshire in April 1920 and then disappeared. Later, a man who was supposed to be a wandering labourer arrived at Tomintoul and began living in the empty cottage; local folk paid no heed until he started tearing down the woodwork for kindling his fire. On 1 June, the Tomintoul policeman and two neighbours went to the cottage. A revolver shot rang out and two of the party were badly wounded, whereupon the man fled. From the description, it became clear that Topliss had escaped from Hampshire to this remote spot in the Banffshire Highlands. Five days later he was seen on the road between Carlisle and Penrith, and when challenged by a policeman he drew his revolver. The constable retreated for armed help and there followed a fight on the road, when Topliss was shot dead.

THE HILLS

Bennachie (528m)

Pronounced baina'hee, the name probably comes from Beinn Chioch or hill of breasts. From north or south the long ridge of Bennachie with its prominent tors resembles a series of breasts. Although not much over 500m high, Bennachie ranks

The Mither Tap, Bennachie, from Millstone Hill

as one of the best-known hills in Aberdeenshire. Standing high over the 'fairm-toons' of the Garioch ('geeree) and the further low farmlands of Buchan, Bennachie is the first hill to be seen by North-East fishermen nearing land on their way home to Aberdeen. Many who have never had the pleasure of seeing Bennachie or of exploring this hill so dear to Aberdeenshire folk will have heard the sad old song that runs:

> Oh! gin I were far Gadie rins,
> Far Gadie rins, far Gadie rins,
> Oh! gin I were far Gadie rins
> At the back o Bennachie

(Gadie, pronounced 'gaadee, is the burn on the north side of the hill, running into the Urie.) Many know the song as a bagpipe tune, the regimental march of the Gordon Highlanders.

Bennachie forms not so much a single hill as a 5 kilometre-long ridge with a series of distinctive tops. The highest is the 528m Oxen Craig, but the best known and by far the finest is the slightly lower easternmost point called the Mither Tap (Scots for Mother Top). A great mass of granite crowns the Mither Tap, which makes it easy to identify from afar and gives Bennachie a character greater than that of many higher peaks. The Forestry Commission has planted the lower slopes with conifers which are hard to walk in if you stray off the cleared paths. Bennachie has always been a popular hill, and in recent years visitors have greatly increased.

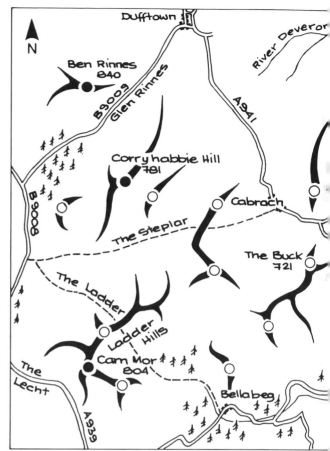

On the north side of Bennachie a public road leads from the B9002 one kilometre west of Oyne (pronounced 'ein) to the Back o' Bennachie car park. From here, a path completed in 1973 by the Forestry Commission leads south through the woods to the top of Oxen Craig (2½ kilometres, 370m ascent). The Commission has also made a path from Oxen Craig direct to the Mither Tap. From the Mither Tap you will enjoy a very fine view of north-east Scotland's windy coastal tip and of vast tracts of lowland farmland, moorland and hill ridges.

A second approach comes from east of Oyne where a public road leads to the Rowantree car park at 692 244; this lies near the old fort of the Maiden Castle and the very fine sculptured stone called the Maiden Stone. From the Rowantree car park a path runs south-west and then winds up to the Mither Tap (2½ kilometres, 330m ascent), the last part passing through a huge 4 metre-thick circular wall of large stones which form the remains of an Iron Age fort.

A third approach starts from Esson's car park at 699 217, from which a path leads up through the forest and then steeply up to the Mither Tap (2 kilometres, 370m ascent). A fourth is from Donview car park at 672 191 on the south side of Bennachie, coming up round the side of or over the top of the Millstone Hill. A fifth approach is from the west end of Bennachie, starting at the top of the Brindy ('breenee) hill on the B992 road from Alford to Insch.

A long-distance waymarked route called the West Gordon Way begins at Esson's car park, runs west along Bennachie to the Brindy, and then continues to the top of the Suie road at 547 231 on the road from Alford north to Clatt and Kennethmont.

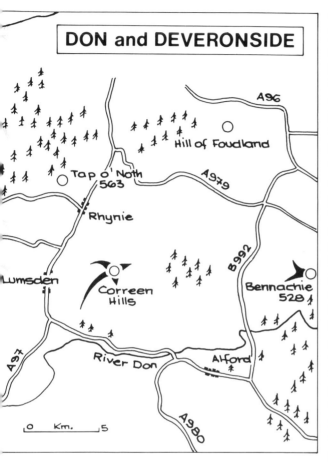

DON and DEVERONSIDE

Tap o' Noth 563

Rhynie

Hill of Foudland

A96

A979

Lumsden

Correen Hills

B992

Bennachie 528

River Don

Alford

A97

A980

0 Km. 5

Tap o' Noth (563m)

Lying between the Deveron and its eastern tributary the Bogie, the Tap o' Noth looks a prominent cone with a flat summit. The blunted top comes from a circular wall of vitrified masonry, where the firing of a wooden Iron Age fort was so hot that it melted and fused the stonework. It dates from the same period as the vitrified fort on the little green hill of Dunnideer near Insch, whereas the conspicuous archway of Dunnideer Castle dates from much later in medieval times, though largely composed of material from the older fort. The quickest way up the Tap o' Noth starts at the A941 road from Rhynie to the Cabrach. From a car park at 480 283 at Howtown, a track winds northwest and then east to the top. The valleys and former moors to the north now form the heavily wooded Clashindarroch Forest. An interesting place is the strange moor with its many weird rock outcrops and little hills north of the B9002 road from Lumsden to the Cabrach.

The Buck (721m)

Local people usually call it the Buck o the Cabrach. You can reach this graceful pointed hill quickly by going to the highest point on the Rhynie to Cabrach road and then for one kilometre south along the B9002 road to Lumsden. From here the Buck's summit lies 2 kilometres along the fence to the south-west (310m ascent). A beautiful fertile green cone over rich andalusite schist, it gives fine views over the vast moors and scattered hill farms of the Cabrach basin to the west.

Carn Mor *(big hill)* (804m)
Carn Ealasaid *(Elizabeth's hill)* (792m)

Both these hills are high points in the long range of the Ladder Hills (from Monadh an Fharaidh or hills of the ladder). From the highest point on the Ladder right of way (see the Ladder Road, below), a short walk south-west takes you to Carn Mor, the highest of the Ladder Hills. These broad hill tops bear a crisp lichen-rich

The Ladder hills from above Glas-choille

vegetation, with vast peaty hollows between them where many golden plovers pipe mournfully and a few dunlins scream in late spring. Carn Ealasaid (kairn'alsitsh) is a fine viewpoint 3 kilometres on the west side of the county boundary on the Lecht. At the Lecht there are ski tows on both east and west sides, a cafe and car parks.

Corryhabbie Hill (781m)
This hill is the highest point of a range of heathery high ground between Glen Rinnes and the heads of Glen Fiddich and Glen Livet. The easiest access is from Ellivreid in Glen Rinnes, on a public road at 269 324. Opposite the farm a track heads uphill, next goes up the Hill of Achmore to Muckle Lapprach, and continues to the top of Corryhabbie Hill (5 kilometres, 470m ascent). There is a fine spacious view over vast rolling hills and moors to the Banffshire lowlands and to the hills across the Moray Firth.

THE LOWER GROUND

Donside. Although less grand than Deeside, Donside from Monymusk upwards shows a soft beauty and much variety. The river continually bends around the base of wooded hills or laps the edge of pleasant green haughs. At Corgarff, some of the highest arable farming in the north of Scotland occurs on the south-facing slopes.

Pressendye Hill from near Logie Coldstone

Here the road goes over the Cock Bridge, across the Cock Burn (from Gaelic Allt a' Choilich or burn of the cock). On Donside you will see scores of interesting little hills and glens and vast moors, with a rich wildlife and fine views. A few good 500-570m hills are Lord Arthur's Cairn and the scrubby Coiliochbhar (kallie'vaar) north and south of the beautiful oak woods of Littlewood to the west of the Howe o Alford; the pointed Ben Newe (nyow) east of Bellabeg; and the Baronet's Cairn overlooking that lovely sweeping bend of the Don beside Lonach. These and innumerable others offer plenty of fine exploration.

The Lecht Road. An Leachd, the declivity. This is now the public road from Don to Tomintoul, which often features in the news after it has been blocked with snow. Although its highest point at about 645m altitude, one kilometre south of the watershed, lies slightly lower than the Cairnwell road's approximate 670m, the Lecht hills usually receive more snow, height for height, than Glen Shee or the Braemar hills. The road climbs steeply above the bridge over Don and then reaches a flat top which gives a very fine and unusual view to the east and north-east sides of the Ben Macdui-Cairn Gorm plateau, some of the Loch Avon cliffs, and the great bulging flanks of Ben Avon. The road drops from this flat top before climbing higher again, and then descends steeply to the Conglass Water. Halfway down on the east side of the road you will see a lovely, reedy tarn called Lochan gun Doimhne or lochan without depth. The road then crosses the Conglass, and near the corner below the bridge it passes the Well of the Lecht on the way down to the breezy uplands of Blairnamarrow (Blar nam Marbh or moor of the dead), Glen Conglass and Tomintoul.

The Ladder Road ('laider). This old right of way is the shortest walking route from Strath Don to Glen Livet and Tomintoul, taking you over an interesting range of rolling hills, the Ladder Hills. Distance: from the public road at 339 158 north-west of Bellabeg to the Chapeltown of Glenlivet 13 kilometres, total ascent 440m. A public road from Bellabeg (Baile Beag or small farmtown) goes up Nochty Water (nochta or naked) and over the hill to Glen Buchat. Leaving this road just before Torrancroy, you turn into the secluded upper glen of Nochty, and walk on a road through a Forestry Commission plantation to the ruined croft of Duffdefiance at about 385m. It got this strange name from a crofter called Lucky Thain who came over the Ladder from Glen Livet to squat here; by the time Duff, the local laird, challenged him, he already had a house up and its 'lum reekin', so he sat there successfully in defiance. From Duffdefiance you climb by a vehicle track for 180m on to a long plateau. The track ends at 595m where you come to the old path leading to the summit at about 735m, near a cairn. On the far side the route drops down by the Ladder Burn to the Braes of Glenlivet, a wide open green basin surrounded by heathery hills, once well-populated but now with most of its farms in ruins. The name Glen Livet ('leevit) comes from liomhaid, meaning polished or glittering.

The Steplar Road. This old right of way goes from Glen Livet over the hills through the Blackwater deer forest to the Cabrach. Distance: from Chapeltown of Glenlivet to Cabrach kirk 17 kilometres, total ascent 420m. From Chapeltown, take the path by Burnside of Thain to join a rough private road along the side of the River Livet to the lonely Suie (Suidhe or seat) on a grassy knoll. To the south-east, the steep narrow valley of the Kymah Burn and the broken rocky face of the Eachrach stand out prominently in this countryside of gentle rolling slopes. Beyond Suie the track carries on up Glen Suie to a col at about 520m, and then zigzags up west almost over the top of Corryhabbie Hill and down into Glen Fiddich and Glen Rinnes. From that col, a track descends to Glen Fiddich Lodge and so down the glen to Dufftown.

However, the old Steplar route breaks off as a track to the right after Suie, climbs easily to between Cook's Cairn and Cairn na Bruar at about 600m, and then contours round for one kilometre. Avoiding the track which breaks off to the left and leads to Blackwater Lodge, you descend straight ahead to the Black Water which winds along the bottom of a wide treeless glen. The chief impression 'here is one of great loneliness, low rolling hills and bare moorlands, with not a scrap of wood or green ground in sight, and the whole scene made more weird by a solitary granite tor, rising like a ruined keep on one of the distant hills' (Alexander, early edition). At about 400m you cross the upper Black Water and then climb up to the summit at approximately 540m beside Dead Wife's Hillock. Ahead now you suddenly see the Cabrach which lies like a huge cup below, surrounded by low hills and studded with many farms that are now mostly deserted. This great bowl is the Hich (Scots high)

Cabrach, whereas the Laich (low) Cabrach lies further down the Deveron. The name Cabrach means 'place abounding in cabers or tree poles', revealing that this now mostly treeless bowl was not always so. Dropping downhill by a track, you come to the old houses of Aldivalloch (Allt a' Bhealaich or burn of the pass), the scene of the song *Roy's wife of Aldivalloch*. Here you come to the road leading to the Kirktown of Cabrach at about 320m, from which you can drive down Deveronside to the Grouse Inn in the more wooded Laich Cabrach, and so to Dufftown. The historic Steplar path continued from Kirktown of Cabrach on to Rhynie by the route now taken by the tarmac road. From Aldivalloch, an old drovers' road goes south to 356 178 in Glen Buchat (10 kilometres, 200m ascent), and another further east runs from the Cabrach kirk south to 411 173 in Glen Kindie (11 kilometres, 250m ascent).

Hills of the North-east Lowlands. Several well-known isolated low hills give fine views over the broad farmlands and coast. Among the more notable ones are the 430m Knock Hill (locally the 'knoke) north of Huntly, a rounded heathery hill easily reached on its south side from the Banff-Keith road.

The more pointed 320m Bin of Cullen at 480 642 stands nearer the coast, a very fine viewpoint to the hills beyond the Moray Firth. It is most easily reached from the 207m top of the public road on the south-west side. The Fourman ('fore-mon, no 'Hill' as on the OS map) rises steeply above the fine broadleaved woods of Mayen by Deveronside. The hills of Foudland and of Tillymorgan carry large old slate quarries beside the Huntly-Aberdeen road. Furthest out of all, in the very tip of windy Buchan, stands Mormond (Mor-mhonadh, 'more mon or big hill) rising to 234m at 964 573 near Fraserburgh. Mormond, one of whose summits has now been disfigured by tracking aerials and buildings, is well known for its white horse and white stag, which are made of white stones on opposite sides (south and north) of the heathery hillside. Many more will know it because of the fine old Buchan ballad *Mormond Braes*.

The coast. The coast of north-east Scotland has a rich variety of fine sea-cliff scenery. In Banffshire, most of the many miles of cliffs are of Dalradian slate, and to the east of Macduff some fantastic sharp slaty ridges run out to the sea. You come to the finest cliff scenery at the 120m crags near Gardenstown and Troup Head, and at the vertical red sandstone walls of Pennan where there are huge steep stacks and spectacular ridges. The higher grounds of Fishrie south of Gardenstown and Windyheads Hill south of Pennan give particularly fine distant views of the hills described in this chapter as well as beyond to the Cairngorms and across the Moray Firth to Caithness.

CLIMBING

On Bennachie a number of granite tors project from the hill. A few steep outcrops on and near the Mither Tap provide short but sporting routes on rounded, weathered granite, from Moderate to Very Difficult in standard. Disused quarries offer the only other substantial inland rocks, mostly short. However, the coast more than

On the Mither Tap, Bennachie

makes up for the scarcity of natural rock inland, and indeed is outstanding. When bad weather comes to the hills you can often have a grand short winter day there. It is also excellent in summer, when the climbing becomes more carefree on the sun-warmed rock and when the smells of sea-thrift flowers, campion, salt water and sea-bird dung all add to the unusual character. Logie Head east of Cullen on the Banffshire coast gives very good climbing on sandstone, and Mull Cleave north of the Mill of Melrose is an unusual rock blade east of Macduff. The rough pink granite cliffs of Longhaven (lang'heiven) just south of Peterhead are well-known for their excellent rock climbing. You will feel quite a mountaineering atmosphere among the varied amphitheatres and ridges, where some of the walls even face inland.

SKIING

Height for height, this is the snowiest part of north-east Scotland and provides excellent ski touring in most winters. Bennachie stands too near the sea to get good snow cover in average winters, but a tour along its summits is splendid in a hard winter. Unfortunately the potential of Bennachie has been reduced greatly by blanket afforestation of the lower slopes, and mass tree planting on moorland has also spoiled formerly good hills for ski touring on the Correen Hills near Alford, Corrennie, Wishach Hill, Clashindarroch, and between Dufftown and the Cabrach.

The forest roads do offer routes which remain snow covered after most of the snow on the hill has melted, and there are waymarked ski trails at Wishach and Clashin-darroch, but forest roads are monotonous linear routes compared with the open spacious free skiing on the moorland that they have replaced.

The Ladder Hills offer good snow every winter, with the possibility of long tours linking the various summits, and fine descents into Glen Livet or Donside. The Buck, Corryhabbie and indeed the whole area of the Cabrach, Black Water and Glen Buchat is one of the better places in Scotland for intermediate-altitude ski touring during snowy periods. There are also innumerable good routes up the long glens and along the moors when snow cover is general.

FURTHER READING

D.G.Gordon (1973). Turriff Advertiser, 4 May. An article on the Bailies of Bennachie.

A.W.M.Whiteley (ed) (1983) *Bennachie Again.* A detailed book on many aspects of Bennachie.

SOME GAELIC WORDS IN CAIRNGORMS PLACE NAMES

abhainn	river	damh	stag	larach	dwelling place
achadh	field	darach	oak	leac	slab
ard	high point	dearg	red	leathad	slope
allt	burn	deas	south	leitir	slope
aonach	height	diollaid	saddle	liath	grey
ath	ford	donn	brown	lochan	small loch
bac	bank	dorus	door	mam	round hill
ban	white	drochaid	bridge	maol	bare hill
baile	farm town	druim	ridge	meadhon	middle
barr	top	dubh	black	meall	lump
bealach	col	dun	fort	moine	peat moss
beag	small			monadh	hill range
beith	birch	each	horse	mor	big
beinn	hill	eag	notch	muc	pig
breac	speckled	ear	east	muileann	mill
binnean	peak	eas	waterfall	mullach	summit
bo	cow	eilean	island		
bodach	old man	eun	bird	obair	river mouth
bothan	bothy			odhar	dun
braigh	upland	fad	along		
buachaille	herdsman	fearn	alder	poite	pot
buidhe	yellow	fiadh	deer		
		fionn	white	rath	fort
cailleach	old woman	fraoch	heather	righ	king
caisteal	castle	frith	deer forest	ruadh	red
camas	bend	fuar	cold	ruighe	shieling
caol	narrows	fuaran	well		
caora	sheep			seann	old
caorann	rowan	gabhar	goat	sgor	rocky peak
capull	horse	gaoth	wind	sidhean	fairy hill
carn	hill, scree, cairn	garbh	rough	slochd	pit
ceann	head, end	geal	white	sneachd	snow
coinneach	mossy place	gearr	short	srath	strath
cioch	breast	gille	young man	sron	nose
ciste	chest, coffin	glac	hollow	stac	steep rock
clach	stone	glas	green, grey	stob	peak
cnap	hillock	gleann	glen	stuc	peak
cnoc	hill	gorm	blue	suidhe	seat
coille	wood				
coire	corrie	iar	west	tigh	house
crasg, crosg	crossing	inbhir	river mouth, confluence	tobar	well
creag	crag			toll	hole
cuil	nook	innis	meadow	tom	hill
cul	back	iolair	eagle	torr	small hill
curra	bog, marsh				
		lag	hollow	uaine	green
da	two	lairig	hill pass	uisge	water
dail	riverside field	laogh	calf		

INDEX OF PLACE NAMES

The names of rock routes, most low-ground features and also most access points, bothies and other such items which are easily available in the sub-headings of the Introduction and the Chapters, are omitted from this index, which concentrates on the main hills, corries, glens and cross-country routes.   Names with the Gaelic definite article (A', Am, An) are under A below.

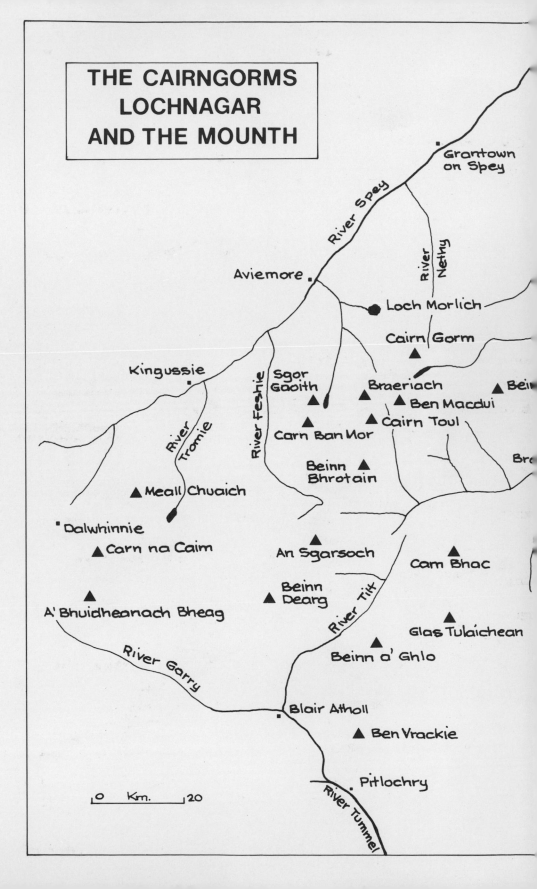

THE CAIRNGORMS LOCHNAGAR AND THE MOUNTH

Grantown on Spey

River Spey

River Nethy

Aviemore

Loch Morlich

Cairn Gorm ▲

Kingussie

River Feshie

Sgor Gaoith ▲

Braeriach ▲

▲ Bein

▲ Ben Macdui

River Tromie

Carn Ban Mor ▲

▲ Cairn Toul

Beinn ▲ Bhrotain

Bro

▲ Meall Chuaich

Dalwhinnie

▲ Carn na Caim

An Sgarsoch ▲

Carn Bhac ▲

Beinn Dearg ▲

River Tilt

▲ A' Bhuidheanach Bheag

▲ Glas Tulaichean

▲ Beinn a' Ghlo

River Garry

Blair Atholl

▲ Ben Vrackie

Pitlochry

River Tummel

0 Km. 20